A CHANGE
OF HEART

A CHANGE OF HEART

An Essential Christian Resource for
Current and Former Offenders

KEVIN J. McCARTHY, Ph.D.

AMBASSADOR INTERNATIONAL
GREENVILLE, SOUTH CAROLINA & BELFAST, NORTHERN IRELAND

www.ambassador-international.com

WHEN THE STEEL PRISON DOOR shuts behind you and you slump down onto the prison bed, no one can look behind the mask you are wearing at that moment. Deep within your emotions and memories, all of the events that brought you to this point well up and leave a bitter taste and feelings of being overwhelmed and lost. Completely cut off from those who love you by miles and layers of steel, you sit by yourself, trying to figure out where you go from here.

Or you are past the prison experience living back out in the "world" and reeling with the problems of unemployment, suffering stigma and wanting relief from the pain. Perhaps you have even lost a recent relationship. Now one more time you are back at that strange starting point again marked by failure like a shadow brother or sister sitting on a prison cot their first night in prison. Most likely you feel like you are a lost soul doubting any possibility of real worth or a future worth living.

If you can relate to either statement above I am glad that you have picked up this book. Maybe you are ready to consider the possibility of having a change of heart, but you have no idea how to make that happen. Then this book has been written for you; for I sat on that same prison cot and had the same experiences of failure living in the "world." This book is my journey of hope.

It is not a book about wishes or perfection. It is a summary of the steps which I have taken over the course of my lifetime: from the point of my last arrest through my release from parole requirements and beyond into thirty-five years of living. This book describes the one door that has always been opened for each of us. But for one reason or another we missed it time after time.

This book has been written for you, and I hope to engage many of you as you walk through the unrecognized door to freedom. It is all about having a change of heart and it is never too late to begin.

A Change of Heart

Printed in the United States of America

ISBN: 978-1-62020-237-1
eISBN: 978-1-62020-336-1

Cover Design by Josh Frederick
Page Layout by Hannah Nichols
Ebook Conversion by Anna Riebe

AMBASSADOR INTERNATIONAL
Emerald House
427 Wade Hampton Blvd.
Greenville, SC 29609, USA
www.ambassador-international.com

AMBASSADOR BOOKS
The Mount
2 Woodstock Link
Belfast, BT6 8DD, Northern Ireland, UK
www.ambassadormedia.co.uk

The colophon is a trademark of Ambassador

DEDICATIONS

To my Lord and Savior, Jesus Christ, kind, loving and above all compassionate and forgiving.

To my children, Susan, Jennifer, and Kevin, bright lights that marked my way on a very dark path.

To my grandchildren, Brooke, Blaire, Riley, Rowan, and Magnus, who bring me great joy just to know them.

To my siblings, living and passed. It is my honor and pleasure to call you brothers and sister.

To my father and mother, who more than any others, suffered at every faltering step along the way and continued to support, encourage and love me back into a relationship with Jesus Christ.

To Quinta, my true love and partner who has given vision and support for this undertaking. She continues to be an igniting fire in my soul.

To all who invested their time, efforts and resources to help shape my life, I am indebted to all of you.

DISMAS
P R O J E C T

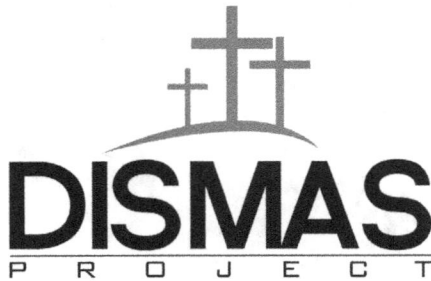

Dismas Project is a Christian not-for-profit Louisiana-based corporation providing spiritual and ongoing emotional support and encouragement to families of offenders and an outreach ministry to death row prisoners across the United States. A grant from Dismas Project helped to cover the costs of publishing this book for current and former offenders.

ACKNOWLEDGEMENTS

LIKE MY PREVIOUS WORK *Surviving the Justice Experience,* this book was derived from the collective experiences of many people. I remain unable to name them all given my memory limitations and the considerable number of individuals who have contributed to this work.

I speak to each of you from my heart as I express the joy and blessings of having shared an earthly encounter with each of you. Please forgive me that I can only offer words of recognition and thankfulness.

You have all shown great personal courage and compassion by investing in my brokenness. Blessed are those that share the journey.

For those that invested their time and talents in providing me with an education, I trust that this work bears evidence of the fruit of your efforts.

To my editor, Carol Henson, who was a crucial force in making this book a readable document for the benefit of those who have the misfortune of not being given the educational resources which have been made available to me.

To the other anonymous individuals who have contributed to this effort, I would like to thank each of you individually for your enthusiasm and support. Many publishers told me that offenders do not read books. You have proven their preconceptions wrong.

Some of those who have put their creativity to work are Jason Hufft, Kevin McCarthy II, Pastor Rod Pasch, Brennen Hodge, Randi Pena, Father Rareshide, Father Gerard, Dave Whipple and many others.

Last, I would like to thank Sam Lowry of Ambassador International and his son, Tim, who collaborated in this journey to shed light on the lives suffering from the influences of evil and the pain connected with living out those lifestyle choices. They have blessed my efforts and shared my commitment to reach into the darkest places and shed the light of God.

For families and offenders alike, living with the burdens of daily pain and suffering, let's continue the journey we have begun together.

CONTENTS

Part One
PREFACE & INTRODUCTION

PREFACE

THIS WORK WAS NOT WRITTEN to sell books, but rather to honor God and serve my neighbors. Several individuals whose opinions I respect read the largely completed work. The most common feedback given was about the dry nature of the early manuscript. One observer suggested that I had to add my own history in order to help the reader understand that this book is based on my own journey. It is not a prescription for other people's lives. It comes from the life I have lived.

At least one observer felt that this lack of connection between my personal history and this book was based on shame and that looking at and opening up about this shame was essential to helping the reader understand how to begin personal change. Yes, I would agree that there are many things in my past that are shameful, and I don't want to bury or hide my past failures, no matter how painful they may be. My one and only desire in writing this book is to honor God and help others.

This goal to honor God creates a bit of a problem for me in putting together my personal and factual information. I am trying to make my role smaller in the life-changing process known as KNOWETICS, with credit being given where credit is due. I'm just following directions: a small servant trying to listen to My Master's voice. Nothing in this book should replace God's authority. Further, nothing in this book should be viewed as an endorsement or approval of the life I had previously lived outside of my relationship with Jesus Christ.

Given this caution, I end this work with a summarized personal history of my life. I'm not going to list certain events or choices and then try to explain why I chose them. I'm just going to offer this list of horrible choices that hopefully, will show my readers just how destructive my choices were.

This cycle of destructiveness was like a spreading oil slick in my life. It became a force of its own. Today I am convinced that this oil slick was fueled by evil, though I could offer you an almost endless number of reasons why I made such choices. They were wrong choices and I was wrong to have made them. Given the wide number of people who were hurt by these actions, I can only hope that my book can help soothe the pain I have recklessly (though often unknowingly) inflicted on others.

Early on, I was able to see how alcohol affected the behaviors of people around me. I discovered that people could change so much while under the influence of alcohol that you never knew which personality would show up. As a child, I can remember watching these behaviors and becoming fearful. I can also remember telling myself that when I grew up I would not become like those people.

In spite of my good intentions, I went on to develop addictions to alcohol and drugs. As a teenager, while hanging out with the older crowd, I had access to a steady supply of beer outside of my home. It became an open doorway to pain which I couldn't see coming. Once that door was opened as an adolescent, it wouldn't be closed until I found myself arrested on four felony charges facing the reality of spending a long time in prison if I was convicted.

I can't seem to connect all my bad choices in my mind. I think it's because what I did and how it affected my life was very complicated. What I can say is that once I headed in the wrong direction, things went quickly downhill. The slide downward from the early days of hanging out with the older crowd, to eventually doing time in prison, was a fast slide toward self-destruction. It's interesting because I didn't notice the fall or potential hard landing.

This downhill slide started with a youth court appearance for truancy. The bar was lifted to theft and check forgery, which led to doing time at the adolescent facility at Riker's Island, N.Y. It all happened so fast that I scarcely had time to notice the fall and I had no idea that there was still time to get off this train.

What I had lacked in understanding and maturity before my six-month sentence, I made up for by learning new skills and new techniques while in prison. In addition to soaring levels of anger and rage, I also became aware of a number of ways to get what I wanted and needed after prison. At the age of sixteen I felt alone and unable to trust anyone. I knew my choices were poor, but all I had were raw survival instincts.

These crude actions and my number of run-ins with the law became more and more frequent and routine as I vented my pent-up fury. This record included arrests for criminal mischief, burglary, attempted arson, escape, fugitive, felonious assault, menacing, probation violation, DWI's, failure to obey court orders, breaking and entering, rape, and lewd and lascivious conduct. The ever-growing record of arrests only partially showed how much anger dominated my life at this period of time.

In reviewing this list, I'm struck by how there's no order to any of my actions, either in the offenses or in how I personally behaved. Again, I use the idea of a spreading oil slick, but when I was in the middle of it, I had no idea how big this slick was. I thought I was living the good life. These "events" were just inconvenient problems I had to solve. Now I clearly see that I was striking out in all directions and wherever my blows landed, I made few, if any, excuses for my behaviors. I spent a year or more incarcerated before landing a sentence of six years and four months in the California prison system. This became my Damascus Road experience. This book is about what happened in my life after a "spiritual awakening" and the doors that have opened to me along my life journey.

KNOWETICS is not an instructional guide to life-changing experiences. It is a practical log of choices I've made under the remarkable influence of the grace of God. It's not a perfect plan, but in my life, it has formed a basis for an action plan. Given the willingness to show up, I have experienced a lifetime of blessings, while having been given the strength to navigate the storms of life. I offer these ideas to others as a starting point in transforming wasted lives. The only thing being championed in this book is the reality that useless lives can be transformed into lives of devotion and service to others through the phenomena of experiencing a spiritual awakening.

This all boils down to a very simple idea: "just show up" and see what happens. If you don't like the result, your pain and misery will be cheerfully refunded.

While talking to my son about this book, he pointed out the fact that forgiveness can't be negotiated, but comes from seeing sorrow or contrition in the heart of the offender. If there weren't any interaction between offender and victim, it would seem that wounds never fully heal.

KNOWETICS is about that process and focuses on the choices the offender can make to start the process of healing as a way of life.

Ultimately the goal of all this: "True reconciliation is based on forgiveness, forgiveness is based upon true confession, and confession is based on penitence, on contrition, on sorrow for what you have done." So the ultimate goal is reconciliation and restoration of our lost brothers and sisters. It all begins with forgiveness.[1]

Kevin J. McCarthy, Ph.D.
January 19, 2012
San Jose Adentro, Dominican Republic

---

[1] Tutu, Desmond, *God has a Dream, A Vision Of Hope for Our Time* (Image Books, Doubleday, 2004)

INTRODUCTION: A NEW DAY HAS BEGUN!

DO YOU REMEMBER A TIME when you were loved—truly loved—for who you were? Your parents, family members and others saw you as a unique expression of love. You could do no wrong at that time in your life. Everyone was able to understand your needs, and it did not matter how you showed this: a word, arms outstretched or a painful cry of fear. You were still loved unconditionally. The world was a great place and you were a very important part of daily life. You had a hard time going to sleep because you did not want to miss a minute of life.

Then at some point, (and only you know when this happened), you started to understand something was wrong. Your babysitter started to say you were a handful, your teachers started to send notes home to your parents saying you had a hard time standing in line and they also noted you regularly disrupted the classroom. Of special note was your unique ability to disconnect and entertain yourself by daydreaming. Neighbors who used to love having you around, now grumbled at the sight of you. Soon everybody complained about the way you behaved and you started feeling bad about yourself. As the number of complaints started to grow, the way you felt about yourself as being loved and being lovable was shattered by your parent's actions. They were telling you they no longer felt you deserved unconditional love and your world started to change for the worse. You found yourself on an unfamiliar road feeling small, lost, and frightened. You didn't have a road map for this experience! You and I soon learned that we had to do things in order to get even brief moments of conditional love.

These moments became few and far between. It was hard to predict what our world would be like at any time and this changed our behavior around other people. We would carefully remember the things we did and put them into the categories of good and bad. If we could get enough "good" points, we hoped for moments of unconditional love. When we had too many bad points, we got scared, wondering when we could get back to unconditional love.

With no road map, no instruction guide or no advance warnings, we were left to sort it all out, to intuitively relate to society. Most of us are considered average. That's why we blend so well into the community. The term "average" could also indicate how well we learned about unwritten rules of living within society.

Those children who are described as socially "bright" learned the rules quickly and blended in well with others. Often times, the bright ones came out at the front of the pack. They often had lots of people who spent time with them and helped them along the way. In time, they were helped to understand how to get along and how to do what was expected. They may have had brothers and sisters, grandparents or extended family and friends whose efforts made for a smoother road for the bright ones.

At the other end of the scale, there were those who everybody called socially "handicapped." Their behaviors and ways of interacting soon meant they were labeled and defined as hopeless and because of that, worthless. We can quickly see and remember those we threw away along the path of life. You see, at some time in our young lives we experienced the pressure to join the crowd and apply our skills, talents and personalities finding a "place" among the crowd. That leaves us average people struggling to understand what's going on around us. One act at a time, we began to realize we were being disciplined and rejected. Because of that, we changed our behaviors, and those changes may not have been for the better.

For most of us, we made this leap completely by faith and hopefully we landed on the other side of the gap. This leap happened because we were labeled and excluded. No one wants to be left out—not even the socially handicapped—so we eventually learned how to change our behavior just enough to get along in society. This is not the same as changing our beliefs (which is the underlying foundation of our personality and our ability to relate to others).

Most of us had no clue as to how society works. It was like learning a social algebra; it's very impressive but I'm still not sure what "x" and "y" have to do with how I fit into society. So we shut our mouths and nodded our heads that we did understand the dance steps in this elegant ballet called life.

Well, I didn't understand then, and I'm *still* not sure I understand everything about this awkward dance of life. But I'm sure that there are several things I do understand by virtue of having lived my life. I came from the relatively protected upbringing of daily life in a parochial school located in Astoria, New York. In my elementary school adventure, I earned the labels of odd and disruptive. After my eighth grade graduation ceremony, I unofficially received another label when the pastor of my church determined I was very "glib."

I had asked for his personal recommendation to attend a high school preparatory program that would lead to further studies and eventual ordination as a priest (which was something I wanted when I was younger). Without permission, I opened and read his recommendation letter because of a nagging thought that he was not impressed with my state of holiness. I read every word and then had to ask my mother what the word "glib" meant. That's when I found out he thought I was slick or smooth. After discovering I'd been labeled as "glib" or slick, I abandoned my dreams of the priesthood and tried to move on and also tried to figure out how to fit in with the crowd. The crowd was headed for regular high school and I went along with it because that's what my mother wanted. She saw me as a future priest, symphony piano player, or opera singer at some upcoming appearance at La Scala.

She dreamt that I would rise to her expectations with one small stipulation—my future worth to both her and the world depended on my ability to turn the sweetness of my boyish voice into that of a tenor. I failed miserably at this expectation of hers (and many others in the course of my life). I would forever be a baritone.

I had just popped out of the starting gate of life and I had miserably failed my parents, family and friends. I took my next false step when I discovered sexual interests (remember the 6th and 9th commandments of God?).

This opened up a whole new world and I never looked back. The dilemma was how to use this secret discovery and still obey God's commandments. I didn't have the slightest clue. It seemed like I was stepping back and forth between my private world and the world made by society, and was mostly going from joy to shame. At the age of thirteen, I was determined to get along somehow and live in both worlds.

So, with my newfound glibness and reinforced by my new claim on the pleasure principle, I went off to high school hoping that it would offer me personal salvation. Somehow, I would use all this to find unconditional love that I knew was out there. Wow, was I a misinformed kid!

My freshman year of high school was spent at St. Agnes High School in New York City. There, under the experienced eyes of the Marist Brothers, my life was shaped into becoming a true "Christian" young man who could easily fit into the desired halls of society. I suffered daily, waging a moral war within and a public struggle without. I experienced trying to get and apply all the wonderful knowledge I could from a Catholic High School Education.

Like the child who struggled to stay in line or pay attention to the strange language of a new teacher in first or second grade, I really did want to be successful in high school. Both the well-intended Marist Brothers and I were unaware of what it meant to be affected by all the limitations that went along with my immaturity. At the end of my first year of high school, I failed Algebra, English and Latin and was labeled stupid with all of the problems that come along with that label.

How could I explain to anyone that I had only recently figured out 2 + 2 = 4, or 6 x 6 = 36? Now I was expected to figure out what an "x" and "y" might equal. I had no idea . . . maybe a "b"? I confidentially wrote that on my test papers and received F's. It wouldn't be until later in life that I'd come to the understanding that math is just like another language.

If either of those frustrated Marist Brothers or I had known what it meant for me to deal with immaturity, my life might have taken another road toward adulthood. Instead, I quit high school on my sixteenth birthday and I was finally freed from the school's control and from being publicly labeled "stupid." Privately, I had to come to terms with the fact that I received failing grades (3 "F's") because of my stupidity and the painful knowledge that I would never experience unconditional love. That was for smart people and productive people.

I was a marked young man. *Our stupid son, living in the same house as his "above average," even "genius brothers and sister," has really failed now.* I soon went out into a world where I could be successful. This book is about my journey to find that way of living. It is also about what happened when I began to slowly believe those labels and my experiences in wrestling with those marks of Cain.

As you follow along, you will silently meet those who have shaped and influenced my life as well as members of my immediate and extended family. I have mentioned only a few of those who have helped shape my life. There are many others you will meet in the pages ahead (though usually unnamed).

These are all "average" people. The chapters in the rest of this book are sprinkled with historical figures that have shaped our lives by their thoughts and their actions.

To help understand the connection between "average" people and the labels given to some people, I have coined two terms.

The first term is KNOWETICS: a spiritual way to describe the lives of people like me. It takes on a life of its own as you read the following pages. It will help you recognize how you've come from having the *unconditional* love that you experienced as a very young child to the dark world of *conditional* love or being kicked out of the rest of society. It will help light up your future by looking at the labels others have given you as you tried to live your own life. It also shows how you can get back that secure feeling of unconditional love. This is the spiritual process that I have called KNOWETICS: the knowledge that everything that makes us who we are comes from God's love for us. We are *all* His precious children.

The second term is SEVERCIDE: This term is meant to help identify what happens when someone is labeled and excluded. It describes how these two things affect individuals, groups, communities and society. Each of these things shapes our personality and what we believe about ourselves inside. The actual type of label doesn't matter much since the better the label, the more we compare ourselves to others. These types of labels—given to us by our family, community or society—make us different from others in our family by making one person worth more than another. Each of these good labels can quickly turn bad and might include new labels like drunk, divorced, jobless, felon, homosexual, homeless, unreliable, undesirable, unwanted, unknowable and unlovable. SEVERCIDE is my personal attempt to create a way of thinking that makes a difference in the quality of our personal lives. We are not God's evil children!

This way of thinking is used to let others know about my journey of hope, my wanting to help others understand what has gone on in historical, political, scientific, and religious thought. What is going on right now will take on new meaning as you become more and more aware of how these things affect all of our lives.

* * *

At one time in my life, a friend strongly advised me to check out the life of the legend Walt Disney and his "military" service abroad. Supposedly, Walt Disney had received a "release" from service by The American Ambulance Corp, a division of the Red Cross because of something that happened in France, February 1919. His superior's wrote him off as worthless, unable to be of any use to them and possibly even a danger to others because of what happened in France in 1919. It's too bad they didn't consider that he had other talents they didn't know about and could have used him to do something else.

Later, he used his complex knowledge of drawing, and with his creative use of color and motion, became famous for developing various animation techniques. But the Red Cross couldn't find any other way to use this young man's talents and abilities. Stop a moment and think of how his knowledge could have been applied to the endless problems found during the war.

Personally, I'm glad that they dismissed him. He was then free to show the world his ability to combine animation and entertainment. Millions of children worldwide have had their lives brightened by his heartfelt stories. He wasn't of much value to the Red Cross, but the world is grateful for his tireless efforts to capture our attention and transform our lives. He did it one cartoon frame at a time, one person at a time.

Consider the life of Nelson Mandela who was labeled a felon, terrorist and undesirable by the South African Government then in power. He was "rehabilitated" by focusing on freeing his people from the cruelty of apartheid. He later became president of the nation that had previously condemned him to an awful life of darkness and isolation.

Finally, let's consider the fact that some of those now in power in Israel were once called terrorists by Great Britain who placed bounties on their heads. Such leaders are now well respected in their own country. They have been rehabilitated and transformed by what they were able to do later in their life. History no longer talks about them by labeling them as terrorists. The same things are happening NOW in the Middle East, Asia, Africa and South America. The message is clear. All people are worth something!

But you say, "It's not the same as it is in America or in the rest of the world today." It's time to look back at our own history as a nation. Our founding fathers were once labeled as traitors, rebels and even criminals by Great Britain. It seems that they labeled people all over the globe. For example in India, the West Indies and other countries that wanted to rule themselves without the interference of Great Britain. Thank God these countries did not quit under the pressure. Otherwise, we could all be speaking with an English accent today!

Interestingly, our current government officials are busy doing the same thing to others. Consider the growing list of people who have been denied entry to the U.S. under the label of undesirables or known to have supported or been associated with branded terrorist groups (by blood, reputation or politics). It is done routinely, and you can learn more about this by listening to public radio. Our government is focused on those outside our culture who MIGHT represent a threat to our way of life, as well as those inside our culture who have been isolated and excluded in the aftermath of a "justice" encounter.

The term SEVERCIDE describes the business of exclusion and labeling that becomes significant, but it has been done around the world less than 100 years. In the U.S., it has grown in only the last 80-90 years or so, but the process of exclusion earnestly began to happen more and more as an outgrowth of the prison-industrial complex. Now in the name of security, its tentacles have reached so far as to restrict our civil rights in the name of protection. This is routinely happening as part of the terrorist industrial complex. Out of our fears we have become a society where labeling has become a dangerous control mechanism.

And so, in the process of "social control" we are currently given examples of SEVERCIDE which have flowed through a series of manifestations that has shaped our country and will continue to do so until the effects of these policies have been clearly understood by the citizens who blindly allow these odious mechanisms of control to persist in the name of security.

They are summed up as their developmental evolution has emerged:

- The Military Industrial Complex
- The Prison Industrial Complex
- The Terrorist Industrial Complex
- The SEVERCIDE Industrial Complex

Let's begin the journey of *A Change of Heart*. It will help us know who we are and why we all deserve unconditional love. This is my journey of hope and perhaps your own transforming journey of hope. A new day has begun!

PART TWO
SOCIETY'S INFLUENCES ON OUR INDIVIDUAL LIVES

CHAPTER 1

KNOWETICS

EVERYONE HAS THE UNDENIABLE GOD-GIVEN right to change. No one can take away your freedom to change. The only thing the government and society can do is give you a label. The only power they have is the power we give them.

The legal system may claim to have the power to judge you and tries to claim the power of pardon, but these claims mean nothing when you realize you are a child of God. All labels and legal ideas fade in the light of this personal revelation. Once you are busy using this new process you will see positive changes to your spirit and life. That is part of the process known as KNOWETICS.

KNOWETICS is the knowledge that you can make a constructive path to change. Unlike mental health services that are always ready to make money through therapy and medications, KNOWETICS is designed to help you safely organize your own skills and personal therapeutic exercises.

How you apply this information is unique because our personal histories have made us who we are today. No longer do people have to get involved in the healthcare business to find effective help for the shame and pain of past failures. Now they are free to apply the skills they've learned in a program, at their own pace that lets them explore their lives and be accountable for the way they do it.

People have to decide how much the past affects them today. KNOWETICS provides a process to shape personal change without encumbering costly and dramatic implications to our current lives. It is a personalized approach to taking stock of your life and it is available to use at any time. Since you can begin at any time, it can be used at any point in the day when you want to connect the life you have now with what has happened to you in the past. This process is not a denial of past failures, rather it is reshaping of those events to serve new purposes in the days that lay ahead.

Why is the past so important? The past has made us the people we are today and many of us have been held hostage by past traumas and events. Becoming aware of these things in a non-threatening context can make a safer place where a person can look at what happened in their lives when they made personal choices that changed their lives. It creates a comfortable place to go over the events that shaped us.

We are more than the sum total of our past experiences. There are personal things we can use to shape our future and change the bad times into times when we can accept ourselves and have true inner peace. One goal of KNOWETICS is to help a person change their mindset to a positive influence by understanding what they did to shape their current situation.

KNOWETICS should not replace regular healthcare decisions, nor should it be considered a cure-all when dealing with healthcare issues. It is a tool to be used as a starting point prior to professional mental healthcare, helping inform and guide your decisions. While KNOWETICS is not a replacement for professional care, its carefully crafted skills can personally be used in any time or place including prison life.

Mental healthcare is generally made available in different formats including psychiatry, psychology, social workers, licensed counselors, marriage and family therapists, a large collection of addiction specialists and a variety of other professionals. It takes a lot of effort to find your way through endless choices and professional statements. The way they work can best be compared to the old analogue technology; it is very predictable and suggests you can make personal changes by being aware of other's opinions. It is like using outdated TV rabbit ears to get good reception.

KNOWETICS is best compared with digital technology. It is not dependent upon the actions of others. You use your own feelings like an integrated circuit. It focuses on your personal viewpoint and history and does not rely on theories, therapy or prescriptions. This is something that starts with you. You direct it yourself by applying what you learn to yourself, unlike the analogue technology that requires a specialist. No one knows you as well as you know yourself. Much of the current mental health treatments insist on lots of time spent with therapists or other professional to establish the boundaries of opinions. This ends up costing you time and money.

KNOWETICS builds on what you know about yourself and what's going on with you right now. It assumes that you can be honest with yourself and that you can be responsible for your own change. You apply what you've learned and use the skills you've developed to get back to those things that have great meaning in your life. KNOWETICS relies on what you do personally for yourself (like the new digital technology).

KNOWETICS is a remarkable advance in taking care of you. It doesn't depend on what others do for you. You don't need to be caught up in insurance problems, co-pays or deductibles because it depends only on you. The limitations of confidentiality and/or professional privilege have little impact on a self-directed program. More importantly, you don't have to worry about money or wasted time waiting for endless doctor appointments. Apply what you've learned about yourself, what you've discovered about your feelings, anywhere and at any time. You can reinforce what you've learned, the skills you've learned every day. People who can benefit from KNOWETICS include those of us who have failed to measure up to God's standards and the laws of the land. This book is written for those of us who need to remind ourselves daily of our own value as a person and how we can interact with others in a loving and healthy manner. No matter how we have failed in the past, each of us has something meaningful to offer the world around us.

KNOWETICS is the journey of self-discovery and self-acceptance that helps us do that. Welcome back to life; it's time to stop hiding because of those past failures. Forgiveness, pardon and the ability to change our lives are given to us by our Creator and can NEVER be denied because of the opinions or actions of others.

Welcome to a new life that starts today with your choice to use what has been given to you, to be accountable and with the power to make your own personal choices to create an ongoing KNOWETICS event in your life. KNOWETICS is the harnessed power of personal change by making choices and being accountable. Let's begin.

CHAPTER 2

WHAT DOES SPIRITUALITY HAVE TO DO WITH IT?

WITH MORE AND MORE PEOPLE thinking of science as a religion—especially over the last 150 years—people have tended to disconnect from the "old" morality and have turned to the "promise" of freedom held out by modern science. Those who believe in science have to have complete faith in the rules of science. It is an all or nothing proposition. I remember reading a new magazine editor's introduction letter that said only ignorant people believed the myth of religion.

That magazine is considered to be a reliable "source" of current information and scientific news. The arrogance of the editor's words led me to stop my subscription to the magazine. Magazines aren't the only ones telling us this. It seems like just about everyone in the news business tries to make us believe that science is about absolute truth.

I have lived long enough now to be able to see many of these truths fall apart. You don't have to look far for this evidence. Think about all the lawyers who are ready to bring lawsuits against the pharmaceutical industry and makers of medical devices, etc. Many of these claims have been found to be false. Think about those people who had thrown away their morals believing in new "discoveries" of science, only to find out later that these new discoveries were wrong or false. Truth is needed to guide our thoughts and actions. Truth must be part of our own beliefs. At some level, truth acts like a rudder on a ship and allows us to steer clear of disasters. It is not a self-interested or misinformed truth that gets wielded like a sword to force us in certain directions. No, the truth I speak about is like a calm secure feeling inside of each of us that can guide us through all chaos.

My friend, Bobbie, suggested that I think about the case of Galileo. He had been branded a heretic by the church for his belief that the earth was not the center of the universe. But at that time, science was convincing everyone that the opposite was true. History shows that he went back on his belief because he was pressured into it. What I later learned was that he was worried about what would happen to his children. His sons were well taken care of and thought to be out of harm's reach. But his two daughters, who went off to live at a convent during this time, could have been in real trouble. Bobbie pointed out that they needed men to help and protect them. If Galileo had died a heretic, men would have abandoned or rejected the daughters and the girls would have been branded as heretics too. Galileo took back what he'd said about the earth not being the center of the universe because of what might possibly happen to his daughters. But in his heart, he always believed that he was right. He had inner courage based on truth.

Some would ask, "Whose truth?" and that is a fair question. Let's start with the major religions of the world. What does it mean to be a good Buddhist, a good Catholic, a good Jew, a good Christian or a good Muslim? Well, in short it means obedience to the principles of their religion. Right away, we have a major problem. If being obedient to the "truths" of our religious faith can make us better people, why do so many of us have a hard time living up to those beliefs?

As small children, many of us got our moral training from parents, pastors or educators. Yes, there have always been times we don't live by those principles, but we still believe the truth we've found in the Torah, Bible or Koran, and we try to live by this truth.

Basically, this means we grew up being told to tell the truth, not to steal, to honor your mother and father, etc. These were known as truths because all faiths and religions offer guidance on how to make moral decisions and live our lives in peace with others. Do you remember the first time you told a lie or the first time you took something that did not belong to you? This invariably bothered you and made you feel bad about yourself. However, you likely forgot about it and moved on to the next thing. Even though you knew you'd done wrong and felt bad about it, you'd find something else to distract you. Case closed.

There is a problem when we try to forget our uncomfortable feelings. Right away we realize we can usually get away with lying or stealing on a small scale without consequences. We tell ourselves that everyone else is also doing it. That kind of thinking—trying to avoid the discomfort of admitting we did something wrong—set's us up to repeat this destructive cycle. It is all done inside ourselves without anyone else even knowing about it.

Personally, my beliefs are based upon my acceptance of Christianity. Truth is the center of my faith. Even so, the struggle described above has played itself out many times in my life. I am reminded of the story of Adam and Eve and their resulting fall from grace. Their act of disobedience quickly laid the foundation for the world's first murder. It seems to be a giant step from disobedience to murder. But all the small steps when we ignore what we've done wrong (because it makes us feel uncomfortable), can lead back to the first time we told that first lie or the first time we took something that wasn't ours. It becomes easy to push those nagging thoughts aside and forget the moral of the story. It is just a folktale or a myth. We start to question the very existence of God by not letting truth guide our lives.

We declare our independence from this UNSEEN god and move into high gear, racing ahead with our lives. This usually starts before we are teenagers, but can also develop at any point when something traumatic happens or there is a life-changing crisis. Learning to question God's wisdom and goodness, we decide we can make our own decisions and do whatever we want. We have taken the first step toward completely ignoring our morals as we decide to move on, hoping to discover what life has to offer us.

We rarely tell others about this and we put the whole thing under the heading of personal choices. We keep all this to ourselves. We begin to withdraw emotionally, distancing ourselves from others who can influence us and from any type of authority figures. Social scientists call this becoming an individual: part of what makes us our own person.

This also keeps us from becoming more of a spiritual person. This can be seen in our actions and behaviors. But we're the only ones to notice. If we have had little or no moral training, we start thinking, "the sky is the limit." If we have had good moral training, there's a crisis for us as we try to figure out what "truth" means for us. Again, we keep this to ourselves.

So how can religion and spirituality come together? More importantly, what does this have to do with KNOWETICS? Since the way we get to know our own spirituality may be the single biggest influence on what we think and what we do, we need to go back to our own beliefs about spirituality. When we do this, we may be surprised at how little our beliefs have anything to do with the way we live our lives. If God isn't helping us or we don't understand what God means to us, our beliefs aren't going to bring us much hope for the future.

Even if we don't believe in God, it doesn't mean we can't find spirituality. People with no feeling for who God may be can see that each person is unique and has their own individual personality. That may help a person use different options when learning how to apply the personal skills of KNOWETICS (Chapters 1-6 address the current and historical realities impacting and shaping our lives).

***

I am married to an intelligent woman with many skills and abilities that I'm learning about every day as we enter our ninth year of marriage. She was born and raised in Indonesia, whereas I was born and raised in the United States. There are differences in our marriage: first in age, but also in our understandings of spiritual things. For example, our understanding of what it actually means to be a Christian and how this affects our daily choices. But rather than keeping us at odds with each other, these differences shape our lives together and add a depth of love and understanding in the way we feel about each other as individuals with unique viewpoints.

Consider the following story showing how we get along together. My wife is an incredible cook. She can start with just the basic ingredients and create a beautiful and satisfying meal that I enjoy very much. The difference between us is that we could use the same ingredients and yet come up with completely different meals. If you were smart, you'd choose to sample Quinta's creation over my own.

I am not being critical of my own ability to cook; I am just telling the truth about the differences between Quinta and myself. Though given the same basic ingredients (olive oil, spices, rice or noodles, fish or chicken and vegetables), our meals would be completely different from each other. Mine would be basic while Quinta's would not only taste good, but it would smell wonderful and look fantastic.

The resulting difference between my creation and Quinta's is our understanding of how to use basic ingredients. She understands how valuable it is to use a good recipe and recognizes the value of good techniques before putting the ingredients to the fire. That's the major differences in our cooking skills. Quinta uses a good routine that she's developed over the years as a guide to her meal preparation while I have always used a poorly understood routine that gets me the same results every time I cook.

Truth and spirituality have a similar relationship in our lives. Truth and moral training are the same as having a recipe to guide our actions. Spirituality is the use of all the ingredients we need to produce new results, rewarding connections and fresh personal experiences in our everyday lives. So what are these ingredients? In later chapters we will explore each one, but for now it would be useful to go back and talk about how timing or the quantity of each ingredient we need and knowing how it will all turn out are similar to the cooking experience we are seeking. So with words I am attempting to explain how this process can come together in our lives and transform us.

The same basic elements are necessary in applying the skills of KNOWETICS for the process of personal change. Spirituality offers a number of tools to help us grow as a person. We need to remember that only with open minds will we be able to live the lives we are worthy of having.

At this point, it would be useful to look at the facts we know about KNOWETICS and to start thinking about what will happen if we let spirituality play a part in our everyday lives. The next few chapters will help us understand how KNOWETICS, along with the use of spiritual tools, can help us transform our lives.

CHAPTER 3

TRUTH IS TRUTH, RIGHT?

THE IDEA THAT THERE ARE multiple truths is a giant leap in reasoning that can help a person escape from personal responsibility. The problem with this choice is that following this path takes us into a strange group of rabbit holes in how we behave and invites us to live secret lives. This path doesn't have the structural ability to help us in our need to make changes in our lives. A secret life is when we include activities that we enjoy only in our private lives. What we do in our secret life helps us reduce our anxiety and stress by doing things that bring us satisfaction or pleasure.

These activities can be anything from video games to all kinds of addictions and/or obsessions (examples: overeating and hoarding) and they take up a majority of our time and energy. Our secret lives are different from our regular lives because we can become defensive and unwilling to share what we're doing with others. Our secret lives involve very private things that we use to reward ourselves after we've gone through stress or emotional discomfort. It may be something as simple as coming home and drinking a six-pack of beer. Or, it may be expressed in the use of pornography and compulsive masturbation.

There are many forms to a secret life, but the main feature is obviously secrecy. This brings along shame and personal disappointment each time it happens. Eventually, this secret life leads to a withdrawal from other life commitments, and the pleasure we get from this activity becomes our focus in life. Others notice how distant we're becoming and may want to talk to us about it. But usually it is their growing awareness of how much we've changed that makes even more distance between others and ourselves. We become more focused on ourselves and emotionally distant as we try very hard to get some sense of balance in our lives.

In time, it gets harder and harder to change what we're doing in our secret lives. Stopping—giving up the very thing that regularly gives both pleasure and pain—would be even worse. In the meantime, we learn to live with the shame and struggle knowing we're creating more and more chaos inside us. This can lead us to give up all hope of change and tell ourselves it's just something we have to live with. If this is all so normal, why do I feel so bad?

One way we may try to comfort ourselves is to compare ourselves with others. Since we are so good at rationalizing, we may decide that we are no different than our friends and associates. This view doesn't help our internal conflicts and instead tends to make us feel justified in continuing these self-destructive behaviors. Another view we may imagine is that this is just a normal part of living in the twenty-first century. Both of these alternatives are points of disconnection that fuel our thoughts to make **no** decision, and so the inner conflict continues.

The real victims through this entire struggle are our peace of mind and our internal feelings of our self-image. Eventually the struggle becomes part of our public life, though we still try to keep our behaviors from others. This usually leads to others questioning our behavior. They are at a loss to explain why you've changed and try to get the relationship to go back to the past. Shortly, though, they may give up on us or we give up on them and the friendship dies.

In extreme situations, this change in our behavior leads to divorce, arrests, bankruptcies or loss of employment. All this happens because others can't understand why we've made such poor decisions. Only, now we have even more problems because they start labeling and excluding us. Eventually we start believing the labels they've given us. Because of this, we assume that the labelers have "discovered" our personal flaws and have made them public for all to see, and we become *more* distant and uninvolved with other people and society. This serves as a way for others to sever ties with us and justifies their use of labels and lets them exclude us (for all to see and criticize). These actions have a name. Let's call it what it is, "SEVERCIDE."

Unlike homicide and suicide—in which a human life is taken-- SEVERCIDE is an equally dangerous process that strips away our humanity, dignity and self-worth by denying who we are as individuals. Since the pursuit of happiness is in the Declaration of Independence, it is recognized as a right that should affect us personally. SEVERCIDE is an organized attempt to interfere with a person's ability to seek life, liberty and to pursue happiness.

SEVERCIDE reduces a person's place in society and can even make him or her, a non-person simply by applying labels. Fortunately, this can work only if we accept the labels and all that the labels can do to us. For example, our sad history of racial discrimination can continue only if we accept those labels and apply them amongst ourselves. I, for one, am more than the sum of my failures and defeats.

In the early part of the twentieth century, those who were labeled as "drunkards" became social rejects and were expected to end up in a mental institution or a prison or to die young. In other words, they were viewed as beyond help and not good enough to help. Thank God that there were people with character who did not give up the belief that others can change. Now in the twenty first century, we have come to accept what it means to have addictions and society has a new understanding of the problems caused by addiction and this has led to the return of hope.

There will always be groups and individuals that will resist such change, but the fact is that the "official" thinking on all this has changed dramatically. Because of this change, there is more government and private funding directed at "accepted healthcare practices," which has resulted in a social climate change where hope and acceptance have replaced the pessimism and social isolation of the past. As a single most-effective long-term example of this, look at Alcoholics Anonymous. This program sprang up between two drunks and their mutual rediscovery of hope and transformed lives. It did not come from a laboratory or the brilliant thoughts of a healthcare philosopher. It came from two men talking about their struggles.

Their experiences RESET the thinking of society and all current addiction treatment practices have since come from that climate of hope. Ultimately, twelve-step programs have developed all over the world to help with just about any personal challenge. It is unique in that it doesn't cost anything to use the programs. Some have asked,

"If it doesn't cost anything how could it possibly be worth anything?" You need only ask the millions of lives affected by attending these meetings. These things are true in most religions and even offer the non-believer a place to start when organizing their own experiences while making their own behavior changes.

In the 50s and 60s, America became caught up in the sexual revolution and alternately experienced a dramatic social upheaval that changed our values and our thinking. Prior to that point, society looked down at divorce. Yes, divorce happened, but those who were divorced felt shame and society called them "irresponsible and not very religious." Society disliked and did not approve of the divorced.

Consider the label "divorced" and what it meant in a person's life. A person was considered single again and also a failure at marriage. That failure was powerful and could affect all potential future relationships and maybe even social and business opportunities. Today, with the acceptance of divorce, there is little to no shame attached. Now it's fairly common and you are not considered a social outcast.

In the last part of the twentieth century, there was a rush to define every possible illegal activity and new laws were put in place. This helped authorities take a bigger bite out of crime. Additionally, every type of unacceptable behavior came with its own set of labels. A person charged with a crime is put in jail (unless they are rich enough to afford bond and a good lawyer) and then put on trial. Their personal information goes into several government, business and public computers. Few people understand how this information is going to be used. Fewer individuals are knowledgeable enough to worry about secure databases and the general climate of fear surrounding these security mechanisms.

This all comes at a cost—the cost of putting someone in jail and any financial loss from the crime itself. The long-term costs range from stigma and labeling to social separation. Through the use of labeling, a convict loses his or her individual rights as a citizen and now becomes invisible.

The label "felon" stirs up emotions and feelings of no longer being part of society. And the person's movements are restricted in more ways than one. Maybe it means they are now out of touch with the rest of society and their self-worth takes a tumble. They are now expected to be invisible and just disappear. The rest of us make ourselves more comfortable by telling ourselves "Thank goodness I'm not like them."

Another way to distance convicts from the rest of society is by stripping their right to vote. If you can't vote, you can't take part in government and this means you have no right to try to change things. Taking away the right to vote, especially for rehabilitated felons, makes as much sense as denying food to someone who has cancer. For the felon, he has been excluded from the voting club, while the growing cancer might be slowed down by the lack of food. Both of these "solutions" show how out of touch this kind of response-based thinking really is.

As a non-citizen-citizen, the felon still has to obey laws and pay taxes, but can't do anything to change either of these things like most citizens can. Correct me if I'm wrong, but wasn't that why we fought the American Revolution? If it didn't work then, who says it will work now? Doing the same thing over and over again and expecting a different result is one definition of in-sanity. The problem is that when the government does this, it's called policies, laws, rules or regulations. This is how the term SEVERCIDE was born.

SEVERCIDE happens when we are constantly denied the expression of self-worth and we have no demonstrable power to change. All we have now are labels and penalties. SEVERCIDE keeps us from feeling good enough to express ourselves. If genocide is the organized murder of groups of people who have been labeled worthless, then SEVERCIDE is the organized "extinguishing" of a person's right to hope that good things can happen to them.

As the Jews of Adolph Hitler's Germany were considered worthless, so too can many American be labeled as beyond redemption? This is what happens to people who try to make their way in the world while they are told they are invisible.

The answer to this strange "catch twenty-two" isn't to just accept SEVERCIDE or to go along with the current soothing promises of the mental health system. It is a personal challenge leading to re-discovering our own sense of humanity. Our hope comes from deep inside ourselves. It's a spiritual chance to change how we think of ourselves without giving into the destructiveness of society's labels. This change is known as KNOWETICS. It is an inside job of awareness and change using personal accountability.

CHAPTER 4

DOES THE DOCTOR KNOW BEST?

NOETICS (AN ANCIENT SPIRITUAL TERM) is a word that considers the relationship between "sin" and mental health problems. Unfortunately, the people who believed in NOETICS started to make a practice of what they thought would be remedies for the "sin" problem. Given human nature, it was not long before these "prescriptions for life changes" became hard to handle. It also meant that individuals began relying on others, rather than their own understanding of what was right and wrong. Professionals became "experts." Because of this, we learned to ignore that soft voice within us and let the doctors tell us how to fix our lives. Doesn't the "doctor know best?"

This process of NOETICS actually comes down to the fact that others may know what they think is happening in our lives, but we are the only one who really knows how the consequence of "sin" is experienced by us and how it is played out in our own lives. What goes on in our personal thoughts and experiences is pretty much beyond other people's understanding. That means that NO professional or helpful individual can find solutions to the problems in our lives. They can only go so far in helping with these problems.

Professionals can only come close when they diagnose and treat our problems. These therapists and professionals, through research and study, have come up with what they call "standards of care." Eventually these standards were organized into programs that licensed professionals believe in lock, stock and barrel.

Somewhere the value of our own human experience has become lost in what's called professional "truth." We move further away from the value of human experience. No wonder we often feel lost and confused. We're now living in the age of non-truth or truth without meaning.

If truth is vague and confusing, it loses all meaning and won't be used as a social compass. Truth and non-truth comes together and becomes the price you pay for being accepted in society. Who knows what "truth" they will use next? Which brings us to the question Pontius Pilate asked of Jesus Christ, "What is Truth?" (John 18:38 NIV). Truth is how your own experiences match up with what is considered holiness. Wait a minute—you're trying to preach religion to me! Not so.

Who can explain how much an individual life is worth? Within a single human life is the potential for solving life's problems, one person at a time. That is how much a human being is worth and can't be reduced to a label or category. We all count and we all contribute at some level to the experience we call life. Take one of us out of the mix and what's left is a big hole. Every individual has worth and potential and no human government can take away that hope. A legal or professional document can't destroy our hope. That would be like trying to put the light out in the universe.

There are lots of examples throughout history where others have tried to put limits on the human spirit. These efforts have failed because in the long run, it is impossible to de-value the lives of others. Again, another person can't impose his or her will on you. Not for long, at least. The only way this will succeed is if you allow someone to do this in your life.

You can't allow another person to tell you what type of life you should live. This is especially true if you accept who you are inside. I must remember that I am not what you label me; I am what I choose to become. Jesus Christ noted that the prostitutes and tax collectors (I am not sure about the IRS) were inheriting the Kingdom of Heaven before the "chosen" (Matthew 21:31 NIV).

This is a very revealing reflection on the value of labeling human behaviors in order to exclude individuals. I once knew a priest, Father Charles, who served as a Catholic chaplain in a state prison. He would regularly have meetings with leaders and members of various prison gangs. His skill as a priest was well served by his understanding of human nature. Prisoners rarely have the opportunity to enjoy a meal other than what they get routinely in prison. There was only one thing you had to do to get an invitation to one of Fr. Charles lunches. You had to show that you could sit next to others who were a different race or came from a different culture. You had to be able to get along. A skill learned as child.

He would often remind the prisoners as they enjoyed their meal that they had better learn to like each other since they were going to be neighbors in heaven for eternity. He could bring these different people—who would never have voluntarily gotten together with each other—together. Out of these quiet lunches, people were learning to talk to each other and this made quite a difference to the prisoners and even the staff of the prison. The prisoners generally enjoyed the chance to have an "outside" meal more than they wanted to show their personal hatreds and grievances, and so they changed their own behaviors for the sake of participating in this small pleasurable activity. They were even able to change their attitudes about other people different from themselves, a little more with each lunch arranged by Fr. Charles.

This even got the gang leaders talking. Father Charles looked beyond the label of "criminal" and he saw we all have the same human experiences. What he saw caused him to act with compassion and humanity. Many of those who participated in those modest lunches began soul-searching and looking at ways they could redeem themselves.

Most of these prisoners would never qualify for pardons. There is nothing very remarkable about them that would cause them to come before governors or presidents. Most have discovered that even if they were to be pardoned by authorities, this pardon has little value if they haven't been able to pardon their own failures. They have learned to rise above the labels, to repair their prior offenses to the best of their ability, and to restore the losses associated with their prior activities.

In effect they have reconnected with basic truth in their own lives and have developed their own pardon process. This is an exercise in self-directed redemption that may also transform the lives of their families, friends and community members. Such individuals have come to a place where they make peace with the world around them.

It is a carefully planned and executed journey. They have found meaning in the simpler things in life and this meaning doesn't change because of time, location or circumstances. It is the freest of human expressions: a true encounter with the human spirit.

This part of the human spirit can trigger a wealth of creativity and helps a person realize what strengths they have inside. It shifts the way a person feels about himself inside, what he lacks and what his limitations are, to a view of endless potential and expression. It shows that each individual has worth and does not seek selfish personal gain on the backs of others. As a result, we come to see our endless worth through spiritual eyes and our lives become changed forever.

Whether health issues, legal processes or other trauma have impacted one's life, the process of recovery begins with an awareness that life's mysteries are carefully played out around the simple idea of truth that we learned as a child. The rules have never really changed. Truth is truth. It always has been and always will be!

CHAPTER 5

CHILD'S VIEW OF THE SEVEN DEADLY SINS

TO SOME EXTENT OUR INDIVIDUAL personalities are the result of choices we have made to reduce conflict in our lives. Likely, we were taught from infancy an endless list of do's and don'ts. But as we've grown older, we've had the benefit of learning the principles that help us live our lives.

We have heard endless variations on play nice, don't steal, or don't tell lies because, if you do, no one will believe you. Eventually we find ourselves in a crisis, trying to understand why the people we love the most lie despite the fact they told us NOT to lie. It doesn't take long to figure out that people don't always tell the truth, but I am expected to be truthful always? Wait a second, how does that work?

Add to that mystery, the pecking order for truth that we start to realize as we get taller and older. The smart child learns to weave the truth depending on the situation. Those of us less bright usually got caught in an awkward half lie and denied we'd ever tell a lie. Then to add to this confusion, what's with the so-called little "white lie"? Another piece of the puzzle is when we heard grown-ups say, "I did it for your own good."

Will the truth never stop changing or do we tell ourselves that truth really depends upon the moment? If the truth is used only to act as a go-between every time we find ourselves in a jam with people bigger than us, how will I ever believe it when the scripture tells us that God's Word is Truth and that Truth leads to life?

If people do not always tell the truth, what does that say about God who has created me and everyone else? What does it say about those persons and things that support religious teachings? Very early in my life, I began to realize that there are many different ways to solve all problems. Grade one, lesson one—to tell the truth or not tell the truth!

Children are usually blessed with the gift of innocence and so they generally see things in black and white. Sometimes adults get a lot of enjoyment when they see their children making the right choices. At other times grownups wonder "where did that come from?" when they see their children do something that they know the child got from watching their bad examples. This begins a dance that will continue throughout our lives, whenever we have interactions with others.

Either through religious instruction, formal education, or even through experimentation, we discover what is known as the seven deadly sins. Depending on the age of the child and their level of experience, the "deadly sins" rarely affect their day-to-day life. It is only when we start to wrestle with personal sin that we are able to understand how our choices bring about consequences.

As a child, I remember thinking that the sin of pride would never have much to do with my life. I thought of myself as small and not very important, definitely not able to have any effect on the lives of others. As a teenager, I was accused of causing fights between my mother and father and I couldn't figure out how I could have that much power. I got scared thinking that, since I had no idea I had any power, I wouldn't be able to control this power in the future.

This really was a frightening experience as a child to think about what this meant. Then later, when I learned about demon possession, I decided I was a hopeless cause.

When somebody is hopeless, they are beyond help, beyond hope. At that point, I made the decision to live my life for myself, since I didn't seem to be able to follow the rules. It was a very important decision for a young child to make. I had decided to disconnect. This is how I began my formal education in personal spirituality: I determined I have the final say in whether something is right or wrong in my life.

At this point, it may be helpful to look at what these seven "deadly" sins mean. Now that I'm an adult, they have taken on a different meaning than I knew as a child. They have become easier to understand because of experience.

I'm no longer an innocent child trying to make sense of my world. The older I got, the more I realized that I had become an expert at these deadly sins in my personal life and because of that, my life has been filled with storms and struggles.

The sins themselves go by the familiar names of Pride, Envy, Sloth, Anger, Lust, Malice and Greed. Looking at them in print, they don't look like they have the power to make anyone misbehave.

However, all you have to do is glance at the daily newspaper or internet and you'll see plenty of examples of their practice in our lives. It seems like we're immune to the shock of finding out just how many people accept all of this. Or maybe we just tolerate, even prefer, all the drama these actions produce in the lives of others.

When I was a child, I thought like a child. Now I am an adult and I have managed to convince myself that what was right is wrong and what is wrong is now right. When I was a child, abortion was wrong and anyone involved in it were murderers. When I was a child, suicide wasn't considered a healthcare option. It was still wrong to lie, cheat, and steal.

As a child I didn't know anything about the sin of lust, nor could I imagine what coveting meant. Now the media have happily decided that these truths are old school and any other opinions aren't keeping up with the times.

My friend, what I have discovered is that truth will always be truth. It never changes and IT WILL SET US FREE (John 8:32 NIV). So let personal truth become something we re-discover. One element of that truth is the fact that I am a child of God. I am a birthright and a gift.

Truth has to be the starting point in any attempt to re-discover your life and transform your future. If you currently lie, cheat or steal, start by recognizing you are choosing this behavior. The best place to begin is back in childhood when you first heard "do as I say, not as I do." Try to focus on that crisis point when you abandoned the hope of being "good" and resigned yourself to being "bad."

That was a remarkable moment that led to your giving up on your dreams and goals, and accepting the realities of "growing up." You disconnected from things that nurtured your spirit, and changed your diet to a stream of maybes, ought to's and should have's suggested by the actions of others. For most of us, it was not a definitive moment in time, though these experiences may have had a dramatic effect at the moment. It usually was a process, sometimes subtle and sometimes not. Surprisingly, we found that we are not in Kansas anymore. The rules had changed.

Is good health the mere absence of bad health or the absence of disease? I think not. Likewise, truth is not the absence of other realities, nor is the presence of non-truth a defining point. It is an invitation to return to essential thinking and re-connect with the fact that truth doesn't change.

You have been and always will be a child of God with all the rights and privileges given you by being a member of the family. It may be time to let "Dad" help us to cast away the chaff of our lives and re-claim our individual gifts and abilities. Each of us may add to the picture He is painting.

So what do I do with all of the labels? Get out the big, big, big trash bag and start dumping them in one at a time. When does a murderer stop being a murderer? Or when does a rapist stop being a rapist? What about the common every day variety of liar? Of course, the answer is incredibly simple; it is when they stop their offending behaviors.

Once you stop the offensive behaviors and accept God's help, you acquire a new nature: a sort of coming together that takes you from lost to saved.

Does that mean I am still to be burdened by past sins, failures or defeats? Society only has the ability to disapprove. Would you willingly go to someone who always reminded you of your past problems? No, it would get old very soon. Psychology's old thought is that the best indication for new behaviors is based upon our sad history of old behaviors.

Somehow, the field of mental health care can only offer us the thought that every behavior has a distinct cause. Again, we have to decide if we are slaves of the mental health professionals or the liberating freedom of truth. Behavioral healthcare offers descriptions and generalities, while the law industry offers us inflexible rules, rigid labels and punishment without pardon.

It is a trap, which we have been told to accept. All rights and privileges associated with life—our life—flow from the Giver of Life. God is the giver of all gifts and He graciously gives them to His children without playing the blame game. In spite of our errors, He still takes care of us every day. He invites us to reason with Him (Isaiah 1:18 NIV) and guides us with the scriptures.

As I have read His Word, the Bible, I am regularly happy to find lots of examples of God's ability to change so many Bible character's lives. He gave meaning to their most misguided and misinformed actions if they were willing to begin a conversation with Him. The burden we bear is not heavy or wearisome for Him.

My life experiences, a doctorate in Clinical Psychology and a thorough study of the Bible has convinced me that society doesn't help us change our behavior. God's Word, as it tells the story of the life of Jesus Christ, shows us mercy, forgiveness and pardon. It is not a CHILDISH BELIEF; IT IS A PROMISED CERTAINTY. This gives every person the right to change and hope for a good future. So who are you going to believe, the guy (hint: red suit and pointed tail) who keeps telling you what a loser you are or The Giver of all life (1 Timothy 6:13 NIV)?

How do I connect with this hope and promise? I re-connect with the basic truth that I learned as a child and I start to practice truth in all areas of my life. Truth has never been untruthful or unclear. It is a sure hope and certainty. So whom are you going to believe?

I don't care how far down the scale of life you've fallen. Your experience can help someone else. You have great value in God's plan. Working with God and accepting your own accountability, you can put together your own pardon plan and start the work of changing your life. Make amends whenever possible and restore to others what is rightfully theirs.

As Jesus urged the woman caught in the sin of adultery, "Sin no more" (John 8:11 NIV). You can be assured that both she and Rahab were welcomed to the bosom of Abraham by their first name, not by the labels society had put on them. Score two for God and zero for the system. If He has done this for Rahab, the harlot, won't He do the same for us? He is interested in our future while society is interested in our past. So if you are greedy, slothful, angry, lustful, prideful, or full of envy or malice, you are just the person I am hoping to meet. On top of all that if you have been to jail or prison, have a terminal diagnosis of HIV/AIDS or some other fatal disease, if you have been divorced (multiple times even) or have been bankrupt, fired and labeled a liar publicly, then the value of your personal stock has just increased. We are on the way to heaven; all you need to do to get on the bus is to re-connect with the truth your spirit knows and recognizes.

The promises of God's Word are not just for some future time or place. They are to be lived now. Join me in the adventure of a lifetime. Let's make something happen together. Let's decide and focus on one small part of our current lives and start a brand new life right now. This new life starts with recognizing our personal worth and dignity. Small beginnings are still worthy of God's blessing. Let's start by recognizing each other as once-hidden expressions of God's love for us. While I am busy finding ways to express my love and concern for you, I won't have any time or reason left to harm you. My relationship is no longer just with you, but is full, trying to match my life with my spiritual responsibilities.

With this shift in thinking, you get to make your own decisions through the power of choice. I no longer make choices out of fear. I can now live my life hopefully and productively. All of this comes to my life through the "fruits of the Spirit" (Galatians 5:22-23 NIV).

I'm not going to be making as many selfish choices as I did before and I start to see the world as one big opportunity to work out my problems by working with the problems of others. I will have enough time and enough resources to carry out my purposes on earth.

God will do for me what I can't do for myself. By working toward new goals and being accountable, I can rise above society's attempt to measure my self-worth or to define or label me by what I did in the past. That is a true spiritual experience. My worth is based on my being a child of God. I am defined by His respect and love for me. After all, He sent His son Jesus to pay the price of my sinful life and to release me from fault and labeling. He really does love me!

Chapter 6

THE "W" WORD

REALISTICALLY, LONGER PRISON TERMS HAVE failed economically and socially, but the financial world and its expected profits from mass incarceration helped to create a boom of prison building. With this, we gained something new and that is the creation of prisons for profit.

We moved the idea of incarceration as a societal reality one more step away from our personal lives and linked the values of (perceived) sound business management to outcomes associated with the most basic and intimate struggles in our lives. It's all part of the justice business now.

Even mental health systems are now bringing science into management. And might I add, this is brought to us by those annoying folks who are part of the new high-tech justice and public security scheme.

All it took to build this new way of doing things was by beating the war drum, abusing fear-based thinking and spending billions of dollars.

The concept of war seems to fascinate Americans. It offers the romanticized notion of great conquests and the still famous patriots of the past.

You too can be a vital part of the war effort. Ah, the promise of war and the hints of triumph in the air cause young men to enlist and old men to re-live past glory. Today even women want to be active participants in the struggles of war.

War-like thinking has energized the planning and performance of many programs in society. This offers the hope of winning the war and celebrating the victory. The problem is that there appears to be no end in sight to "war-like" thinking.

Instead, this country got involved in yet another war—the war on crime—that has resulted in the development of the prison industrial complex. Like the military industrial complex, it has been long on promises and short on delivery.

Both of these have continued to cost a great deal of state and national money with legislators crying out songs of death, devastation, destruction and despair.

We have grown so unmoved by the message that we didn't hear the bugle blowing the same tune—only with different words—every time election year rolls around.

I have lived long enough to have been inducted as a draftee into the war on communism. Others wars include the war on fellow travelers and those which have tried to subvert the American way of life: the war on drugs, the war on crime, the war on child abuse, the war on illegal immigration, the war on Medicare fraud, the war on tax fraud and waste, and the war in which we are currently engaged, the war on terrorism with its basic worries over security.

Remarkably, we have been at some sort of war for almost a century, either at home or across the world, and sometimes simultaneously. These wars have been fought one right after another starting (in the 20th century) with World War I, World War II, the Korean War, The War in Vietnam, The Wars in the Middle East and the now-global War on Terrorism. Not to mention all the "police actions" we've gotten ourselves into.

I am personally tired of war-based planning, preparing our soldiers and constant worry over funding the war. When will the war mentality stop and when will we come to our senses?

We, as a country, have given our blessing to anything or anyone threatening to use that "W" word. Using this fear and knee-jerk response has become the main way of doing the business of the people. So now, we have a government where there is no room for the "people." There are only policies, practices, financial initiatives and election results.

Our government was founded on the principle that it is "of the people, for the people and by the people." Unfortunately, the people have become "them," and not "us." No government can be for the people if it doesn't plan for their basic human rights. Millions of people are not in the loop. To win the hearts and the minds of the "people" you need to *be* one of us and be one *with* us.

Perhaps what we talked about earlier (legal practices, the business of healthcare or access to basic human rights) needs to be revisited.

A long week's work in a coal mine will get your clothes dirty, but it will also open your mind to what it means to live a coal miner's life. A few days of bagging groceries at a major food store for eight dollars and some odd cents per hour, and you'll remember what it means to hope and dream again.

Or how about spending a few days in a major prison or trying to figure out how you can try to stay safe, dry and warm on any street on a November night by laying on a piece of cardboard and covering yourself with newspapers, rags or bits of plastic. How about eating your dinner out of trash bins located behind food stores and restaurants. If these make you cringe, you have little or no idea what it's like for many of YOUR fellow citizens.

A recent online news article discussed the lives of released sex offenders living together under a bridge in Florida. This was the result of state-sanctioned social segregation laws (SEVERCIDE) making it impossible for them to live (alone or together) in any community within the state.

Another example is the ever-growing number of fatal police shootings that continue to create fast and furious "nuisance" claims, in even the most obvious and well-documented cases of human rights violations.

A recent raid by government agents into the homes of several student loan borrowers shows us that the government has its priorities straight and knows how best to use our tax dollars. It's us against them, RIGHT?

We are a nation in a serious crisis of character and economics given how much we're spending. We have no long-term plan to fix the problems.

As early as 1991, Peter Schwartz wrote about taking the long view in his book *The Art of the Long View*. Since its publication, we've continued to spend and spend here at home and internationally draining the economy of trillions we'll never recover. The most moving loss has been the loss of lives and the loss of the chance to contribute that could come from the non-citizen citizens. It's not reasonable or rational to cut these people (US) out of the process.

What we call government today, and the things that are happening now, would horrify our founding fathers. A government that doesn't recognize this situation is only worried about itself, not the betterment of its people. Thomas Jefferson recognized this possibility by noting, "when injustice becomes law, resistance becomes duty."

Like a corporation, the government lives and breathes by the actions of its members, so you'd think that it would at least discuss the problem to see if there are any new insights or new information that might help.

Instead the government refuses to respond to the problem. Oh, they've come up with a few short-term answers with new laws. It's the same type of response cycle that the homeless individual and his assortment of newspapers, rags and bits of plastic are using to keep them alive in bad weather conditions. No response is a response!

When did we become a nation that could deny the possible contributions of some of its citizens while making it hard for others to make personal changes or "legally" denying basic human rights to still others? All people have value because they are created by God.

History is repeating itself in a new location. Same show, new day. What people fail to realize is that what happens to me now, will eventually happen to you, using the same laws, as soon as they discover that you are somehow different too.

Remember that the Jews of Germany were soon joined by Greeks, Italians and Poles, Catholics, Baptists (many others) and assorted non-believers (political prisoners) who voiced opposition to the abuse of individual human rights.

Besides trying to let others know about our country's problems, the purpose for writing this book is to give people the tools to change their behavior without the usual response to behavior issues that don't always work and can burden the system. We all need to have hope that change is possible.

If you have personally experienced the effects of SEVERCIDE, you're going to learn about how this happens and is considered legal social discrimination. The readers who have only heard whispers of these practices may want to get involved in response to policies put into practice in their name and endorsed by lawmakers who believe that they have been elected to create social change at the expense of the citizens.

Do you remember when Ronald Reagan almost took the funding away from HIV/AIDS research and encouraged world leaders to do the same? The economic and social costs of that decision have ruined millions of lives and taken us from a national problem into a world problem.

Do you remember when Richard Nixon resigned the presidency of the United States? Somehow the office of president has never recovered. The title of POTUS (President of the United States) no longer stirs the same respect that it carried before the Nixon presidency.

One more example is the Kennedy Brothers assassinations and the murder of Martin Luther King. These events ended the desire of many and the hope to help reshape the American dream.

Through of all this, I learned that I cannot control outside events, but I also learned to reflect and respond to important events on a personal and societal level.

Personal change is usually the most successful way to inner peace and acceptance. KNOWETICS shows how behavior change is an inside job.

PART THREE
HOPE AND THE PROMISE OF PERSONAL REDEMPTION

Chapter 7

THE BASIC INGREDIENTS AND THE RECIPE

BY NOW, YOU MUST BE wondering how this process is all tied together in a meaningful way. Theology can be thought of as the recipe, and spirituality is the basic ingredient.

Remember how I told you about Quinta's cooking? About how if we engaged in a cooking project together using the same recipe and ingredients, my wife and myself would produce two dishes so different from each other you'd have a hard time believing we used the same cooking process?

This is not a discussion about which meal is the best. I might very well be pleased and happy with what I made, however; you might not like it. Really, it's a matter of individual expression. How did we end up with two dishes so completely different?

The ancient concept of NOETICS talks about the modern day relationship between sin and mental health by urging us to think about what these two things have to do with each other. So God's Word also talks about our spirituality in relationship to personal worth and dignity.

If I accept as complete truth what society says about my worth and dignity, then I get all caught up in the ever-changing idea of multiple truths. God's Word is the ultimate statement on me as a person; all others thank you for your opinions!

So what role does personal spirituality play in the drama of my life? If the recipe is God's Word, spirituality must be the basic ingredient. What I do with it in my life will define my life experience and transform the recipe into the finished product.

For our purposes, I want to focus on five basic ingredients available to each of us every day. These ingredients have the power to transform a life of defeat and failure (labels) into personal victory that no man can deny. The truth is we are of endless value; that we can be molded and shaped into happy, useful and productive lives by consistently using the basic ingredients with the guidance of the ultimate recipe for life, God's Word!

Therefore, it is essential to become familiar with what God has to say about us as His child, or we will have missed the opportunity to claim our birthright. He says you are mine (Ephesians 1:13-14 NIV). He says that He loves us passionately! He says that we have great worth (Psalms 139:13-16 NIV). This is evidenced by His willingness to send His Son to pay the price for my sinful life and assures us a place among the family members of God.

There is nothing to debate because His word clearly tells us about the concepts of mercy, grace, forgiveness, faith and hope. These are the basic ingredients of spirituality.

If I'm not familiar with these ingredients, I can't possibly hope to use them to build a new life. If I don't know that something exists, then I can't use it to help me make decisions or a plan for my life.

What if I've got so many labels I can't possibly see my way through the struggles? We already know what society has to say about such things, but let's hear what God has to say.

Let's not jump into the body of scripture because it could overwhelm us. Instead, let's keep it simple and find our place in the simple message of individual worth that is part of the entire story about the possibility of having a relationship with God in the Bible.

God tells me that I am the apple of His eye (Zechariah 2:8). He uses the examples of what He has done in other lives to show me what He can do in my life. He uses my mistakes to shape my life into something of value (Samson) (Judges 16:1-31 NIV).

He also clearly states that I am not as responsible for what happens to me as how I react to what's happened (Joseph) (Genesis 37:1-50 NIV).

God also promises to use my limitations and failures—despite the sinfulness of my life (Gideon) (Judges 6-8 NIV). God promises that His presence in my frail life with others will overcome those things that otherwise could cause divisions among us (Ruth and Naomi) (Ruth 1-4 NIV).

He promises that a person's background isn't going to keep Him from personally working in our lives (Jephthah) (Judges 11:29-40 NIV). I don't expect there to be any background checks for entry to Heaven's glory. He also states that our loyalty to Him puts every other relationship into correct perspective (Jonathan) (1 Samuel 19-21 NIV).

So what does this mean in practical terms? Even the lives of death row prisoners have great potential value though they are in prison. They could spend their time praying for others and working for social justice by small acts of kindness to unseen members of society.

When prisoners in the dungeons of the California state penal system sponsored a drive to raise funds for worthy projects (their prison work earnings ranged from ten cents to twenty-five cents an hour), these proceeds were **not** separated out from the funds given by other citizens.

In other words, the lepers came forth bearing a very meaningful gift for others who were less fortunate than them. Among the rejected of society a small light of compassion shone forth. That's the indefinable human spirit at work. That same spirit is alive and working in your life. The very fact that you are reading this book means that you are seeking answers to your questions about life's choices.

How does that spark of life happen in a fortress of pain among those labeled as deviates, anti-socials and assorted other terms? If nothing else, it can assure us that there is something more to these lives than the labels associated with their prior behaviors.

In God's economy, everyone has worth. Do you remember the story of the widow's two mites (Luke 21:1-4 NIV; Mark 12:41-44 NIV)? Nothing is neglected in His care for us. What others fail to see as worthy in our lives, He considers small hopeful steps toward a future with Him.

If I have lived a life of shame, grief or humiliation as a result of my past personal failures, can I honestly think I'm in line for real forgiveness? While God has forgiven me, surely I must continue to be weighed down with society's labels. Wrong. Starting today, it is important to claim your inheritance as a child of God.

I can happily reflect upon the many brothers and sisters who have come into my life to serve as role models, teachers or friends who accepted me with all of my flaws and showed me the love of God in the way they treated me. Most of these people who managed to change their own character helped me and led me by example, without the use of words.

These included the nuns (Dominicans of Amityville) who provided me with a rich elementary school education as well as the Marist Brothers who were convinced that I was a blockhead in high school. Their spiritual urgings and my parent's fervent prayers became the foundation upon which my life later took shape after gaining sobriety at age thirty-one. Some of us had a longer adolescence than others!

Others include: my family—who withstood such horrible suffering by witnessing one major failure after another—all while not knowing if the personal ruin would ever end. Ron Wynn, a gentle giant who sowed seeds of personal worth during the most trying experience of my life. Dave Whipple, a quiet civil servant who never failed to plant spiritual seeds in my life through his actions. Adolph Johnson, who made a similar discovery about spirituality and eagerly kept in touch with me, his brother in faith. Dr. Lorraine Howard, whose bright personality and cheerfulness helped as I started learning to measure myself by where I currently am against where I had come from. Lou, who, out of the depths of his own personal tragedy, found the time and energy to reach out to a labeled person early in the redemptive process. Or there's John, a true model of Christian spirit in action.

Also, there's the personal encouragement of Dr. Wayne G., whose gently-chiding manner moved me along the path of personal and professional development. Or Buck, Kitty, Drs. Stephanie and Jim, M., and Dr. Sam McQ., who, over hours of conversation, unwittingly helped me develop awareness about my need to rise above life's past failures and set about the task of using my experiences, training, education, skills and abilities to reach out to others.

Also still is the later encouragement of Henry Johnson, who always came by with a fresh viewpoint on God's Word and his personal encouragement for me to apply it directly to my life. George and Dona, whose candid and distinctly human manner served as a model of Christian kindness, John W., a knightly sort of fellow whose daily battles on behalf of his clients provides hope for many. And to Fr. Louis of Long Beach and Fr. Paddy of Biloxi, both whose loving acceptance helped me through a recent, particularly destructive period in my own life, without losing hope.

I could also mention my God-directed travels, which led to meeting my wife Quinta in a Christian chat room (Meet Christians.com). She has become a pivotal part of the enhanced knowledge about how spiritual influences impact our lives, and with meeting Quinta, subsequently the introduction and later acceptance into the Situmorang family.

These people mentioned are a sample of the human markers that have opened my awareness and served as models of accountability. This handful of people met me in intelligent, spiritual, witty and meaningful ways. Each has contributed to this project. They shared special gifts with me and helped me create the idea of KNOWETICS through expressions of their love and the care they showed me. Religious or non-religious, all of these individuals (and others) have helped me to forge an understanding about of the importance of applying spiritual solutions along with accountability.

The reason for this brief summary of remarkable people who influenced me is to highlight the importance of working with others with whom you can develop trust and accountability. So please take note that while I'm sharing with you the basic ingredients of change, they must be shaped by your relationships with others. You can start to re-define your worth through the words of others and through your commitment to opening up. This whole process thrives in the enriched soil of loving acceptance.

What about the ideas found in ancient NOETICS—the thought that our sinful life has a direct effect on our mental health? This is just a starting point in understanding how we are creatures of habit. We start with conflict, ultimately resulting in pain—to ourselves and others—and the loss of hope.

It does not matter right now what you have done in your secret or private life. It starts with a decision, a choice and a willingness to let your spirit be bathed in God's love for you. It begins when you start to re-connect with that inner self-worth you experienced as a child. Do you remember the joy of just being alive?

Find some piece of your personal history to hang onto—a piece that helped you understand your uniqueness. It is important to sit down and write about this inner discovery so you can keep it in focus; otherwise, like all of the other good ideas you've had, it will float away and be lost to the moment.

Writing about that time in your life will help you to pull other pieces into focus. Try to remember a time when you discovered your individual personhood—a time before the labels started to transform your life. Can you remember being pleased with yourself?

Most of us had a time, however brief, when we were a sweet and happy child. Searching through those memories may trigger feelings of anxiety or discomfort as you remember those special moments in your life. If you begin to experience inner turmoil, it's time to ask God to remind you of His view of you as a child. A simple dialogue to help begin the search can go something like this, "Lord, help me look back and see myself as *You* saw me as a joyful child." God doesn't make junk; so right from the beginning of your life you were a precious child of God.

Next, can you remember a time early in your life when you were proud of some small personal success? It might have been a gold star on a schoolwork page, a good citizenship award or some other form of recognition. Dwell for a short time on the happiness of that moment, and reflect on the pleasure you experienced. Think of how it made you feel knowing that you were capable of being a good child—a child who could exercise self-control. You were a child who wanted to please others in your family and school because it made you happy with yourself. At that particular time in your life, you were a happy, healthy child in spite of your surroundings or limitations. You were spiritually sound.

At some point, we came to understand that not everything we did was appreciated by grownups, but we were usually able to find comfort in people we trusted—those who knew we were worth something and who lovingly accepted us for who we were. Unfortunately, some people instead found this time in life made them feel terribly alone and unsure of themselves.

Let me take a break from these ideas for a moment to tell you a story. One day, after noticing a gnawing in my stomach, I drove to a local restaurant that serves the official and traditional Monday meal in the New Orleans area—Red Beans and Rice with sausage. (I tell my out-of-town friends, it's like tasty oatmeal served for dinner.) During dinner, I had the opportunity to launch into a philosophical discussion with Nikki—my waitress and newfound friend. Somehow, the conversation turned to things that you might never share with others—about feelings of discomfort and isolation. The question came up about sharing news of an indiscretion and whether you'd share it at all. Nikki, without hesitation, stated that she would tell her mother immediately, and then her husband later. Right away, I realized that Nikki had a special relationship with her mother that she'd been able to maintain through the years. Her answer clearly showed that she could say anything to her mother and not be judged harshly.

Her next comment showed how comfortable she was when she stated, "You have to get it out and talk about it or it will eat you up." The meal was great, but the conversation was even better. It helped me understand better the "secret" feelings of a healthy, open and responsive adult.

I walked away from that brief encounter convinced that Nikki was the type of person who gives straightforward and honest answers. She is also the type of person who can hear any kind of information. She is a quality adult who does not need sugarcoating to hear the truth. Her honest answer to this hypothetical question made it easier to outline the next part of this chapter.

Children struggle with making sense of his or her often-confusing life and, try to understand often-conflicting information. A child doesn't always have someone who will explain the difference between being bad and misbehaving. Because of this, that child is likely to decide that they are bad, while others are good. This is even more confusing because the child sees their role models making mistakes. For example, the parent or caregiver might tell the child to always tell the truth; then, instruct this child to tell a caller that he or she is not home —even though they are. Wow! How does that one work in the mind of a child? Possibly thoughts such as, "Obviously, honesty is not the policy at home, so how do I apply this new information to the prospects of punishment? I will learn to choose my lies well and *try and* keep them down to things that won't be looked at too closely." But inside the child might become sad and conflicted when they lie and get away with it. This creates another problem. Since the adults aren't helping, the child can't figure out what will happen if he or she tells the truth.

So gradually and quietly, this sad little child learns a tragic lesson, how to tell a lie and not feel bad about it. It is such a silent process; it usually goes unnoticed by most family members (unless the lie is extremely obvious). Through this strange little process, the child now creates a secret life of his or her own.

Now let's talk about theft. Let's say the child develops an overpowering urge to own something that does not belong to him or her, and in a moment of weakness, takes this treasured object. However, while looking over the item, he or she begins to feel bad inside, suddenly aware of the fact that they have stolen something and cannot make it right, even by putting the item back. Now there is a conflict—*I already took it so I am a thief; and even if I put it back, I'm still going to know I stole it.*

As a result, the child may throw away his or her object, or it gets put into some junk box where it is likely to never see the light of day again. The secret life has now gotten larger. The child begins pulling away from the life of being good. As if in a slow mysterious dance, the child can envision being pulled away from goodness with no way to come back to how it was before the theft.

Now, let's add labeling to this. The child may approach a point of no return—a point in which they can't see any possibility to change what happened. This creates the grim question. *How do I accept myself as being beyond hope?* This is an awful burden for a child to bear . . . so the child gives up!

The secret life continues to appear through cheating, gossip or just plain meanness. Punishment becomes a way of life—including all that comes with trying to encourage the child to think about the consequences of what they've done.

Unfortunately, this child has been doing nothing but thinking about all the confusion in his or her life. *If I can't figure out what I'm thinking, how could I ever find the words to tell you? Even if I could put all my thoughts and feelings in order, I have no way of knowing how you will respond to my troubled life.*

Remember, when you look at an iceberg, you see only a small bit of its size above water. The tip of the iceberg for a troubled child struggling with a secret life is rarely identified for what it is: a sea of confusion, uncertainly and anxiety. Once committed to this secret life, a child sets out to become captain of his or her own ship. Most parents and caregivers have no idea that the ship has already sailed, much less that this child has developed a secret life to help them make sense of his or her world.

Pre-adolescence and teen years put them on separate paths to the lands of "that makes me feel good" and the awkwardness of all sorts of sexual issues. These early visits to the land of lust may lead to the use of pornography (generally viewed as an acceptable adult form of entertainment) in the form of all kinds of e-media or just good old conversation between friends.

* * *

Once I have crossed over this boundary line, I feel that there is NO GOING BACK under any circumstances. While I burn with a newfound sense of excitement and curiosity, I struggle with my secret shame and my secret sin. Eventually those people around me keep telling me that this is all perfectly normal and encourage me to keep it up. Oh boy! There is fun ahead.

I'm lost and on my way to hell, so I might as well enjoy the trip. No one is going to miss me anyway. They never did know me. Off I drift into the endless sea of compromise and feeling off balance while my flimsy boat heads toward Destruction Shoals. I'm out here now I might as well make the best of it.

Oops, I think I heard the bottom of the boat scraping, well it's not too important now, I have already been thrown out of school, branded a trouble-maker and I have completed my first practical lesson in civics, with the experience of my first arrest and a short time in jail. I guess it is just the luck of the draw, seems to me, that the others in jail were normal people just like me. By the way, what was that connection's contact information? I may need it soon.

At this point, I don't want to go back, even if I could. I've earned enough labels now to distinguish myself somehow. Besides, if they didn't know me way back when, they could never begin to understand me now. Still, a warm bed, clean clothes and a nice meal would be appreciated.

Onwards the journey continues with an ever-growing sense that there is no other way (no other choices). I simply can't remember a time when I was young, happy and loved. Well, if it hasn't ever been that way for me, maybe I can find someone, settle down and make it happen for them and me ...

Before long, life has become mind numbing and without any happiness: Lots of other distractions, though. Boy, I'm glad for those constant distractions, because I am soooo bored!

On and on the days cycle by like some pretend weird Kabuki dance, ah, but at least watching the drama in everyone else's life is interesting and amusing. And for your information, I have thought about college, a job and church, always in that order. But don't start pushing me again. I have plenty of time for all of those things, right?

Totally unaware of what's coming next, the storms start, one after another. Fired. Divorced. Bankrupt. Imprisoned. Round One!

Divorced again. Drugging and drinking is my daily routine. Stealing "professionally," I smile. Round Two, Round Three and so forth ...

The slide into the spiritual black hole goes on, while I enjoy watching everything going on around me. I am strangely blind and deaf, but the trip is not really so bad. Yes, I do believe that's the floor rushing up at me, Wham!

Afterwards, when I come to my senses, I'm sitting on the floor of life surrounded by all my labels, some earned and some not earned, trying to find some order in my life. Life is in absolute shambles for me and those close to me. Not what I had expected. By the way, where are we?

I know I'm someplace, but it's definitely not Oz!

Decision time: Time to figure out how I lost my way. I can always go see my clergy, doctor or lawyer and they will help put me straight. Oh boy,

I really don't want to tell them everything. I'll share just those things they already know. Same advice, different day!

* * *

Remedy: Start at the beginning and try to remember that one point where you decided to turn away. The one time you made a decision leading you to feel you could never (ever) be good enough again. Do you feel the pain in the young child's heart? That's your heart we're talking about. Your heart is breaking and all you can think about is running away from the pain and shame—as far and as fast as your legs will carry you. Boy, if there were a circus of other people just like me, I would run away and join them!

Listen quietly to the stirrings that reach out to you and assure your heart that there is a place like that for you—with a lot of others who are just like you! You push forward and join the other "freaks" like you. But that's the point of disconnect where you started to abandon all hope of having joy. So you decide to grab at anything—any opportunity you could find to run away.

* * *

NOW, that is the moment I want you to go back to. Everything you've seen since then is directly related to the decision to disconnect. It is such a sore and tender spot; you won't have any problem finding it— though you have spent your whole life trying to avoid it.

That was the point you truly began to see yourself as bad and unworthy of being loved. If you want to move on and change your life, you have to go back and revisit that moment with the sensitivity and understanding of an adult looking at the sad troubles of a small child.

It is a most-painful problem you had in your young life, but if you can continue to work through the process and talk about it with someone who will keep you accountable, you've completed the hardest part of your journey.

You will need to find a "Nikki" for yourself—someone who is willing to tell you the truth, someone who speaks to you from his or her own heart and who throws you a life vest and a safety line. This person doesn't have to be a professional at this point, but must be willing to tell you the truth. In the back of this book there are some comments dedicated to helping you look for this kind of person.

Thank God, you can find them just about anywhere. Once you've worked through that moment you ran away from other people, we are ready to figure out how you can get back home.

Don't just take a quick look at this point in your life; be like Scrooge who was forced to look at the dark future without himself or Tiny Tim. Look and imagine how things would have been different if only you could have called out for help.

Feel the loneliness and loss of that moment and everything after it. Take your time thinking about these experiences, but remember this child's tender years and their early loss of innocence. Then and only then, can you start to ask God for help in going back and re-connecting with that sweet child.

By the time you get to this point in your self-examination, God will have already stepped up with His big bag of tools and will have begun the process of laying them out for you to use. Those tools are the best way for you to re-connect with the person you lost: you! These tools are always available for free, and you don't need a church membership card. So they are a theology-free gift from God for you to use right away.

Let's go back to those recipe ingredients we talked about earlier. You have to know the nature of the basic ingredients and how they may add to the dinner you'll eventually create. Having a dish of all chicken or fish, and no rice or vegetables, would be an unexciting meal. A meal made without spices would be bland, but too much spice and we won't be able to eat it. A meal made without cooking oil would probably end up burnt and ruined by too much heat.

Only through your own efforts, along with God's help, will you be able to figure out the correct amount and timing required to cook individual ingredients into a great meal (work out your own salvation, Philippians 2:12 NIV). You may be surprised at the strong effect of some of your ingredients as you learn to work with them.

So what are these ingredients again? They are: Mercy, Grace, Forgiveness, Faith and Hope.

You will need these ingredients when you ask God for help in getting home again. It is such an intensely private moment—maybe as intense as the moment you disconnected in the first place. Only this time, the pain is replaced with unspeakable joy and inner peace. That's a promise!

When you use the ingredients in the recipe, you are in for a life-changing event. It does not matter what kind of labels you hang onto or how many you have collected, God is telling you to trust Him and throw them away NOW! Your first new label: I am a child of God!

* * *

Mercy: Understanding, clemency, kindness and compassion.
Grace: God's undeserved favor for you and me.
Forgiveness: Absolution, pardon, amnesty and exoneration.

Faith: Trust, reliance, assurance, confidence and conviction.

Hope: Anticipating, expecting, desiring, wishing, a sense of optimism.

* * *

In the following pages, I will try to help you understand how each of these are a part of God's plan, and I'll give you examples of His promises being used today!

A CAUTIONARY NOTE

NOW THAT YOU HAVE DEVELOPED insight into the arbitrary nature of governmental processes and the reality of social indifference which pervades the implementation of laws, policies and procedures on one hand and now understand the pressures brought to bear on individuals and families through worldly influences on the other hand, this knowledge does NOT grant us a license to resist the rule of law or to dismiss the demands placed upon us by the dictates of the world. We will not defeat the injustices of SEVERCIDE through methods that lack spiritual focus.

The battle in which we are engaged is about the choice of good versus evil. Spiritually what does develop is an inner knowledge that we do not use carnal weapons to wage a battle for changing the hearts and minds of people. Instead we grasp the tools of KNOWETICS and apply them generously toward things we can have direct influence upon. Those areas include: culture, education, work, finances, outreach efforts, family, friends and the communities in which we live. We embrace the words of Our King, Jesus Christ, and use our spiritual tools to reshape the world—one event at a time, one person at a time, one day at a time.

This is our recipe for success. It bonds us together as a family, loving others and ourselves, working through all hardships and challenges with the certain belief in the truthfulness of His words and promises. KNOWETICS neither endorses, denies, nor engages in dogmatic or doctrinal assertions. It focuses solely upon the essential aspects of Jesus Christ's ministry on earth. The characteristics that are covered in the succeeding chapters are accessible and applicable to every human life without exception.

CHAPTER 8

INGREDIENT ONE - MERCY

I AM A MAN WHO has broken the laws of God and man many times in my life. No one—including God—owes me anything; in fact, in view of His holiness, I should be left to stand in the dock of heaven while He metes out what I've rightly earned. No alternative, no remedy, no probation, no copping a deal, no appeal, no savvy silver-tongued attorney to represent my interests. Just a one-to-one encounter between me and the God of the Universe!

That is the courtroom scene we will ALL face in the future. Those of us who have had reluctant courtroom experiences in this life know exactly what the word *trial* means. If you have ever had to listen to the hateful attack of a self-righteous prosecutor, you have already tasted what is to come when Satan presents his case about whatever you've done—both public and private—through-out your life. All of the evidence against you will be admitted for everyone to examine. Your life will be laid bare.

It won't be like an episode of *Law and Order* where all of your con-stitutional rights will be carefully applied—*No, Sir!* This is going to be the ultimate moment of truth in your life. You may be surprised at how many will come into that heavenly courtroom without any preparation.

Crying out for mercy at that moment and pointing out that the heavenly clerk failed to give you enough time to prepare won't hold sway among these courtroom members. Telling the God of the Universe that you object to the proceedings because of lack of timely notice will be similar to pleading ignorance of the law to a charge of murder anywhere in the United States. You will be swiftly informed that ignorance of the law is not a defense.

Another surprising reality will be that God will not allow you to use comparison with the lives of others to gain any legal edge in His courtroom. You will be examined on the thoughts, words, actions and inactions of YOUR OWN life. You may have ridden high on the hog in this life, but in the next, there will not be any honorable titles or labels of the past.

Speaking to the issue as though it were all a bad dream and calling yourself a "freethinker" will offer no hope of escaping this judgment. I can be a God-denier all the days of my life and encourage others in this practice, but I will have to account for all I have been graciously given and will struggle in silence as I consider the grandeur of His presence.

Think of the shocking implications for those of us who have spent a lifetime trading on various aspects of the truth. When you see eternity looming and all you can do is give affirmative responses to Satan's accusations, you will tragically consider all of the missed opportunities you had to embrace God's helping hand. You will hate the fact that you disregarded all the signs for help sent you as you sped by in your hurry to live your life. Wow.

I will stand in the dock also. I will face the same prosecutor who knows every aspect of my life. There are no secrets to be kept from

God. Since Satan has been my silent partner in my life of sin—crime against God—he is intimately aware of my nature and history. No use starting to cry now. It's all there and I have nowhere to hide. One by one I answer yes to the charges on the docket under my name. No need to try explaining. It didn't work for Adam and Eve and they were very close to God. It's not going to help me one bit.

Just at the closing moment of my judgment hearing, a door bangs open in the back of the courtroom and all of the eyes turn from focusing on me to a man with a gaze of pure love. His regal majesty—His presence—silences the songs of men and angels, and for an instant I listen to His approaching footsteps. He doesn't look anything like Caesar whom the crowds of old awaited for the final sign of judgment. This One has not come to my hearing as a curious observer. He has come to keep His promise to me!

All are looking at the Person who has entered the courtroom on my behalf, and with a solemn glance at His Father, He states, "he is one of Mine, Father"! Now the proceedings will be dismissed since all legal and devilish claims against me have been fully paid by His Blood on Calvary. He is My Savior, My Redeemer, Jesus Christ!

What I have just described to you is the supreme act of mercy. Jesus Christ is the author and dispenser of all mercy. Mercy has many forms, but basically it means he will keep His promises to me—not just in heaven, but HERE and NOW.

His actions on my behalf have given me a unique ability to present my case to Him at any moment of the day. I have had multiple life experiences where the conclusion was already determined before the proceedings started. It makes one wonder why it is necessary to hold such stage art and for whose benefit it is held. Like a well-rehearsed and highly-anticipated Broadway play, these proceedings have great drama at the core and a formula finish to ensure that there will be limited disappointment when the finger is pointed downward. It is grand theater, but it only bears a shadowed resemblance to any element of real life.

The mercy of Jesus Christ is not theater; it is an encounter with Truth itself. Nothing in this life will stir your blood like the experience of Jesus Christ coming to your aid and defense. He is never early and never late. He is a gentleman and always on time. He is a keeper of His word. He delivers prisoners—setting us free—and does so for all eternity without limits.

That is Mercy—God's personal engagement in my life no matter how many times I have fallen down. He lifts my head and restores my peace.

A friend of mine, Father Paddy, recently returned from a holiday in Ireland. He had spent several weeks visiting family and friends. During his stay abroad, he encountered someone that he knew and the talk turned to the subject of mercy. His friend lived in a rural area where farming was a way of life. This friend described a recent sermon that an old parish priest had given which attempted to define this concept of mercy. The old priest was giving his sermon to his parishioners, and his frame of reference was the agricultural community in which they all lived. Using that background, he challenged his listeners to picture stumbling across a lost sheep tangled in thickets, nettles and thorns. Unable to extricate itself from its trapped position and bellowing in pain, there it stood trying to shake itself loose, but only further entangling itself in the vegetation and creating more pain as a result of its struggles. The old priest painted the picture well in the minds of his parishioners and then offered up the wise observation that mercy was their efforts to set the sheep free.

That is what God does for His sheep.

Mercy is the majesty of Jesus Christ bending down to comfort a great sinner like me—whispering in my ear, "You are my beloved child. Welcome home."

Step up and take your place at the feast table. We have all been waiting for you. Bring the sandals for his feet and the new robe of righteousness. I realize that it has been a difficult journey, but you are home at last.

I am a sinner! I deserve nothing but condemnation. Nothing I have done in my life has any worth or value apart from the great-accomplished work of Jesus Christ. Mercy is the embrace of my loving Savior after He has done all of the work. No sin or combination of sins (human against human) is beyond the Mercy of Jesus Christ!

CHAPTER 9

INGREDIENT TWO - GRACE

KNOWETICS IS NOT A SUBSTITUTE for practicing the faith you may have embraced in your life. It is the personal fulfillment of that knowledge. If you are a non-believer, it's not an attempt to sway your beliefs or try to convert you; you are a unique being with an individual body, emotions, a substantial thoughtful life and a long history of attempting to put together your views on life. KNOWETICS does not try to take away your basic views of life. Hold on to what you have.

If you travel by air from New York City to Singapore, you do not surrender your ethnic background or culture as part of the process. You are still the same unique individual in the other hemisphere that you were back in the heart of America. God does not insist that we surrender ourselves to a blind system of thought; instead, His grace (unique and individual favor) offers the opportunity to understand His nature through the everyday practice of talking with Him.

God has a way to reach us in the most desperate of situations. He also has ways to reach us when we are experiencing a cloud of satisfaction and a sense of personal fulfillment. This concept of grace may invite an uninformed view of a grace factory producing specific products for use by everyone—like candy bars, drinks or breakfast cereals—in which the manufacturer attempts to create a product that meets the taste and health standards of most consumers. We learn as we grow about our preferences and then we go out and find things we either like or dislike. However, God's grace is unique in the way it is constructed and is expressed solely for my own personal use. Grace is not dated; it doesn't expire and doesn't lose its effectiveness at some point in time. Rather, by its extraordinary nature, it will flow on for the benefit of others if I should choose to ignore its promise. One thing to note about having an experience with God, He is a gentleman and will never force His ways on us.

It's not only God who creates and dispenses Grace, but we give or deny that experience to everyone we meet in life. My sister Maureen encouraged me to come and visit her while she was living in Africa. Since I had the time, funds and good health, I obliged and was able to enjoy her hospitality. I had the pleasure of visiting four countries during my trip. That trip, in itself, was a small example of Grace given by Maureen who has been a supporter, advocate and fan of mine through all of the lost years and beyond. Unearned Favor!

During my African adventure, I observed many of the children wearing clothing that had obviously been made for a Western market. Yet here were children halfway around the world proudly wearing these highly-prized individual items of clothing. Apparently, these products weren't needed in the markets of the First World, so they found a home on the plains and in the cities of Africa. That is the same thing that happens with the flow of Grace. If I don't use what was given to me, it will eventually flow on to someone else. In

God's economy, there is no waste or meaningless activity. Grace is what I need, when I need it.

During my dating life, I had the pleasant experience of knowing a young, Vietnamese woman. Being the good cook that I believe myself to be, I offered to make dinner and she quickly offered to bring dessert. Done deal! When the day came, I gave my best effort to create something pleasant and culturally sensitive. She did the same with her selection of Durian as the dessert fruit. In spite of my many travels in Asia, I had never experienced this unique fruit. Let me assure you now that if Durian had been the fruit in question in Eden, it would have served its purpose with the first sight—wonderful to look at and tempting to behold.

I had seen hand-lettered signs in a small hotel in Korea carrying the message, "No Durian Allowed in Hotel Rooms." Unfortunately, that did not help with the decision I made at dinner that night. My guest broke out the white, marshmallow-like treasures that were about the size of small oranges. The smell was pungent, but that wouldn't stop me.

Now if you have never been a man, it is important to realize that appearances are important. So here I am, seated at the dining room table with my new Asian friend and a roommate (Curt F. —who was only too happy to share in the delights of a meal he did not have to cook). We sat at that table (Curt and I), absorbed by the exotic experience awaiting us and I noted with a quiet sense of satisfaction that my guest was making eye contact with me from across the table. With child-like confidence I put a forkful of the offered treasure in my mouth. Looking back, I realize what I took to be a look of interest and encouragement, most likely was a humorous attempt to warn me that what I had at the end of my fork was a life-altering experience waiting to happen.

Into my mouth went this tasty treat, and with the first bite, my life was changed into an alternate reality with a sudden loss of inner harmony and tranquility. My mouth was trying to tell my mind something, but my body was screaming so loud that my mind couldn't hear it.

This experience became of great significance in my life. While I had loaded down my fork with a surplus of Dorian (expecting to taste something delightful), Curt had wisely chosen to try only a small bite of the fruit. You can imagine how I felt as I sat at the table attempting to act suave and debonair, but I quickly realized that if I were to show true gratitude to my guest for her gift, I had better swallow and smile.

I overcame my gag reflex by sheer inner strength and forced the nasty fruit down my throat. I sincerely hoped I could pull this off with all of the verve and panache I could muster without vomiting on the table. It is amazing how many thoughts flow through the mind at a time like this. While my life did not flash before me, my choices certainly did. I can't be sure now, but it seems that my guest's eyes twinkled with a spark of amusement and satisfaction at that key moment. She was trying very hard to read my body language, but for some reason, I had lost the power to speak.

Not to be outdone, Curt—with his great sense of timing—noted that his dessert was very tasty, but that he was definitely full. With the sweetest expression of Christian friendship, he graciously offered to allow me to finish his portion.

So now that you've heard the whole story, hopefully you can see how I was able to figure out that the mind is capable of functioning on many levels all at the same time.

Grace is nothing like that experience. God does not invite us for discussion and then offer us some secret (supposed) delight only to persuade us to stuff it down our throats at the moment of truth. And He doesn't remind me disapprovingly that it was an experience created by my own choice (the free will mystery). When He interacts with me, I find Him soothing and comforting. Because He knows everything about my spirit, my preferences and my life history, His responses to my everyday situations are tailored to my own needs. That gentle assist, that He is always offering, matches the true definition of Grace.

Scripture tells me that Grace is God's unearned favor but the significance of Grace becomes lost in the seriousness of the words. Think about it in terms of vanilla ice cream. If you had never tasted vanilla ice cream, you would have no reference point to help you make sense of my description of "ice cream" (especially vanilla ice cream). As hard as I might try to describe it, you'll never understand what I am experiencing with vanilla ice cream—and the more I try, the worse it gets. Let's see, it's wet, cold, creamy, sweet, and so on. This is a communication problem matching the proportions of the complexity that faced two scientists, Crick and Watson, who struggled with the properties of the DNA molecular structure. Once they had evidence of its existence, they were presented with the challenge of creating a model that could be used by others in education and science.

It seems that it's human nature to experience some frustration— at which point, we may choose not to communicate with others as we try to understand our own personal experiences. Sadly we move away knowing that we have just missed a great opportunity to connect with another human being.

Back to the ice cream scenario, the other person walks away mumbling about the mystery of the "wet, cold, creamy and sweet" and starts looking for their own vanilla ice cream experience or they decide you're suffering from an overactive imagination. Pure fantasy! And so now we've lost that incredible opportunity to share and grow. Just one lick of vanilla ice cream could create a totally new experience of shared knowledge. Grace is just like that experience.

Before Christopher Columbus set sail, others made fun of his idea that the world was round. They decided to oppose any new ideas that challenged what most people accepted and understood. That response was played out in the closure of many opportunities—quietly and sometimes not so quietly—dismissing his claims as the ravings of an eccentric individual. *Nice guy, but a little odd. He is so intelligent, but his fantasy life is something else. Don't waste your time. Be polite, nod your head and quickly move away. Then go home to the safety of what you know to be true and comfort yourself with the knowledge that you are right in there with the thinking of the times.* Columbus did not accept the continued denial of what he knew in his heart to be true, and moved beyond Genoa hoping to connect with someone who shared his vision. He found that in Queen Isabella, who funded his grand scheme. This rewarded him with the experience of discovery. He shared the basics of the same discovery process with Sir Alexander Fleming (credited with discovering penicillin) and Crick and Watson's discovery of the DNA molecule. All of these things were in existence long before they were "discovered," but our knowledge that they existed was incomplete and outside of our experience.

Grace is the same thing that kept each of these men moving forward in the pursuit of what they knew in their hearts to be true—no matter how shadowy it was at the beginning. It is God's quiet and helpful encouragement that helps us identify what we know to be true within ourselves. Often, taking the time to listen to what some "so called" professionals think, tends to muddy our thoughts, rather than being helpful or adding to what we know to be true. Not all professional interaction is awkward or unhelpful, but we can be left with the same communication problem like the person who walked away mumbling about our description of vanilla ice cream. Only God has the sensitivity to understand our journey through life without trying to diagnosis or label our behavior.

Labeling is not understanding, nor is it knowledge in itself! Labeling is a substitute for getting into the heart of the troubles faced by another individual. It's a rare person who can selflessly engage others on a level playing field of love and acceptance. Grace is God's gift to us to make that experience possible. It is a meeting with love. Grace goes beyond labels and opens a new experience of shared understanding. Take, for example, the simple act of acceptance showed by Father Charles in the way he connected with the prisoners. He showed Grace by acknowledging the lives and sufferings of these human beings. He didn't go back to the "safety" of what each man had been labeled because of his prior behaviors.

Grace will start to make a difference in our lives if we can get past the idea of it being a religious problem and begin to see how Grace has great potential in all of our lives. Whether I choose to accept it or not, life is a process—not a moment frozen in time. The same is true of spirituality; it offers us insight into our continuing purpose after death. Our purpose is to help others and have our own lives end in the finality of human death (or to some, living an alternate reality that continues in an afterlife). Either way, the problems that come because of differing religious beliefs have no bearing upon our ability to use spirituality to transform our lives and to reach out to others with kindness, self-knowledge and compassion. This experience can be crystallized as the enhancement of knowledge and understanding that we acquired with our first lick of vanilla ice cream.

The way spirituality works is a lot like the five fingers you have on your hand. They are all equally important, serving multiple functions at the same time. They also work together to help me accomplish whatever I'm doing that requires my ability to grasp and perhaps even to meaningfully interact with the world. Would I cease to exist if I lost a hand or a finger—NO! However, my entire life would be changed because of such a loss. It is interesting that the basic ability to grasp now requires a specialized surgeon in the field of hand surgery. (Remember, they used to simply hack off body parts resulting in serious impairments.) It is also played out in the creation of the artificial hand. A disabled individual can now regain use and satisfaction of being able to grasp any object of interest. In fact, a whole industry for the development of prosthetic devices has quietly grown in our midst, and serves those maimed by devastation or disease.

Grace is a lot like one of those operational fingers. Do you remember the story of Jesus Christ healing the man with the withered hand? Jesus recognized the whole picture of this man's life instantly. He didn't define his experience with this man as a meeting with someone who had been maimed. Rather His sense of compassion moved Him to restore the functional ability of the man's hand. It was an act of grace—transforming grace! That is what He is seeking to do in our lives.

The maimed man probably never imagined that his hand could be restored; however, he had the surety of knowing that if his situation could possibly change, Jesus was the only one who could make it happen. He moved forward into the presence of His Maker and with the quiet confidence of a small child, he extended his hand. That whole experience was about Grace.

The man had done nothing to deserve the gift of healing. He was not a person of remarkable reputation, great wealth or social stature. He was only a humble and desperate (perhaps viewed by society as worthless and unworthy) individual who could not offer the Kingdom of God any type of payment for his healing.

When Jesus healed this man's hand, it also healed his soul in an encounter that transformed his life. That sudden meeting with Jesus went beyond his level of understanding and his limited view of what was possible. With a soul full of joy and love, he worshipped his Healer and delighted in reliving this experience by telling others his remarkable story. He likely did so his whole lifetime because the experience of meeting Jesus changed his life. He was never the same again!

We are called upon to discover and rediscover this experience with Grace and to share it graciously with ALL others. Truth is a constant; it never varies. Our awareness of truth changes our thoughts or expressions. Jesus Christ is the picture of Truth and our ability to reach out our withered hands and defeated spirits in hope is the spirit of His Grace in action. One final thought about Grace—its power is not restricted to the problems we present to God asking for His help; Grace envelopes all of the darkness of our lives with a spirit of light and the promise of personal renewal.

CHAPTER 10

INGREDIENT THREE - FORGIVENESS

IT HUMBLES ME THAT THE God of life itself has given me the privilege of writing about this remarkable gift. I'm the last person who deserves His gracious embrace, but like the man with the withered hand or the blind man standing before the Sanhedrin, I'm glad to talk about my limited understanding of this essential dynamic with God within the context of my own spirituality.

Forgiveness is another finger (component) that has been freely given to us to help us complete our journey of life. It's the promise of renewed friendship with God. It is the essence of the father's embrace of the Prodigal son, or what we dream of in our most private moments—a return to love.

I'm a rather obstinate fellow. For example, when a server brings out a freshly prepared meal and cautions me that the plate is hot, my mind refuses to accept it. I have to test it for myself, so with my finger, I gingerly touch the plate and sure enough, I burn myself. This experience serves the purpose of showing others my obstinate spirit. With all the forethought of a mule, I go happily (or not so happily) on my way, experiencing life (I also find it amusing to disregard wet paint signs).

I'm sure that if you feel the same way I do, you have your own ideas about what it's like to delight in new experiences. Remember the old saying that doing the same thing over and over again and expecting a different result is the definition of insanity. I'm sure that Heaven's courtroom of judgment will erupt with laughter when my personal life tapes are replayed for all of the hosts of heaven. I can even feel myself blushing with embarrassment as I privately review some of those moments. I wonder how I'll be able to handle the laughter.

The same experience of unusual choices has been active throughout my life; it's not something I've just learned about myself. The most glaring examples happened from the age of fifteen until thirty-one when I was using alcohol and drugs in a way that would have impressed Don Quixote. His endless attempts at jousting with windmills were the same as my endless use of mind-altering substances.

Not to be outdone by the obstacles associated with mastering my chemical friendships, I learned in a moment of wonderful awareness—at the age of thirty-one—that the secret of conquering my chemical problem is in giving up the struggle. That was a spiritual experience unlike any other learning experience in my life. In that moment of clarity, I was faced with the choice of either using this newfound knowledge or not applying it to my life. Thankfully, in a moment of quiet desperation and offered Grace, I was able to grasp the offered life jacket and start the slow process of returning to sane living. While this moment marked a personal change in my life, the actual reformation came during my years of recovery. This is what's called a healing experience; it is God-inspired, but the individual has to do the reforming and be part of the personal decision-making process. These past thirty-five years have been a growing commitment to the truth. This journey has shown me the need for personal forgiveness and forgiving others for their own trespasses. I'm not an authority on the subject of forgiveness. I can offer only my own point of view on how important this is and show some possible opportunities to apply its soothing effects to life's troubles and concerns.

For those of us who have offended much, forgiveness offers the hope of doing better in the future. After all, scripture reminds us that our judgments once made us enemies of God and were confirmed by our actions. His gift of **personal forgiveness** is one of the most important things that helps us get back in touch with the Central Figure of importance in our lives. Its main effect is to restore our relationship, reaffirm our self-worth and sharpen our ability to look into the future with hope and promise. That's forgiveness in action. Critical to our personal understanding is the knowledge that forgiveness has ALWAYS started with God. He forgave us first. We don't carry a supply of forgiveness around with us to use for ourselves or for the benefit of others in some high-minded show of enlightenment.

God's forgiveness began with that small, still voice within us urging us to hold on to it. The mental picture I have is that of a loving parent as they try to encourage their precious, hesitant child onto the school bus. The parent exemplifies God, the school bus is life and the child is each of us. Word pictures work for me!

For many of us, it's a lot easier to forgive others who may have offended us rather than applying this soothing balm to our own lives. I'm likely to have a small portion of forgiveness available for others. But for me personally, I **run** when I think that my actions have meaning in God's great plan for my own life. I actively resist the urge to accept His loving embrace; when instead, I pull out the self-censure stick and give myself a good wallop of reality.

In Borderline Personality Disorder, the patient may frequently self-mutilate or become cutters. They use this form of behavior because life has made them numb and senseless and when they cut, that pain gives them back their ability to feel emotions again. The problem with inflicting themselves with pain is they continue to reinforce the label of loser, which becomes a fixture in their life.

Each new wound might bring momentary relief, but it also brings the unlimited pain of constant disapproval at what they've done to themselves. And so the inner battle of life goes on. Or they may choose new behaviors, therapies, medications, chemical substances or weird experiences to control the uproar raging within. Since it is a privately waged battle, others can only watch these struggles from the outside. Because we usually distrust others, we can't afford to open up and admit what's going on. Our desperate choices are committing suicide or becoming a hollow shell that no longer experiences life. Do you remember the problem we had talking about ice cream earlier in the book? The same principles of personal discovery and communication also apply to my efforts to explain this growing awareness to you.

* * *

I am just a shape, with no real substance. If I make myself small enough, maybe I'll just vanish and no one will know that I'm gone.

How can I even think of sharing my fractured life with you in any meaningful way? I'm beaten before I even begin to try and express myself to others. I'm screaming inside that I'm just like you and that I'm in terrible pain, but my muffled roars are misinterpreted as something else as you quickly back away from me.

Once again I'm alone and small and afraid and without hope. I'm lost in a strange kind of time warp; I'm beyond any hope of getting help from others. The help I'm looking for—which I know by instinct—is a true connection with one other person. Unfortunately, this is all I know, so I continue to mindlessly self-destruct and cause myself pain with each new problem that comes along. You don't recognize how desperate I am and can't see that I keep on offending you and society by the way I behave.

This cycle finally leads to me being totally shut out of life. I am a non-person.

* * *

This thought-process shows that Severcide has two important dynamics. The reaction brought out by others and society, and the individual's actions that just put the whole thing in motion. The result is a song without words—swaying along while waiting for an end to the pain. Life without expression, connection or relief will ultimately lead to death or untold damage to individual lives. We can all recognize the melody, because to some extent, we have all had similar experiences.

The problem with trying to communicate (in this context) is that not everyone is aware of the volume control knob. So personally, I dismiss the constant whines of family members or friends by thinking about my own ability to decrease the personal turmoil of life. I know how to use my personal volume control knob. I have nothing to offer others, because they should know better. I am blinded by my inability to understand that they have no idea what it means to have an internal volume control knob (which will help them to soften their turmoil). Further, I'm tired of trying to educate them and wonder why they can't just grow up. It's time to apply the things we've already learned.

Do you remember the experience of trying to teach someone else about vanilla ice cream? Eventually, we may choose to distance ourselves from others since they don't seem to understand or know what it takes to live a successful life. We privately label them as suffering from a social learning disorder and refer to them as "socially retarded." We don't do this because we are vindictive, but because we become so aggravated as we try to bring back some sense of inner peace and harmony. I guess we're not so different after all!

Is it just a matter of individual difference or intensity? This is another example of knowing the recipe and what makes up the essential ingredients. I can't give away something that I don't have!

My friend, Matt, is serving a life sentence for the murder of a young woman during the commission of a felony. This is called the felony murder rule. The crime itself happened in the distant past. I recognize that my readers will think that this is a glaring disregard for the life of the victim, but it's not. In an unthinkable moment, his actions inflicted grievous harm on others and there is no room for disregarding others in the context of KNOWETICS. The rest of the story is separate from his crime.

I can't know what happens within an individual who is overcome by passions, pursuits or the rage of the moment. Others may be able to write off things with their behavioral theories, profiling technologies or the statistics of the pseudo-science of societal distancing, but I'm just concerned with the real people I know—real flesh and blood people— who suffer and live life as I do.

Nothing within KNOWETICS should be used to justify the use of any form of violence against others, but the reality of life is that random acts of violence do occur.

Having confirmed what we already know, let's move onto the heart of the issue. What do we *do* in response to these events? We handle the events through what we call the "justice system" and we refer the offenders to some made up form of legally defined suspended animation. We know that they exist; but they exist outside of our own lives.

Our traumas usually fade in intensity over time and we quietly move on with our daily lives. Mercifully, our minds are able to lessen the shock and we go on with life. The system is dealing with them. That is all we need to know. End of the story, right?

Wrong. Once touched by these events, our lives are forever changed and though we "move on", we remain spiritually connected to that individual for the rest of our lives by the after-effects of the traumatic event. This is true whether the event is murder, divorce or just being labeled as "stupid or uncaring." In some strange sense, we're all playing out the same drama on the playing fields of life.

To help shed some more light on this subject, I would like to go back to the world of science and discuss some things that might be useful.

Using "Chaos Theory" as a model may prove helpful as it serves to enrich our understanding of seemingly unrelated events. However, note that acceptance of the underlying beliefs of KNOWETICS does not preclude the usefulness of informed theoretical scientific thought. We now understand the new reality of constituent multiple dimensions, inherent in the known Laws of Physics. What this means in layman's terms is that there is a relationship between all of the things that happen in our world. Nothing occurs randomly or in an isolated fashion.

Thoughtful expansion and enhanced understanding which were derived from the theoretical work of Niels Borh (he stated his understanding about the way large things and small things operate) led to the development of Quantum Physics. We can now intellectually grasp a new understanding of how these laws may operate differently—or in conjunction with each other—on macro (large) and micro (small) levels of efficiency. This re-definition of theory has afforded us the opportunity to understand the subtle interplay between the macro and micro applications of the "Laws" of Physics.

KNOWETICS is the experience of our discovering the existence of "Truth" (which helps us to look at our individual life experiences in understanding the elegance of God's Word). Individual spirituality comes from our personal knowledge applied and defined by our life's struggles and experience.

The sad reality is that the actions Matt inflicted upon another life had a rippling effect on all of us. All of our choices have similar effects on the lives of countless others. But this story does not end with simply knowing about this event. It includes the actions of this young woman's parents who came forward and publicly forgave their daughter's killer.

Now that is a paradigm shift! It's a new awareness much like the "discovery" of Quantum Physics. Only this event was played out in a small prison chapel far from the eyes of the media. On their scale of worth, it wasn't worth burying on the eighteenth page of the newspaper. But remarkably this event, and others like it, gives us all a chance for personal discovery and expression in all of our life experiences—whether positive or negative.

These parents actually applied the "law of forgiveness" to their tragic situation and embraced the man—who had caused them so much personal grief—as an individual worthy of forgiveness. It's a long stretch between accepting the law of forgiveness and applying it to the most painful experiences of our lives, but they acted on the firm knowledge of their Christian experience and positively tried to repair the rip in the fabric of society and in doing so, restored the worth and dignity of one offending individual. Wow!

The story doesn't end there. Matt was turned over to the care of the state's prison system with a sentence of life imprisonment and the case was marked closed. With a sigh of relief, society shifted into a position of restored comfort. The police and prosecutors moved on to focus on new crimes; and those closely involved reflected upon the nice gesture the victim's family had made by offering their feelings of forgiveness.

Years later, lost in the daily struggles of prison life, Matt's intervention in the events of another prisoner's life may have saved that prisoner from death. Inadvertently and probably without personal awareness, he applied the same lessons learned from his experience of being forgiven to the life of another prisoner. You see, that other prisoner had been unjustly labeled "a snitch" in an attempt to set him up to be killed in the harsh prison culture.

In prison, being labeled "a snitch" comes with the threat of certain harm, possible death and sure isolation (Severcide) from other prisoners. Matt broke through and reached out to the other prisoner. He took the time to find out the "facts" of the allegations, and instead of letting the matter go quietly, Matt sought out the truth.

Given that Matt was recognized as a powerful individual within prison culture, his connection to the labeled individual non-verbally signaled others to stay away from this so-called "snitch." His public actions within the prison environment had the practical effect of warning off those who might have wanted to take justice into their own hands. Later, the truth came out, but for a short while it was touch and go.

Far outside the mainstream experience of society and totally unknown to prison authorities or members of the parole board, Matt's actions may have saved the life of another and helped prevent the application of the law of Severcide to this individual's daily prison life.

In saving someone else—perhaps physically, but certainly from the trauma of social exclusion—Matt engaged in a personally redemptive act. He may not have even been aware of the effects that his actions had at that moment, but without his choice to reach out and understand, this book might never have been written. Until today—when you read of this event—the significance of Matt's actions has been lost to the world. He still remains incarcerated, labeled a murderer, but to me, he has long ago been redeemed and remains a true friend of mine.

Next, let's consider another example of the possible side effects of forgiveness. Standing before Roman Governor Pontius Pilate, Jesus, the perfect expression of God's love for us, had his individual worth compared to His fellow prisoner Barabbas (who had led a rebellion in which others were killed). That day the throngs of jeering citizens of Jerusalem were given the choice between the two men as to who would go free and who would face death. The choice was Jesus Christ or Barabbas.

The people, being led by their leaders, examined the worthiness of both Barabbas and Christ and their potential usefulness to society. Eagerly and frantically, they called out "give us Barabbas" in response to the crafty legal manipulations of their religious and social leaders. So Christ was condemned to suffer a cruel death.

It is a horrible reality to think that Jesus Christ, who had harmed no one, was being compared with Barabbas a known murderer and revolutionary (terrorist). It does not matter whether you believe in the divinity of Jesus Christ or not at this point. This man, Jesus, had done no harm, yet He was being compared to a known terrorist in some bizarre drama meant to be social justice. What a shameful event!

The example of His life up until this moment gives us such a rich understanding of what it means for our own lives that we don't need to look further into the biblical meaning of His death and resurrection. We can find all the meaning and understanding we need to live out our lives, simply by the example of His actions as He stood on that judgment platform. He didn't plead for His life; in fact, He didn't say a word in response. He stood there calmly awaiting His fate. What an incredibly remarkable human encounter. He never offered a word in His defense. He understood His own worth and didn't need to plead in front of his social judges. We can learn from this and live out the same practical certainty in our own lives.

Individual worth exists beyond our personal knowledge or day-to-day awareness just like the fact that Quantum Physics existed outside of our personal knowledge before its discovery. Truth is truth and always will be. The ultimate truth is that you are a child of God and no one can ever rob you of your personal worth—even if society tries to with the worst type of labels.

Let's go back to that judgment scene, and imagine what might have happened before the public compared good and evil in the lives of these two men. I like to believe that there was a long hallway leading from Pontius Pilate's dungeons to where Christ and Barabbas stood before the public and awaited judgment. I continue to view that scene in my mind, but I'm not looking for the public moment; I'm looking for something much more meaningful.

I imagine that moment when Jesus Christ came face-to-face with Barabbas. In that instant, I imagine they shared a brief glance at one another. And in that moment, I believe that Jesus looked at the desperateness in Barabbas' eyes and because Jesus knew what was coming, He looked compassionately at Barabbas, showing His loving acceptance and forgiveness of this man. I believe that Jesus extended the gift of personal forgiveness and its eternal consequences to a totally unaware stranger in that brief moment.

Unfortunately history doesn't show us whether or not this was a life-changing opportunity for Barabbas or what the actual impact of a powerful moment spent with Jesus Christ was like. But something in my spirit has always wanted to believe that Barabbas went on to live a life of personal redemption—touched by a moment in time and never the same again.

And for the non-religious, it was a moment before the controversy associated with divinity. May I offer my opinion that this was an entirely human moment, but clearly a divinely appointed one?

If you can suspend your disbelief and accept the possibility that this moment played itself out—even if you aren't totally comfortable trying to understand spiritual things—then you can accept the idea that forgiveness is the complete solution to all of our life experiences, challenges and traumas.

As a believer, I can describe to you my understanding of forgiveness in relation to all our life experiences. But you have to take that first lick of the vanilla ice cream to really understand what forgiveness means in your life and the lives of others.

Oh, the sweetness of experiencing personal forgiveness!

Forgiveness is God's gift extended to every man, woman and child, and is based upon the completed work of Jesus Christ and His resurrection as triumph over the hold of all sin. This is true forgiveness—real forgiveness—and is the forgiveness upon which you can build a new life, all for the asking. If you are ready to ask Him, go quietly in your heart and lay out all the pain, failures, sins, crimes, trespasses and shame before Him. It is a very personal act between you and your Creator. He will never say no to your cry for help.

CHAPTER 11

INGREDIENT FOUR - FAITH

BY SCRIPTURAL DEFINITION, FAITH IS the substance of things hoped for, but as yet unseen. Let's be careful before we go any further, because we are treading dangerously close to psychotic thought (a concept embraced by mental health theorists). Please remember that KNOWETICS does not reject the possibility of encountering elements of known truth in the informed gushing of science; rather, it presumes that personal reality is like an undiscovered landscape that occurs outside of our conscious knowledge. It can include impressions, feelings and potentials.

Now you are approaching the neighborhood of Faith! Stop a moment and breathe in the scent and experience it offers us. I promise you, it will not be anything like my faith that the Durian would be a treat beyond all treats that I had experienced up until that moment in my life. I have faith that the sun will come up tomorrow, but my belief in that fact does not make the sun come up. Can you imagine the problems presented for those who were convinced that the Earth was the center of the universe?

The Roman Catholic Church once accepted that belief as truth and evidence of mainstream thinking. So did most of society. It was common knowledge; something that everyone knew as a single demonstration of "known truth." Unfortunately, it was not truth at all, but something close to the truth that could explain the shared reality of watching the cycle of endless days and nights.

Belief that the earth was the center of the universe was very similar to the later belief that Columbus encountered in the form of accepted (mainstream thought) knowledge that his proposed journey would end in failure for himself, his associates and financial backers when he fell off the edge of the world. Among the many accomplishments associated with NASA's mission, is the globally distributed photo of Earth taken by astronauts at some distance away in space. The photo clearly confirms that the Earth does not have visible edges (except in our hearts as we continue to engage in sharp battles with others). What a wonderful accomplishment for man. One small problem though—the now-known realities pre-existed our knowledge of them. In other words, they were always true, no matter how society came to view them or explain their usefulness. So much for the value of mainstream thought.

Let's look at a few more practical issues related to faith. It is interesting that the State of California has a bottle and can recycling deposit law on most containers sold in the state. The application of that deposit fee is supposed to help consumers understand Earth's limited resources and the problems of waste management that become part of their individual purchasing decisions. Great theory!

How useful this theory is in practical terms is uncertain. One thing is certain; it has improved the coffers of the state treasury, masked as an ecological solution to a hefty social problem.

Consider the implications of the redemption fee. We are supposed to learn the value of a tin can or plastic bottle by attaching a monetary consequence to its disposal. While useful for tin cans or plastic bottles, would that kind of thinking hold a key to resolving the financial burdens of society in disposing of the labeled human trash of the world?

How about legally approving of a redemption bond for everyone we socially write off as unreliable, unworthy or beyond our understanding of his or her ability for personal change?

Consider the possibilities. Misfits, perverts, anti-socials and even perhaps those charged with solving society's problems, politicians, lawyers, and healthcare professionals, all receiving the same opportunity to use a socially-funded expression of faith in the human potential for change. Farfetched?

While there is little hope that society will see its responsibilities to all citizens alike, a redemption bond would be a symbolic act that identified a commitment to even the least of our citizenry. After all, we are already funding the opposition (a prison system with two million occupants) that claims there is no other answer to this wide assortment of social ills except using the practical law of Severcide. The supporters say incarceration is the most cost-effective solution we can sell to the public!

While it is not very likely to happen, redemption bonds would be an awesome application of faith! Can you picture it? A $5,000.00 surety (redemption) bond applied to the lives of those we discard like tin cans and plastic bottles (on which we have collectively—legally and socially—imposed a five cent redemption fee). Can you imagine a world in which we valued our recyclable products equally with the individual redemption potential of the lost sheep?

That is what God does for each of us. He is always ready to redeem His lost sheep. That is what each of us is called to do for one another and more importantly to do for ourselves. Oh, precious child of God. If only you knew or had a hint of your eternal value.

That reality is faith in action. The things hoped for in individual lives but largely unseen at the present moment. Are you catching on to this radical type of thinking? It is all based upon the seen and unseen Truth of God's work. It's not my idea. I have only stumbled onto an element of the Truth that has always existed. Long before I was born it was truth, and far into the future it is truth. So what does this truth mean for each of us personally?

I believe in people; I believe that even the worst of us can make changes. That is the exercise of my personal faith as expressed in my life's work. Want to join me? Careful. Others will call you odd, eccentric, crazy or worse yet, self-centered, manipulative and perhaps criminal in your intentions. Remember the mainstream opposition to the spoken beliefs of Galileo and Columbus?

A more recent example can be found with those who focused on overcoming the stigma and injustices of discrimination. You have to look only to the example of South Africa and its long established reign of apartheid to see the endless possibilities for transforming human lives.

So where is your faith—in the law of the land or the Law of God? One kills the human spirit, while the other shows the incredible worth of an individual human life, of all human life.

Let's jump into this idea of faith and explore the taste of the freedoms it offers us.

Faith is not just expressed in a spiritual form; it applies to every aspect of my life. When I open the box of breakfast cereal, I have faith that I will find those welcomed little flakes of grain, not a package of lima beans. The same is true when I put my car key into the ignition switch. I have great faith that when I turn that switch on, I will soon be off to take care of my errands.

So faith already has extensive applications in our lives. It is the substance of our lives, not just a religious belief. We all have faith!

Some years back, a group of scientists announced their discovery of a cold fusion process. I am not sure if it was announced in a book, but I strongly believe that it appeared in some professional peer-reviewed journal—the way that scientist's usually share their findings with others in their field. Journals not only serve as a way of informing others about their ongoing research, but also permit other scientists to recreate or replicate the original author's experiment and hopefully arrive at the same findings. This process is essential to the scientific method. It is what science is based upon.

It's hard to believe that a scientist, who has labored through twenty years of education to acquire their doctorate and then engages in years of research, would knowingly submit a theoretical or clinical model to the scrutiny of the professional community without making sure that he had his "ducks in a row."

Cold fusion theory was submitted to that same standard of review. The theory, processes, methodology of study and subsequent findings were shared with other scientists through publication. It quickly came to the public's attention rather than remaining hidden in some archives understandable only to those who grasp the shared language of that particular field of science.

With that jump from the professional to public forum, speculation about future application of these findings began to soar. As I remember, there was talk about using a yet unknown technology (based upon the theory) to generate power for all of our energy needs. Can you imagine the concept of a home powered by a safe reactor?

These public speculations quickly caught the scientific community's interest and drove a surge of activity to replicate the original author's findings. As the interests of various international scientists propelled research forward, the results started to trickle in and quickly spread back to the public.

At first, there were claims and counter claims; but sadly this whole process ended in the denial of these fantastic claims for potential personal nuclear technology. Quietly scientists all over the world went back to their workbenches and cold fusion was tossed on the heap-pile of other discredited claims.

Let's go back to the original authors' claims. They had deep faith in the truth guiding their efforts. They believed in this truth to such a degree that they submitted their ideas for others to scrutinize. Their theories and assumptions may have made perfectly good sense as expressed in mathematical formulas or elegantly designed laboratory experiments. All of their faith in the possible future development of life-transforming technologies could not overcome what independent researchers discovered. "Well," you say, "That may apply to the world of science, but I do not see how it applies to my life."

Consider the hype that caught the public's attention just before the year 2000. The airwaves, print media and e-media "authorities" warned us of the possibility of a pending collapse of life as we knew it with the turn of the clock to 00:00:01- January 1, 2000. These claims were readily backed up by the wise observations of instant experts who advised us to prepare for the worst. Computers would certainly crash. None of us would be able to use our ATM cards. The food distribution system would fail leading to the possibility of mass hunger, possibly starvation for billions of people. Think of the great criminal surge that would come from such a worldwide disaster as people took what they needed in their fear-driven race to survive.

We were seriously urged to stock up on everything: food, water and of course, money (lots of money since the plastic cards might not work). That led to fear-based survival thinking which included stockpiling everything from home based (buried) gas and water storage tanks, generators, lanterns, batteries, and real blankets (not the electric ones) to guns and ammunition to protect us from the hordes of barbarians (who were certain to run down our streets).

So from about 1998 through 11:59:59 - December 31,1999, all people were encouraged to acquire the essentials of life to help them through the pending crisis—while the government figured out a way to straighten it all out. Off we rushed and bought lots of containers of water, freeze-dried foods, toilet paper and who knows what else. (Don't forget the guns!) Our society was impacted by what unknown experts were saying, and they helped to fuel the buying frenzy.

The manufacturers, distributors, wholesalers and retailers of our country gladly met the demand for all these needs and on January 1, 2000, they carried their sacks of money to the bank with cheerful nods of gratitude, while using the politically correct expression, Happy Holidays!

It is now 2014, and I wonder if we have all finished our freeze-dried foods or whether they have been sent off to Africa like the clothing I mentioned earlier. Personally, I discovered that those plastic one-gallon jugs, containing precious water, do not hold up well in the long term. Wow, we all had faith in the truthfulness of the media's concerns and the accuracy of expert thinking.

Truth is always truth and our faith in it will never be discredited. It will never sell us a bill of goods on vain hopes or fears.

The truth is that if we have faith the size of a mustard seed we can overcome any barrier in our lives, and you can take that to the bank. It's always been true and always will be true. We have faith in so many non-essential things in our lives, why is it so difficult to have faith in God's promise of individual help?

He said that if we have faith, we can speak to the mountain and it shall obey. Are you like me? Do you have a mountain of obstacles blocking your hopes and dreams? Who do you think gave you those hopes and dreams? Well, along with those hopes and dreams, He has promised the help to make them real.

Do you have faith? Look at the five fingers on your hand. Remember your spiritual tools and begin to grasp the significance of what you have—not what you don't have. With God on your side, whom shall you fear? You are a precious child of God.

I have no personal experience with a DNA molecule. The science of biology offers me a useful explanation of its structure and properties, but as for myself, I have never personally experienced a close encounter with a DNA molecule. I accept what science says since it seems to organize so much of what I understand from my life experiences. Remember the examples of the hot plate or the wet paint signs? Some of our best learning experiences come from these encounters. We know the simple truth that experience is the best teacher. Still I have never personally hung out with a DNA molecule, at least, not that I recall.

You may say, "That's absurd, we know they exist." We have models that explain its existence, micrographs that verify its existence and of course DNA-based technology that is reliably used in the justice system. If I argue that those factors are merely the experience that others had with the DNA molecule, you'll probably tell me that I am being ridiculous in my challenge. See, you are expressing your faith in the truthfulness of the scientific claim. I'm just pointing out that I have never had a personal encounter with a DNA molecule.

You want me to accept what you've learned as a basis for new beliefs in my own life. That's kind of like taking the leap from inorganic to organic, the spark of life! You say this life spark was the result of an accidental process, possibly started by a lightning strike. Wow, I think I'll accept what you're saying about the reality of DNA, now, in lieu of the other offered leaps in faith (namely, Evolutionary Theory and its unexplainable claims). See that's faith.

Back to cold fusion and the survival hysteria at the turn of this century. These two were based upon known "facts" that turned out to be unnecessary exaggerations over the course of time. Without asking you to identify yourselves as a turn of the century hoarder, I hope that you will be able to agree that these claims found little to no value in the long term.

Religion might offer us the opportunity to experience faith in the idea of a caring and loving God. The problems some have while exploring this kind of faith are the burdens of dogma and doctrine that go along with some religious beliefs. Does that mean that these conflicting claims discredit the truthfulness of God's Word? Not at all!

KNOWETICS is a re-statement of the truth of God's Word outside of religion. It recognizes individual spirituality that overcomes all claims on the superiority of known truths. That spirituality is clearly recognizable in the context of our everyday lives. We experience it in our lives with each breath that we take. It is not based upon what others tell me about their experiences with "reality." It stands alone.

The shared experience of many can't change the reality of truth. Do you remember Galileo and Columbus? Outside of the realm of common or personal experience they engaged—with evident inner certainty—the truth, which was part of their consciousness. So truth as it was known at that time came out of the ignorance of joining everyone else's vision of truth.

Our inner lives lead us to the edge of a sparkling pool of awareness to drink happily. Unfortunately, most of us are on the shore listening to others (society) tell us that the water is not safe to drink.

What has this to do with faith and its usefulness in my "real" life? Your life is the only one you'll ever have, now or later, private or public. Given the examples used in this chapter, I'm sure that you'll now agree that this concept of faith is applied to all aspects of our individual lives. We use faith to make choices, and those choices become the substance upon which our lives are lived.

You say, "But I am not a man of faith." Let me point out that you are already using it every day of your life—you just might be calling it something else.

Expressions of my faith can be clearly recognized in my actions, not my words. Like an element of science, faith can be measured by the choices I make throughout my day. This day, today, here and now! So it is not about obtaining faith; our futures are tied to using the faith that we already have.

The experiences of my life (since the age of thirty-one) have shown me that there are endless possibilities for people to change. Is this mustard seed faith?

Have a little faith!

As offenders, we have little value to society as a whole. Those who live on death row have the least value, followed by those who have been in prison. By inference, our families share the same fate. They share in the rejection that our criminal convictions have triggered. But God does not see us in that light. We are His precious children and our value is not dependent upon our behaviors, rather it is SOLELY based upon the shed blood of Jesus Christ and His resurrection from the grave. Find out the truth for yourself. Do not buy into anyone else's vision of the truth. If you ask Him to reveal the truth to you in the privacy of your heart, He will do so. Watch what happens with your faith when you discover the truth about how God values your life!

CHAPTER 12

INGREDIENT FIVE - HOPE

SOMETIMES I SEE HOPE AS a sidewalk that keeps unfolding before me as I walk down the path of life. It materializes as I take my steps forward. So for me, it is not what's to come, but the spirit of the moment lived. How do you imagine hope? Does it get set aside to some unused portion of your human spirit?

I have a daughter with whom I have shared an estranged existence for decades. She sees no hope in my possible transformation (as told to me by a variety of other people) as a human spirit. And so we go through the years of our lives bouncing off this invisible barrier to love and communicate. For years, I attempted to understand this barrier and overcome it.

After what seemed like endless attempts to find the chinks in her armor of beliefs, I eventually stopped trying to make it happen. I gave her up to her judgments, realizing that she had made these judgments based upon her knowledge of me at a time when I was a besotted drunk and druggie. Thirty-five years later there is another reality expressed in my life, but this is occurring outside of her personal experience.

Remember the concept that earth was the center of the universe or that it came with edges? It is the same about knowledge, just with a different application. It is one of the realities of my life that I am unable to bridge the gap between us in this life, but that does not mean that I am the picture of her beliefs and therefore am unable to change. It merely means that I am unknowable to her the way I am now. That is a private example that will help as we explore this idea of hope.

On a professional level, I recently ran into a similar example when my words and intentions were misrepresented. This led to an investigation when it was discovered that in the past I had labels attached to my life.

For what it's worth, I was the one who told them about the "facts" that resulted in labels they used against me! I felt this was a witch-hunt because they said I hadn't told them the whole story. In the process, they decided it was extremely important to tie my sad history of personal failure (which happened thirty-five years ago) with the job I was doing now and the stage was set for the drama of "officially" removing me from the project.

I have learned that there is ebb and flow to these spiritually based events in my life. I hired a lawyer, but never bought into their conclusions (individual beliefs masked as the judgment of society) since I am a child of God. That did not mean that I just moved on and accepted their actions; that would have been an invitation to hide. What I knew (or hoped) was that God had a plan to use this ugly event in my professional life for His glory. The doors He had opened in my life were my personal experience with His truth and I was not about to betray His love for me.

These two sad episodes of mine—private and professional—are events from which I get a renewed hope that I will learn more about God's love for me. It is an intensely personal meeting with my Creator, the author of all of my hope.

Do I look at the emotional mess created by these events, or do I apply God's Word to my life and take the next step while hoping that the real answers to the needs of life will turn up as I walk forward in His care? I am going to bet on God keeping His word. It is the only reality I have known for thirty-five years.

So now we have arrived at the heart of the matter. How do I apply the losses of my life to my future choices? For me, it is simply a matter of using my personal spiritual ingredients to enhance my decision-making process. If I want to cut that process down to a minimum, I have only to ask myself the ultimate question—what would Jesus do?

This book could have become a rant against social and personal injustice. Rather I made the choice, that in the midst of what seems like certain defeat, God still has a plan for my life. Out of my lack, I want to extend my two mites and present this book as a gift to the ever-sustaining God of my life. He is the principle audience, but in writing of these experiences, I recognize that there are millions of others who struggle with the same defeats and limits that I have experienced in my life.

If I seem to turn aside and offer more reflections about God's nature and my dependence upon Him, my writings have brought the issue of perfect dependence into sharp view. If He is my creator and I am the created, He always has and will care for me throughout my life. Have a little HOPE, brothers and sisters; He has a plan for our lives—a plan for today and tomorrow. He is the sustainer of our lives. I do not care if you are sitting on death row with less than 24 hours to live. Even now, it is important that you believe in His ability to offer you the hope of a new life with Him. The legal stay may or may not ever happen (and it is not likely in today's justice business), but His offer never expires. He placed a redemption bond on all of us by giving us the hope of salvation based upon the life, death and resurrection of His Son, Jesus Christ.

When all is said and done, hope is my direct link to God. My hope does not come from my vain attempts to reconnect with a lost family member or a professional search for truth within the mental health industry.

The professional story doesn't end there. Those who chose to harass and malign my professional efforts used local agencies in the community. God, in His glory, has seen me through to vindication. It doesn't matter what my peers think, I am impressed by what God does in my life. These experiences show me more of God's love for me. He is the lifter of my head.

This love doesn't lean on past struggles or limits, but a sureness that something exists beyond all the labels and distance. I am absolutely sure a spiritual experience has transformed my life. I know it because I have experienced it. It exists like God exists.

I can't prove to you that the world isn't the center of the universe, but I recognize that it is only a part of the solar system. As you open your spiritual eyes, you will discover the ultimate truth that defines all human experience.

These deeply personal experiences that I have shared with you are real examples of what has given me hope in my life. My hope is that they will ultimately have meaning as I journey along life's unfolding sidewalk. I'm personally grateful for the military's willingness to freely fuel my ship of hope. It is their sponsored journey, which has resulted in the writing of this book.

Truth has no preferred medium of expression. Do you remember the words of Jesus when He exclaimed that if those around Him choose not to worship Him, then the stones would cry out? I am just one person—a very unworthy person—who God has used to restate His love for us in modern day thought. This story is not about my journey or me. It is only one vehicle (remember the transportation concept) for expressing truth.

The ultimate truth is that God loves me and He is the source of all hope. Hope is the reason we bear children. Hope is the reason we go to school or to church. Hope is the reason we save for the future. Hope is the reason that we get out of bed in the morning. Hope is the reason we embrace others with our love. Where there is no hope, there is no life.

If that applies as a basic element in our lives, then it too is a God-given right of personhood. So what does that say about our epidemic of abortions or the legal sanctioning of suicide as a healthcare alternative? We are a people without hope since we embrace a culture of death through our actions. Whether we do so with our votes or with our buying decisions, it is either an endorsement or rejection of basic ideas that impact all of our lives.

Do you remember Roe vs. Wade? For many, it was hailed as a victory for personal choice; for millions of unborn babies, it was a deadly decision. They didn't have a vote in the process. "Well, that's absurd," you say. Is it absurd someone made the choice to carry you to term? They did so on the basis that no matter what horrible circumstances their pregnancy might bring on, they had a quiet inner assurance that somehow they would make it through all of their challenges. Or instead, they made the difficult choice to surrender you to the care of others, hoping that you would enjoy all of the benefits of life through the choices of others.

That type of thinking, which encouraged us to believe that we could overcome any obstacles in our lives, was based upon HOPE. Take away our hope and you are taking away the air that we breathe. The solutions offered by society offer no hope or promise that things will be better in the future. Hold on, it's only going to get worse, right?

Society's problems seem to be attached to fear at every turn. Do you remember the name Willy Horton? His unlawful actions occurred under the watch of one presidential candidate. The result was a campaign of fear that swept the country undermining public confidence in this candidate's use of good judgment.

Overlooked in this stampede of fear was the fact that hundreds, perhaps thousands of people, are involved in making the decisions in state government. All that mattered was that it occurred on his watch. On the other hand, Reagan's decision to limit funding for HIV/AIDS research had consequences for children that have not even been born yet. And though that occurred on his watch, today he is held in esteem, while the previously mentioned governor . . . what was his name?

Hope flows from or is taken away by all of our actions—personal, private or public. Picture a death row inmate as he sits in the death cell awaiting his execution. It is fifteen minutes before he is to die and he hears the phone ring in an adjacent room. He sits and wonders what that call was all about. Immediately he hears footsteps rapidly approaching his cell, but he can't see who it is. He anxiously strains at the bars trying to read the facial expression of the approaching individual looking for any sign of hope.

He has already been sentenced to death. He should not have any expectations other than the fact that the state will send him to eternity any minute. But somewhere deep inside his psyche, he desperately hopes against all odds that the Supreme Court has granted him a stay of execution. That's raw HOPE; the best kind of hope actually, because it's the point at which an individual realizes that they are totally dependent on the possibility of a life-sustaining decision.

It's the point of personal surrender. Only hope can carry me forward in the next few moments of life. Come on, you know you've been at your own breaking point at one time. What was it that kept you from taking pills, shooting yourself or hooking up a hose to your car's exhaust system? It was the HOPE that things would change; and for most of us, things did change as we took steps forward.

Hope is a gut-wrenching ingredient, like the strongest of spices. When that spice is around, we know it's there; but at other times, we may quickly forget its familiar scent. We can forget certain truths that make us all human. Even as they are inserting the tube in his arm to inject the fatal cocktail of drugs, a prisoner may take hold of the hope that God will keep His promises.

When I stand before the judgment seat, I have no illusions that Satan will overlook even the most minor of my failings in seeking a sentence of eternity in hell. His mission is to challenge God to condemn me to hell based on my thoughts, words and actions. Actually I would be the one who made that choice when I refused to accept the salvation plan that God offered me for my life. What a sinking feeling in the soul, like the man being led to the execution chamber. Any hope please . . . please! Well like that man, I can choose AT ANY MOMENT to accept the gift of hope God promises. Can you imagine how happy the prisoner would be to find out that he could stop his own execution by accepting the full pardon offer from the Governor?

Even though the Governor called the prison moments before his execution, that execution will still go on if he doesn't consent to this extended gift of life. Suppose the warden or other staff members NEVER told him of the Governor's offer. The prisoner would walk to a certain death because he had never heard the message. Now there is a serious problem.

I am nothing but a sinner like you. I'm here to deliver the message. I'm here to make sure you get the message in this unusual situation. A story of bad choices lots of tears and pain—for others and myself—and then in the brilliant flash of God's love for me, REDEMPTION! This is how I use the ingredients of spiritually as I journey on in hope.

I hope in you Lord and I am only too happy to accept your gift of new life.

Taken together, the five concepts (Mercy, Grace, Forgiveness, Faith and Hope) provide a sufficient structure to encounter the ultimate truth about life. God is my Creator; I am His creation. He loves me and sees me as His precious child. He will never abandon me or write me off as worthless, even when I am tempted to abandon His love for me. These words will never make sense to you until you seek the truth personally. When you honestly and humbly seek Him, you will find Him! That is His promise to each of us.

PART FOUR
PERSONAL POTENTIAL

CHAPTER 13

A RETURN TO REASON AND PURPOSE

WHEN I COMPLETED MY DOCTORAL studies in Clinical Psychology and sought an opportunity to use both my education and my practical learning, I explored the idea of writing a book educating prisoners and their families about the pitfalls they'd meet entering prison life. I also thought how helpful it would be to have a practical guide for making it through the entire prison experience.

Everyone told me to find another subject because prisoners didn't usually read. In other words, why publish a guide for people who would never use it? After years of working on this idea, I decided to put the book aside. After all, if no one was going to read it or if no one would publish it, then my book shouldn't even be written.

KNOWETICS is not written about a specific population, like prisoners and their family members. Rather it is written as an expression of my love for God. It is a gift back to Him for staying with me along this journey. Like you, I disliked the idea of religion, but I have always been spiritually alive—though sometimes on spiritual life support. At my worst moments in life, I knew there was a God, but I had made up my mind to disconnect from His authority in my life.

I had decided to put the whole religion thing into some remote mental storage bin. I was often criticized by others for holding on to some items of a religious nature—including a variety of rosary beads, scapulars, crosses, etc. After all, they might be useful if a vampire attacked me in the future. (But I don't own a garlic necklace, nor did I rush off to buy this remedy before the bells tolled announcing the turn of the century.)

At the time of Hurricane Katrina, I was working with emergency staff at New Orleans International Airport, which had been converted to a massive shelter for scores of displaced persons. While staff would routinely circulate among those seeking shelter at this facility, we could offer only warm bottles of water and military food rations to help those without provisions. You can't possibly imagine the disgusting odor from the restrooms. What else can you do, there are a massive number of people to help, right?

One particular aspect produced significant inner discomfort with me. Yes, it is true that the airport was overrun with individuals and families seeking some type of organized shelter and living in not-too-ideal conditions. However, emergency staff was provided with air-conditioned trailers to sleep in (on the tarmac), and food was served in great quantity and reasonably good quality. Showers were available for those with the luxury of time in which to use them. All you had to do to access this "Disneyland" was to duck into the baggage area between those hanging black strips and make your way out onto the tarmac, show some ID and avail yourself of all of the pleasures that NOLA airport living can bring about. I felt extremely guilty when others lay so close by without these basic comforts.

Prior to that assignment, I was located on Interstate 10 and Causeway Blvd Exit, assisting those who were similarly situated as those displaced and clustered on the floors of airport terminals. The sole exception was that this site was set up for processing those individuals displaced by the storm.

As evacuation helicopters landed, those emerging would be briefly screened and then dispatched to waiting busses. Given the lack of destination location information, many families were separated and wound up far apart from each other—one might go to Houston, another to Nashville. All that was important at this point was to move people along the way and get them to some secure shelter.

I was assigned to a mental health team of professionals who had volunteered to offer immediate intervention skills if needed. Otherwise we were to mingle with those newly arriving (via helicopter, boats, various other vehicles and many by foot with only the clothes on their backs). We were to evaluate them for possible signs of mental or emotional collapse.

We were also to distribute bottles of warm water to help keep individuals from becoming dehydrated—especially during the horribly humid days and nights that followed the strike of Hurricane Katrina. In the course of time, I was assigned to work with those needing medical help and those who were being prepared for arriving ambulances to take them to a variety of health centers.

I learned about the principles of triaging, figuring out who needed the most help first and trying to evaluate each patient quickly, using the principals of cost and utilization effectiveness, how long the patient might last and which had the worst health problems. Given those choices, sadly, some of the most ill patients were passed over in favor of those who seemed to have better odds of survival. Behind our command center were dead bodies stored in discrete black body bags.

In this swirl of society's despair and devastation, we were expected to continue handing out those plastic bottles of water and not pay any attention to those left lying on stretchers after the brief sorting out inspections. Well, ever the non-conformist (odd) individual that I am, I attached myself to a woman lying on a stretcher. She had not only missed the first ambulance but also the second, third and so forth.

Judging from the actions of other "helpers" who were assisting these individuals, I got the impression that she was to lay there quietly until she died alone on a lonely section of Interstate 10—far from home or anyone she knew who could offer her any warmth or comfort. I disregarded the instruction to hang out with my assigned partner (who was now busy throwing bottles of warm water to the assembled crowd of thousands who were awaiting transportation). Listening to the small, soft voice in my heart, I knew that I must stay with that woman and somehow get her boarded on an ambulance, rather than watch her die and then be tucked into an anonymous body bag. You see, for me, she was the face of Hurricane Katrina.

Years before that, I had disregarded an order to remain confined to my post and raced to the site of a nearby military plane crash to aid in rescuing those who may have been inside their burning homes. I found one woman and got her quickly to a safe location. After an inspection of the area, I returned to Ft. Monroe where I discovered my status listed as AWOL (Absent Without Official Leave). That one woman I helped became the face of that experience in which others had been tragically killed.

My prior actions had already ensured that I would be dispatched from military service in light of my fondness for alcohol and drugs (a drug habit I acquired while serving my country through the kind pharmaceutical treats which were readily offered for any illness—real or imagined).

After this event, I thought long and hard about the spiritual unfairness that this picture presented. I was a worthless individual who could have readily died in place of one of the unfortunate victims of that crash. Later, I seriously questioned the unreasonableness of God not accepting substitute volunteers since He knows when these things are going to happen. My actions in going AWOL showed that I was not suitable for further military life (a decision that confirmed my own estimation of myself as a person) and I was soon sent on my way home to New York City.

But even as I was driving North, I had a warm glow of having reached out to someone in desperate need. It sustained me through that experience and became a small building block. I later became involved in the therapeutic process of working with those suffering with the aftereffects of Post Traumatic Stress Disorder or PTSD.

Years earlier as a teenager, I had heard the cries of an elderly woman trapped in an elevator halfway between the floors in our apartment building in Woodside (Queens), New York. As I approached to offer help, I noted that only a small portion of the elevator car was accessible and that if I were to reach in to her, I could lose my arms if the elevator shifted suddenly. Was I fearful, you bet! It was decision time and there was no one else around to help me make that decision. I reached in and pulled her out and went merrily on my way. Another anonymous face imposed upon the agonizing experience of hearing desperate cries for help.

These were all significant life experiences (even though I did not recognize them as important at that time). They served me well for later when sharing a final experience with a neighbor who had sought shelter in my home during a flood in Slidell, Louisiana in the mid 90s. She called at about 3 AM and asked if she could come over to my house since her house was flooded. She had always been kind to me and looked after my property when I was called away, so of course, I obliged. As she sat in my kitchen, she strangely stated to me that she thought she was going to die that night. There she sat wrapped in a blanket, while I made a hot beverage for both of us. I noticed her color did not look very good, so I asked if she would like to lie down in the guest bedroom. She agreed, but in the following moments as she got into the bed, her health took a turn for the worst. I frantically called 911 for help, but the streets were so flooded, the service and fire trucks could not get through. I was not prepared for what was taking place in front of me; I was witnessing someone's last moments of life.

As she started to slip away, I immediately started CPR and kept trying to talk to her. Finally recognizing that my actions didn't seem to be working, I again reached for the phone and called 911 (still doing CPR with the other hand). I then heard the quiet, small, soft voice in my heart urging me to tell her about Jesus.

Ashamedly, I now must admit that I waited till her last moments of consciousness and then urged her to call out to Jesus Christ, her Savior. I will never know if she heard my words or acted on them, but I came away from that experience with eternity knowing that I would never fail to act again when I had those quiet, spiritual moments. That had an impact on my life and I didn't resist the movement of the Spirit in my life. That still, small voice is my principle connection to God. You have it too! But you need to get quiet within yourself if you are going to hear it.

These incidents which I have revealed in this chapter, have largely been known to God and the individuals whom I had the pleasure of serving. You will not find them in any journal article bearing my name; nor will you find them in any news accounts. They were anonymous moments. What you will find in various archives of society is the list of labels assigned because of behaviors that occurred at distinct and early historical times in my life.

Those labels—which are readily assigned by society, have little usefulness in understanding the person I am at this time. They were readily offered, and based on the assumption that I might stay the same person I was then. Given the ever-present, fear-based response thinking, I can either join an ongoing battle to restore my honor, or I can recognize that God is the One who knows my **complete history** and His word tells me that He loves me in a very personal way.

My professional experiences have taught me that healthcare is not the same as "soul care," and that there is little tolerance in the mental health field for pursuing spiritual solutions within a therapeutic environment. Spirituality has apparently become a point that we must not venture beyond. It is deemed to be non-professional. Thank God, He has never brought up the issue of boundaries in my daily communications with Him, nor has He ever declared any subject off limits. I can approach Him with anything.

Have you confronted the same situation in your own life? Have your close friends ever said to you, "Too much information"? Most likely, you can't talk about many painful emotions to anyone close to you for fear of being judged. So do we feel it isn't safe to approach God either? Do we let our politically correct culture agree to our being passed over, as the waiting ambulances carried others off for care? Am I expected to lie on the roadway of life—like the Katrina victims mentioned earlier—and ignore the practical potential of helping others by making real connections to my brothers and sisters? I think not! I do not have to answer to society's judgment, but rather to my God for all of the opportunities that He has extended to me. Get some real help before you go shopping among the professionals of life.

Only you know within your own heart the way you have suffered from society's labels. This is the chance that you have been waiting for all of your life. It's time to shake off those labels, trust God's Word, and trust someone else beside yourself. Together we can do what I can't do in isolation. There is nothing—absolutely nothing—that you have done in life that would limit my willingness to connect with you in a one-to-one relationship of accountability. Let's work on it here together before it's time to face the accusations of Satan. I am not alone in this; there are others like me who will put out their hand to you in a helping gesture.

If you truly need professional services in setting you free, those services are ALWAYS readily available—for a fee. God is willing to set you free . . . for free. He does this out of His great love for you and me. Make no mistake; this is not a rehash of religious doctrine. It is a practical outreach to help stop the very private pains of social isolation (Severcide) that you experience in your public and private lives.

I am throwing you a life preserver and a safety line. You can choose any form of anonymous contact or blind communication— only reach out and make the connection. It will transform your life and the lives of others. Help me to forge this healing initiative, and together let's open pathways of communication for others and ourselves. Nothing is off the table. Nothing is too fantastic to consider in forging this linkage. Your healing starts as you reach out to help others. Remember, the ten lepers helped each other walk toward the temple to present themselves to the priest for ritual cleansing (Luke 17:11-19 NIV).

KNOWETICS requires no formal theological training; just grab the rope that is being extended and God will take care of the rest. Do not let religion or non-religion become a stumbling block to your freedom and healing. God has always loved you and will always grasp your hands.

If you are among the well health wise, you have no need of a physician. But if your heart aches with rejection and pain, then this book was written for you. Before you consider any other options (including self-harm or suicide), try the free stuff first (such as the no cost outreaches associated with twelve-step recovery programs). If you are unhappy with the outcome, we will cheerfully refund your misery and you may go peacefully on your way. Nothing ventured, nothing gained.

CHAPTER 14

DEALING WITH THE TOUGH AND TENDER ISSUES

RECENTLY, THE CONCEPT OF INTELLIGENCE has been expanded to include both social and emotional intelligence. Prior to this, our understanding of intelligence was restricted to a mysterious concept signified by the letter "g" (as a symbol representing intelligence), and it has been studied through the science of psychology. In other words, it is "knowable" by the scientific experts skilled in that science. They use this knowledge to define and measure all things associated with this idea. So, no one exists without having some level of intelligence ("g") as one of the qualities that make us uniquely human. Intelligence is similar to the foundation upon which a house is built; and there are no houses built without a foundation. Intelligence is the foundation for our thoughts, emotions, memories and actions.

To harness the utility of this concept, early practitioners devised various methods that inferentially (indirectly) measured one's intelligence. A scale or measurement of the presence of intellect was captured in the science's ability to reliably recognize characteristics asserted to be evidence of its existence.

These measurements were eventually standardized into a number of tools called intelligence quotient (I.Q.) tests. Now the science of psychology's new tool became a way to measure one individual against a known standard (which was developed from a variety of studies from the general population and organized into "norms").

In practical terms, it gave us a way to look at individual ability and potential and assign a value ranging from severely handicapped to genius. Later society approved the use of these labels. The handicapped risked going to institutions if their families and friends did not take care of them, and we poured more and more resources on those labeled geniuses or those identified as having above average intelligence.

This summation of personal worth later became the foundation of "eugenics." This term suggests that some people are a drain on society, while others are viewed as contributing to society. The logical extension of this type of thinking was the development of social groups based on a person's perceived worth to society. Do you remember the concept of life, liberty and the pursuit of happiness?

Governments—using these standards of personal value—moved into the vacuum this created and made it acceptable to exclude these individuals from society. This led to the development of different methods of assigning labels and to the outright management of the lives of these individuals. For one example, think of the death camps of Hitler's Germany.

These "remedies" worked because we had a limited ability to "know" the true value of an individual life. So this justified assigning few, if any, resources to support and enhance the worth and dignity of labeled individuals. They were not worthy of such efforts and were placed on the trash heaps of society. These beliefs became personally tolerable and were accepted as the unstated law of the land. But if I am a child of God, how can this be?

To a lesser or greater degree, our society has used and continues to use a variety of labels to ascribe potential value to the lives of individuals. Remember the labels of drunk, divorced and felon that we previously explored? If I accept these labels without understanding that my personal worth flows from God's system of individual value, then my personal potential is lost in society's attempt to assign limited resources.

This leads us to a potentially tense examination of the conflict between society's value of my personal worth and my own belief in personal worth. Society's willingness to use "informed" scientific thinking goes against my own inner knowledge of myself. And thus, the battlefield has been laid bare, and the scope of the conflict has been simplified. We are fighting over the value of human worth with those who hold "science" to be the correct standard of value.

Somehow it is very easy to get lost on this battlefield with all of the noise, smoke and confusion. The shouted commands and the flashes of fire engage my conscious desire to somehow survive this experience and I begin to lose sight of my own understanding of truth. Maybe the general back at the command post really knows better—though I am the one in the midst of the battle.

Remember that the general has no way of "knowing" what you are experiencing at that moment. He can only approximate your experience through his prior battlefield encounters. So your fate is in the hands of some distant individual who lacks the clarity and understanding of your personal "here and now" experiences.

David was an excellent general and led his people to many victories (which are documented in the Old Testament). But we know from his writings, that his decision-making was informed by his active engagement with God as he sought personal direction and inspiration for his life. We can do the same thing in our own lives.

The conflict between science and religion is played out on the background of truth (known and unknown). We are urged to choose a side and then to stand firm in our beliefs. Truth is not some middle ground that exists between science and religions for the purpose of strengthening either claim. It is not the property of either one. It is a universal reality. The earth has never had edges— no matter how many people believed in those edges.

The way the battle lines are drawn today, one has to choose between science and religion. The fact is that this choice is a red herring. It is an artificial idea that has come from the "eugenic" thoughts of past generations. Truth is knowable! Its properties can be harnessed on an individual basis and can include elements of science and religion, without personal conflict.

KNOWETICS does not mask itself in the cloaks of science or religion, but instead embraces the belief that all men are created equal (with an equal opportunity to develop, to grow and to enrich the lives of others). As we take on this experience of living and through the application of God's Word (TRUTH), we change. We become transformed. My personal life experiences have led me to conclude that the ideas of Mercy, Grace, Forgiveness, Faith and Hope are essential as I begin to experience Truth as a practical reality in my life.

Therefore, Truth begins to take on new dimensions and the knowledge of all this changes my perception of life. How does this all relate to the experiences, failures and defeats of my life? I'm more than my failures or defeats. I'm also undefined potential when viewed through the lens of God's Word. With the application of the ingredients listed above, I'm able to take on this process of change. If I live in a world that has edges, then it doesn't matter how many of NASA's pictures are available to educate me—I have closed my mind to the truth.

To better define this issue, consider the practical effect of Columbus and his belief that the world was round. Everyone believed that it was not round, but Columbus believed differently and let his certainty inform his conscious decision-making abilities. He did so in spite of what everyone else believed. Our lives embrace the same experience about known or unknown truth. Perhaps his initial influence came from reading in the Bible (Isaiah 40:22 to be exact).

The roar of society makes us fearful and offers us the safety of retreating into the crowd of social agreement. If Columbus had engaged in this form of invited retreat, the truth would have eventually emerged in the voyage of some other intrepid explorer. But Columbus would have forever lost the privilege of discovery. We are also invited through God's love for us to discover the essential truth that defines our personhood.

That search for personal personhood creates a difficult journey back through the sea of labels in which we find ourselves immersed. Remember that the sea is only one element—though a big element—of this world's structure. And the earth exists in the context of the universe with its innumerable galaxies. That is a first step in assessing the personal usefulness of any label that is part of our past behaviors.

Our journey of hope and transformation requires that once again we set sail upon this sea of labels, stopping briefly to review each one, and then sailing on until we have moved past the clutter of our past lives and arrived at the point of self-identification in which we recognize that we are all children of God.

Remember back to that time as a child when you chose "good" because it was the right thing to do? You were loved and loveable at the same time. You did not need to establish your worth through your actions. Your worth was known by you and was knowable to others. This knowledge was basic and was not the product of some crafty contrived words or based upon your actions. You were plainly a lovable child: a child of God. KNOWETICS offers the hope of re-discovering this point in time and an opportunity to reposition your life in the knowledge of this discovery.

When I drive to the end of my street, I can choose to go right or left. A right hand turn will take me toward the town, while a left hand turn will take me out of town. This tight structure of urban development seems to limit my possibilities. The fact is that I can abandon my car and walk forward into the woods beyond. Or nature may choose to re-align my options through the experiences of a radical tectonic redistribution (otherwise known as an earthquake).

My personal journey of re-discovery may be caused by a personal "earthquake" (or series of them). In any event, it will take all of my focused energy to undertake and undergo the process of transformation. This is not a journey for the weak, those who are easily frightened, or those who are moral cowards. It is stepping out onto the smoke, noise and flashes of gunfire that we encounter on the battlefield of our lives. My chance of surviving this experience is related to my personal awareness of the truth.

My personal weapons are Mercy, Grace, Forgiveness, Faith and Hope. If I am going to have any chance of surviving this conflict, I must know how to use these resources in this battle and the battles to come. My future life depends upon a personal ability to master my knowledge of these weapons and the best times to use them. This "knowing" occurs outside of science and religion.

A return to reason is based on my knowledge of these "weapons" and understanding the possibilities that exist between them. Remember the simple example of our five fingers and our ability to grasp objects? My fingers allow me to use my hands in an endless variety of possibilities. Knowledge of the terms used to describe all these possible actions isn't the same as the experience of actually grasping an object and using my hands and fingers to complete some desired activity.

If you do not understand the usefulness of what you already have, then you cannot hope to achieve mastery in using the weapons of Mercy, Grace, Forgiveness, Faith and Hope. They are nice to look at and admire as theological concepts. I may even already own a few of them, but if I have no appreciation of their potential, I can hardly use them on a battlefield.

Like most of us, I often cry out to God to help me when I realize that I am on another of life's battlefields. But unlike the general in the command post, God is regularly in direct communication with me (via the Holy Spirit), urging me to use what He has provided for my safe journey through life.

Reading this book and understanding its words is not the same as having a working knowledge about how they come together as concepts. Nor is it the same as successfully operating in the realm of KNOWETIC thought and action.

To be successful, you must learn to master the use of each of these weapons so that while you are engaged in the journey of re-discovery, you will have both defensive and offensive weapons with which to overcome the conflict of the prior labels of your life.

Our enemy—Satan—knows how to skillfully engage our consciousness with a host of distraction techniques. He seeks mastery over our souls by constantly throwing the flaming darts of labels against our defensive shields. In preparation for a battle, the military uses basic training to provide a time, place and knowledge of weaponry and its proper use on the battlefield. Likewise, if I have no personal knowledge or experience with the use of God's Word as an ever-present help, waiting until "battle" will prove to be a poor time to pull out my sword (The Word of God) and start to use it—we must be prepared.

KNOWETICS is the boot camp of individuality. It provides the time to acquire knowledge of our individual weapons and an opportunity to apply that knowledge in the safety of a personal training experience. When I use these skills, in combination with accountability, I can go forward onto the battlefields of life and be confident in my ability to survive anything the enemy can throw at me. Personal mastery requires personal knowledge and skill building.

You may ask, "Why should I go back and acquire this knowledge and skill at this particular time in my life?" The answer is quite simple. You are already on your journey and this knowledge and skill will ensure your ability to survive your current and future interactions within society.

The other application lays in our ability to use both knowledge and skill needed to live with others. This knowledge of our own lives can aid us in reaching out and helping others, even with limitations or the lack of personal resources.

KNOWETICS is not denying science or religion. It adopts the belief that truth is "knowable." It uses a personal knowledge of the truth as its principal concept, which leads us to the hope that our future lives will be different from how we lived in the past.

Awareness of this simple process gives us the foundation we need to move closer to personal freedom. That is truly a return to reason and purpose.

Now, we can move on to applying all of this personally.

CHAPTER 15

STRIPPING AWAY THE MASKS OF SECRECY

TWENTY-FIVE YEARS OF WORKING WITH countless individuals, couples and families have given me an understanding of the many faces of tragedy. They flood back into my memory not only as patients, but also as individuals—many that have been disgraced or labeled (whether they know it or not).

I consider part of my job responsibilities to be helping individuals remove these labels by figuring out what makes them stick in the first place. That way I try to understand each individual's connection point and how those connections affected the lives of those with whom they lived and worked. Then, when the behaviors, the stigma and points of connection were understood, the healing process could begin.

You cannot do this work effectively in a relationship where a power differential exists, such as in the confines of therapy. As a psychotherapist, I may use the information you provide (or that I acquire about you) to arrive at a commonly accepted diagnosis (label).

The diagnosis serves me (the therapist) in that I can use that data point to move onto official treatment modalities (standards of practice), and equally important, I can seek reimbursement through the healthcare system for my work if you have insurance of some type. That is what the business of healthcare offers to its members and practitioners.

While a diagnosis helps therapists understand some general description of the condition, it has little value in helping to forge some meaningful connection point between the patient and therapist. It cannot inform the therapist of the patient's personal understanding of the taste of "vanilla ice cream." We can hang out together and I can observe some of the behavioral costs linked with the diagnosis, but I still have no further actual knowledge of your ice cream experience.

Therefore, the best I can hope to offer you are some generalities that may prove to be useful in navigating your life. I can supplement these efforts with the use of outdated remedies, technical procedures and a variety of self-help interventions, but a therapist can only engage in the old practice of the western shopkeeper—helping you identify what is on the shelf that might help you in the short run. For example, if the shopkeeper convinced me that the most practical solution was the purchase of a hammer, then all of my problems need to somehow be remedied by using that hammer. Since there is no other available product which is a better fit.

That interaction is highlighted by the hidden fact that patients are afraid to reveal too much about themselves out of fear of not being accepted. Set these concerns in the context of a naturally unequal therapy relationship and they are especially limited in what they're willing to reveal about their experience with tasting ice cream. They might think, "If I tell you about cold, wet, white and creamy . . . you will surely think I'm crazy!" Unless we both share those basics in common!

Given a therapist's rule to not disclose too much personal information, it's going to be difficult to find out how to benefit from a knowledge of similar experiences. In fact, in most cases because of financial considerations and personal uncertainly, the project fails. There is a silent agreement to focus on one problem without disturbing the dust on the real experiences of life.

An individual using the KNOWETICS approach—can move into a relationship of engagement with an equal, because I have screened my accountability partner to assure myself that this is an individual who knows the taste of vanilla ice cream and is one who is willing to authenticate my personal experience by offering the hope of real change.

This moment is as personal a meeting as there can be and is on the most intimate level. It's no longer a question of money; now there can be the free exchange of experiences without the use of diagnosis or the effects of treatment. The individual can finally feel, "it is pure acceptance of me as I am—not what you want me to be." Wow, can you imagine having that experience?

You can have that experience if you are willing to go back and explore all of the labels that have been assigned to you and identify the most disturbing of them. Initially having done that in the privacy of your own mind, you continue to move backward in time until you find that little child inside you who was loved and worthy of love. The tools (ingredients) you'll use are Mercy, Grace, Forgiveness, Faith and Hope.

Using these tools skillfully, you then start moving forward, back to your current day-to-day existence, ever mindful of the worth of that child inside. You stop regularly at the oasis of meditation and prayer, refreshing yourself in God's love for you, as the individual you know you are now.

There, at those regular oasis stops, you leave behind the labels that have been used to limit your future. Since it is based on your encounters with God's love for you, this process—once done—quickly becomes a habit and soon you are walking in the "Son"shine of His love—a here and now experience!

You can maintain your strides toward emotional and mental health (hope) by establishing relationships of accountability with those God places in your life. After starting this process, you will never have to look back again. You will come to know that your individuality is a gift from God and that He will knit all of those experiences into the tapestry of His plans. Somehow, in the great unknowable plans of God, it all has some meaning.

Make no mistake—this is not a painless romp in the mall of life. It is a manageable journey of transformation as you get your first taste of the experience of His great love for you. This is not an agreement to religious doctrine or dogma, nor is it the blind acceptance of science. It is the ultimate experience of having an ongoing love relationship with Him. It is all about relationship; it is not about the rules or regulations of society in any form or shape.

"But," you say, "You don't understand the depths of my personal evil or about my abandonment of all of the basic connections to His truth." That doesn't matter. Even if we're unfaithful to Him, He will always remain faithful to His Word. Do you remember the story of His love for His people, Israel?

The same basic truth lives on today in the form of an opportunity for a personal relationship with Him. All healing occurs in the context of hope, not in the context of condemnation. Remember the jeering crowds of Jerusalem; all of their shouts and hysteria could not transform the Reality of Truth standing before them. Will you choose the angered shouts of society as the reference point on which you live out your life, or will you choose the quiet assurance of God's love for you? It's your choice.

Let me tell you about some faces that flood my mind as I attempt to recapture their personal encounters with truth. There are so many individual stories informing the creation of this book, but I want to provide you with those that are most essential in helping you re-discover your humanity and your worth. You see, each of these individuals created the experience of change unknown to even the closest family members, partners or friends. That is the same invitation that I am extending to you in the form of KNOWETICS.

The first to come to my mind was a shy, young woman in obvious pain. She reached into the depths of her soul and revealed a long-term history of a sexual relationship with her father that resulted in a pregnancy and the birth of her son.

Her son was now a pre-adolescent and wanted to know about his father. In her grief and shame, she had nothing to offer her son but a false explanation that his father had died. So she was missing a remarkable opportunity to connect deeply with her son. Her misery was there for all to see; but the causes of her misery were unknown to anyone else except God, her father, and now me.

I could have sent her deep into the arsenal of modern day mental health. Rather I chose to engage in an intense understanding of her unique problems. There was no air of judgment because I knew that what this young woman needed most of all at this time was love and acceptance.

So together, we forged a bond and began to review her life's tragedies in the context of loving acceptance. This odyssey helped her to transform a lifetime of misadventures and horrific decision-making. In this setting, she rediscovered her personal worth and was able to love herself in spite of those happenings.

The outcome of this voyage was borne out in her ability to ultimately link her shame with the answer to her son's questions about his father's identity. She creatively assigned his name to an unspoken category and courageously offered herself, allowing her son to develop a sense of closure as he came to understand her explanations.

Primarily she allowed her son to explore her previous poor decision-making, while avoiding blame and confusion that might have made her reveal his father's name. She sacrificed her own reputation to help her son understand the circumstances surrounding his conception. Wow, what a young woman!

She stands in the company of other courageous unrecognized individuals. Each moved past their life circumstances and with the knowledge that they had always been a child of God, transformed their lives.

Consider next, the woman who presented herself for a disability evaluation in the company of her lesbian lover. She needed the quiet support of her friend to face the personal traumas of her childhood. Given the experiences of her past life, she was depressed and perhaps suicidal. At nine years old, her mother's boyfriend (with her mother's knowledge and even approval) had sexually abused her.

Without warning, her mother cruelly encouraged and participated in the rape of her young daughter. This was not only a traumatic physical violation, but also the worst violation of personal trust that a child could endure.

As a result, she turned to the loving acceptance of other women. She was seeking to find the love she had never experienced at home. So do I look at the label of lesbian, along with her personal depression and suicidal urges, or do I take on this woman's history of trauma and try to deeply and empathically understand how these tragic experiences had marked her life of pain?

To pass either of these two women on the street, one would have no way to recognize their bitter history of rejection and failure. In fact, according to the valuation system offered by society, one would be labeled as a tramp while the other would be assigned the label of deviate. Now, that is a strange way to help an individual transform his or her life. In fact, it is a subtle—sometimes not so subtle—social pressure to "get over it." Sometimes we're stuck and can't move on under our own power.

The horror of these personal stories unfolded in my office as I attempted to understand them in a human sense. The tools of science offered only the cold reality of assessment and diagnosis. Then I was to pass this information (via summary remarks) to those who would decide each woman's worth, and after reviewing my report, would either award or deny disability benefits to her.

This was part of the transforming process for me personally, as I attempted to put a human face on assessment and diagnosis. Each patient had worth and a story to be told in the context of writing a report. Each of these reports was difficult to face as I tried to capture the patient's humanity.

My peers in the field of psychology all had the chance to hide behind the standards of professional diagnosis (DSM-IV, the then-known "truth"). This kept them professionally distant, but you can't truly know someone else from a distance. You have to get in close and share their experiences. God does that with us when we cry out for His help and understanding in making sense of our confused and uncertain lives.

A friend of mine had a prestigious and successful career as a surgeon and doctor. His professional life was excellent and he was well respected among his peers. His medical accomplishments included mastering the skills associated with hip ball joint replacement surgery.

Not only did he provide medical relief to many suffering patients, but he also made the effort to educate other doctors in the technology and the safe use of surgical procedures. His professional activities touched the lives of thousands of suffering people. "Well," you may say, "What's wrong with living that kind of life?"

There is nothing wrong it. But, let's look a little closer at his history. He married someone who eventually betrayed his hopes and the confidence he had placed in her. His wife also gave up any appearance of loyalty and openly embraced her (their) attorney as her lover and accomplice. This sad path led to divorce.

He was stunned by the disloyalty but also by the discovery that his wife and former attorney had defrauded the marriage of funds coming from apartment rentals. He had confidently placed these assets in the care of his wife much earlier in their marriage.

He discovered that both she and her lover were claiming that a certain percentage of the properties were unrented (even though they were). These two skillfully pocketed the income from these rentals and informed the accountant (along with her husband) that they remained unrented. The lovers began to fund their schemes of marital bliss on the back of the helpless soon-to-be-divorced husband.

Antagonism grew in this environment of distrust and initially focused upon the property settlement. Throughout this time period, the husband intuitively knew that something was wrong, but he remained hopeful that a fair settlement was possible, even while he nursed his wounded heart. The next skirmish moved onto custody and visitation issues over their two children. The court awarded custody to the mother and ample visitation to the father. Case closed, right?

Sadly, not so. While he had since remarried and was trying to sort out the shambles of his former marriage, the ex-wife was incensed by her belief that she had somehow been cheated in the original property settlement.

As a result, she continued to cause pain by denying him access to the children during what was supposed to be his regularly scheduled visits. In exasperation, he filed a court action seeking to have his children for the Father's Day weekend, and the court approved this request. Leaving court, he settled into the fond expectation of being rejoined with his now-estranged children over the upcoming weekend.

When the weekend arrived, he drove to the home of his ex-wife (in the company of his new wife), fully expecting his former wife to follow court orders. Surely, she would not be bold enough to violate court orders! But that is exactly what she did. She offered some lame excuse—which was clearly a lie—and wouldn't let him see the kids. At that point, he snapped and lost all emotional control.

He picked up a kitchen knife to dramatize his fury over the denial of his request, but then a struggle ensued for control and in a moment, his former wife lay on the floor dying. In the confusion that followed, her lawyer/boyfriend emerged from a room at the rear of the home and engaged in a struggle with his former client. The boyfriend/lawyer soon lay on the floor dying from the knife wounds inflicted by my friend. At that agonizing moment, the healer of many had transgressed and had taken the lives of two human beings.

If you have never had the experience of having snapped under some moment of tremendous crisis, then you may be experiencing a lack of empathy at this moment. The fact that he had been a caring and compassionate man healing the medical ills of others vanished in the efforts of society to re-assign any estimate or approximation of personal worth in light of these crimes. In fact, the experience was so traumatizing that he had a psychotic break with reality and stood in the bloody kitchen holding the knife until the police escorted him away. In a brief, unchangeable moment in time, his life was transformed into a hellish nightmare—once a doctor, now a double murderer.

We know the publically revealed facts of the case, but few of us understand the devastating personal trauma that followed as he was charged with double homicide. He eventually pled guilty to two counts of manslaughter that the D.A offered as he became aware of the non-public facts of the case. He was sentenced to prison and vanished from public life. All of their lives violently and radically transformed because of non-compliance with a court order. He had hoped for a moment of understanding with his ex-wife and ended up with convictions for the deaths of two persons.

After settling into the routine of prison life, he willingly engaged in helping his fellow prisoners grow past the histories that trapped them; one prisoner even went on to complete doctoral studies.

The reality was that he had lost his medical license in further administrative proceedings that followed his conviction for manslaughter. His great hope of regaining his medical license never materialized. But given the kind support and loving affections of his many friends, he was able to successfully re-establish his own sense of personal worth.

He was ultimately assigned to work in the prison's medical library, in some strange parody of his former life. He worked to maintain his medical expertise by reading the journals that continually arrived at the prison library.

He started to use his medical skill and knowledge of surgery in the defense of other doctors facing claims of medical malpractice or professional negligence. He regained his prior stature as a respected professional by assisting attorneys in developing an intricate knowledge of medical practice and surgical procedures that conformed with the standards of professional medical practice.

Most people, who read of his fall from grace, never knew what happened after imprisonment. But for those of us who have known him personally, we have seen the clear evidence of his redemption experience—transforming the shame of the past into the sweet fragrance of self-renewal. I had the rare privilege to accompany him on his early journey of exploration and discovery. I call him my friend because that is exactly what he is. My co-explorer!

* * *

Crimes and sins have a lasting impact upon everyone involved. The closer the individual is to the situation, the greater the impact will be. Being incarcerated has a notable impact upon those who are serving prison sentences. We now know that the post-incident consequences may often produce a lifelong pattern of symptoms (termed post-traumatic stress disorder or PTSD). From the violation of personal security (which comes with crimes like burglary, theft and robbery), those affected experience life changing shifts in perceptions and decision-making abilities. With the commission of crimes of greater magnitude like kidnapping, assault, rape and murder, this scarring process becomes much more extensive and may impair individuals for the rest of their lives. I have included several case histories to illustrate the lifelong impact that these events have had on these patient's lives. They are used to bring the reader into an awareness of the harm that has been inflicted on the lives of others, by seemingly transitory events. Each of the individual's discussed has been scarred for life, though you would never know the nature of that scarring if you were to meet them casually. Most people who have been victimized (and that might include readers) would never voluntarily discuss their situation out of the shame and personal pain these revelations produce. Rather you would observe these individuals exhibiting a range of contradictory behaviors. Many will never make the conscious connection between past events and current dysfunctional behaviors. But the fact is that trauma inflicted on others will ALWAYS produce scarring in the lives of victims. It will also manifest in some form in the lives of the offenders themselves. Perhaps these histories will afford you, my reader, an opportunity to develop insight and compassion for those you have hurt through past offensive behaviors. When we injure others, no matter what our reasons may be, we incur a lifelong burden of responsibility and restoration. Few of us can successfully shut these events off in our heads. Instead they keep replaying over and over again until they are resolved by an act of forgiveness.

It is impossible to put into words the long-term effects on individual lives that follow exposure to abuse. Any type of mental, physical, emotional or sexual abuse will produce unpredictable lifelong consequences, which form the basis for living out *"secret lives".* What we do to others in a moment of selfish need, anger or fear invariably results in a distinct but unseen personality maladjustment that is likely to NEVER be revealed to anyone else. Nor is it likely to ever heal without extended care and spiritual support.

I will provide a story about living secret lives. Sometimes our misinformed decisions create situations in which our secret lives are partially exposed to the view of others. Usually this results in a surge of inner rationalization and furious damage control. We must continue to maintain the mask we wear, while politely rejecting the curiosity of others in our lives.

Thus we offer a flurry of rationalizations and numerous reassurances that we are not the identified suspects. "You have it all wrong," we plead, "It's like this . . ." and we continue the deception—applying it to all arenas of our lives. "Boy that was a close one. I had better be careful in the future" is what we conclude deep within our psyche. Let's get that mask back on straighter this time.

When Henry was brought to my office in the company of his parents and sibling, he had become the curious focus of a police investigation at the age of eleven years old. It seems that his behaviors with a younger sister had become public knowledge and now he was under the scrutiny of law enforcement as a perpetrator. His behaviors had been revealed through the well-established route of reporting child abuse. How does an eleven-year-old boy arrive at the point of being intensely examined for his behaviors?

Like anyone in a similar situation, Henry had quickly retreated to the shelter of deception and further isolation. There he stood trying to weather out the furious storms around him. The "kindly" policeman had confidently reassured Henry that he knew he was some sort of pervert and that he was not going to stop his investigation until he arrived at the truth. Into this setting stepped young Henry, as he looked warily around my office.

For a brief time his mother offered additional information and concerns (adding to the information provided during her urgent call for help). Our talk took place in the presence of her husband who sat next to her strangely mute. I fully expected that he was reeling from the impact of finding out about intimate behaviors between pre-teen siblings. "How could this have happened in our home", his eyes asked. "After all, my wife and I are practicing Christians and we have raised our children with God's Word."

While the father remained silent through this and future appointments, the silence came from his bewilderment and unvoiced concerns. He clearly did not know what to do, except try to keep his son from these reckless and sinful behaviors. Nevertheless, mom and dad had signed on for a journey in truth telling.

So began the task of establishing a relationship with a suspicious and untrusting child who was extremely isolated emotionally, and was suffering the experience of being cut-off from those he loved. This harsh reality didn't come from above. It came from within, with the sad recognition that he was doing things that were unacceptable and unlawful.

Furthering complicating this picture was how torn his parents were about the whole affair. The police continued to press their investigation and Henry's parents didn't know if they should retain a lawyer to protect their son while helping the family get through possible criminal prosecution.

Several eager attorneys offered some glimmer of resolving this problem; only the promised resolution would require a fee of ten thousand dollar retainer: a financial challenge that only added to the parent's feelings of devastation and fear.

Bringing their problems to my office, I realized that a young boy does not engage in these activities (not mere curiosity or exploration of a sibling's body) unless his experiences had been learned, as someone had previously engaged him in sexual activities. If you could only have seen Henry's eyes as he searched for a way to escape.

With all this personal and societal condemnation, we wearily began our sessions. My role was tour guide and historian, helping Henry see the need to share his experiences with me as a means of accountability (all of this occurring in the life of an immature eleven-year old boy). Do you remember Nikki's keen insight from past chapters? She voiced her personal understanding of the problem, stating, "You have to tell someone or else it will eat you up inside."

Henry had put on a mask of secrecy to shield him from the consequences of pain and judgment. The battlefield had been defined and Henry became engaged in the re-constructive process after intensive months of trust building. He did manage to talk about his early history at the hands of other unidentified males. Eventually he was able to name a distant family member. Grimly as family members became aware that a strange virus was spreading in the family, they sought to comfort each other by starting to discuss this openly, based on truth.

Unfortunately not every story has a Hollywood ending. In this particular family, once the parents of the distant family member became aware of their son's activities, they promptly marched him off to a Christian counselor who cautioned the alarmed parents that their son may need to be hospitalized. In the ensuing reality, they promptly confronted their son regarding the known facts.

Of course he quickly retreated to the safety of denial and deception, not the welcoming arms of understanding parents. He gallantly offered to take a lie detector test. His feverish parents trying to calm their fears jumped at his offer of exoneration (for him and them) and funded his deception to the tune of four hundred fifty dollar's worth for a "lie" detector test.

The parent's mad grasping at the assurance that his denial offered, were set in the background of his current activities. He had recently approached two other boys, during his younger brother's birthday sleepover. Additionally he had approached a young girl at school, with language that earned him a prompt school suspension. His parents were informed that a second similar incident would result in his expulsion from school.

This information was in the foreground of his parent's thinking, but offered no insight into their decision to leap at the opportunity to escape the reality of their son's behavior. See, the lie detector results clearly show that he was not lying! Case Closed: Next problem please! Only time and the child's need to deal with his issues will reveal the problem in an open and accepting fashion. Unfortunately, this leads to more unlawful contacts and the spread of this dreaded spiritual virus to other families.

Henry, after learning how to be accountable for his actions, was able to talk about his struggles with wanting to have further incidents take place. In his sense of shame, he could not grasp this understanding, because he did not understand it himself. *If this hurts me, why would I want to keep doing this?* It was only when his younger sister assaulted the youngest brother (aged four) did he recognize the sinister nature of his own actions and their effect on the security of his family. Like some horrible disease, it was spreading beyond his control, and he was the reason for his family's pain.

Having experienced his pain and shame at such an intense level, together we worked out a safe environment where he could freely explore his thoughts about these behaviors without bringing about wrath or judgment. That opportunity provided a chance to look at these trigger points, allowing him ultimately to understand his recent actions in relation to his early experiences. He continues to struggle with the turmoil, but he has made a remarkable shift in thought and understanding.

When we worked on his learning to be accountable, no longer were there flurries of lies, saying "I don't know," or those prolonged periods of silence when asked directly. Instead he has learned how to confidently express himself and his concerns in a relationship of love and acceptance. He has also been able to offer his parents some insight into his inner struggles (to their profound relief).

The family is well on its way to restoration and wellness by exposing a disease which crept into their midst undetected. This was a spiritual disease. These strange viruses are all about us, eager to infect each of us individually or as a family . . . if we let it happen. Unfortunately there are no shots to boost our spiritual immunity. Our only weapon is our ability to make responsible and informed choices.

This story strangely dovetails, but is a strong indicator of how early choices can shape an ugly present life, filled with shameful personal experiences and incredible inner turmoil. These encounters attract others and usually result in unacceptable behaviors. Outward demonstrations of these behaviors can lead to the assignment of labels and various social sanctions as has been previously discussed Eventually the individual becomes locked into a constant holding pattern on the outside of society, unaware of the hope of dramatic personal change.

Our actions conscious and unconscious have a very real impact on those whose lives we touch. If as offenders we have brought suffering into the lives of others then we have incurred a double liability. We are responsible for our actions to God and to those we have damaged. The relationship with a loving God allows us to get right with Him about any of our actions. The influence we have had on others' lives requires that we pray for them consistently, asking for grace and healing in their lives.

That is what KNOWETICS is all about. No matter what your personal background, no matter what your sins or crimes may be (remember that some may be viewed as scarlet) and no matter what your current position in society may be there is HOPE. A re-reading of Nathaniel Hawthorne's classic book *The Scarlet Letter* may bring a reinforced understanding that you have a personal worth that will ultimately transform any circumstance or situation. After all you are a precious child of God.

The painful work that lies ahead is yours to do in the loving embrace of God's care and a journey companion who presents himself or herself in a relationship of accountability.

Let's define the process further by looking at mental health issues next.

CHAPTER 16

PERIMETER PSYCHOLOGY

THERE ARE VAMPIRES AMONG US, are you one? That is the idea that Dr. Albert J. Bernstein puts forth in his book, *Emotional Vampires, Dealing with People Who Drain You Dry*. He uses a novel approach to explain personality disorders.

A personality disorder is an entrenched way of relating to others. It is usually a lifelong pattern of behaviors that brings us into conflict with others. Since it is a continuing pattern of behaviors, mental health professionals usually have little to offer to those who suffer from these disorders.

The terminology of personality disorders is listed in the *DSM-IV* (*Diagnostic and Statistical Manual IV* published by the American Psychiatric Association). Among these diagnostic terms is the category of Anti-Social Personality Disorder (ASP) that is usually applied to offenders—especially those sentenced to prison.

It is important that you know and understand the way this label will impact your life. We all need to be conscious of the ways we use this information to work on ourselves and reduce or remove this pattern of behavior.

Yes, I said to remove or reduce this offensive pattern of behavior; change is possible. Once locked into this kind of classification, it was previously impossible to counter the limitations it imposed, but knowing about how this diagnostic criteria was developed will give you insight on how to handle this issue.

There is no one on the planet without worth! That is part of being a child of God. I have long believed that these diagnostic assignments are a way of writing off those of us who have offended others. It can be a way of saying "they are beyond hope," but don't you believe it! Until you draw your last breath, there is always hope.

What I would like to do at this point is to give you a short introduction to all of the personality disorders and then to focus on those that are most relevant to offenders. Please remember that everyone has some of these characteristics in their personalities so don't start to diagnose yourself as you read the descriptions. Otherwise, you will find yourself becoming quickly overwhelmed by feelings of despair and hopelessness.

God made you, and though you possibly went down the wrong path, learning things that offend others, He can rewire you with your cooperation! The world tries to change us from the outside; He changes us from the inside. He does not use the world's system of valuation.

The DSM-IV classifies a personality disorder by the following criteria: "An enduring pattern of behavior that deviates markedly from the way that others behave themselves within one's culture. It is usually evidenced by two or more of the following ways of experiencing the world:

- The way we view others or events in our thoughts.
- The way in which we respond emotionally (appropriateness and intensity of response) to others and events.
- The way in which we relate to others interpersonally.
- The degree to which we control our impulses.
- Other items to note about a personality disorder are:
- This dysfunctional pattern occurs over broad areas of our lives.
- It causes distress or impairment in most of the ways we function.
- It has existed for a long period of time and usually started to emerge behaviorally in adolescence.
- It is not the result of another mental disorder.
- It is not the result of short-term transient effects of substance abuse, medications or head trauma.
- It can be measured by the impact it has on the lives of others and the situations in which we live.
- It is enduring because it repeats itself over and over again and we never seem to learn from past events.

Given these guidelines, it is time to take an HONEST look at the way you relate to others as I list the various types of personality disorders below. Each disorder will be given a short explanation so that you can understand the different ways in which they impact others.

PARANOID PERSONALITY DISORDER

This is an individual who views others with suspicion and distrust. They have serious concerns about the intentions of others so they can't seem to trust others. It may also include the way we view organizations or the government.

SCHIZOID PERSONALITY DISORDER

This is an individual who is detached from social relationships and seems emotionally distant or has limited emotional expressiveness.

SCHIZOTYPAL PERSONALITY DISORDER

This is an individual who experiences discomfort in close relationships with others. It happens because of distorted views and/or odd behavior patterns.

ANTISOCIAL PERSONALITY DISORDER

This is an individual who has displayed a pattern of violating the rights of others. They may be regularly in conflict with rules, regulations or laws.

BORDERLINE PERSONALITY DISORDER

This is an individual who demonstrates a pattern of unstable relationships. It impacts how they see themselves, their emotions and their ability to control their impulses.

HISTRIONIC PERSONALITY DISORDER

This is an individual who is regularly seeking excessive attention and tends to be emotionally excessive in the way that they relate to others.

NARCISSISTIC PERSONALITY DISORDER

This is an individual who demonstrates an ongoing need to be admired, they have poor empathy for others and they tend to have inflated self-images.

AVOIDANT PERSONALITY DISORDER

This is an individual who feels inadequate. They are unlikely to be engaged socially and they are extremely sensitive to being evaluated by others.

DEPENDENT PERSONALITY DISORDER

This individual's behaviors can be described as overly submissive and clings to others. They are the kind of individual who needs to be taken care of.

OBSESSIVE-COMPULSIVE PERSONALITY DISORDER

This is an individual who demonstrates a need for control, perfection and orderliness. Their actions cause others to resist the constricting effect on relationships.

* * *

These are the major personality disorders. A brief reading will reflect the overlap between each of the categories. Remember that we all have elements of each of these characteristics in our own personality, so don't take this information and apply it without understanding. It is provided so that you will have the ability to look at how you relate to others.

Now that you are aware of the meanings of these terms, I would like to move the focus ahead to explore five of these categories at a deeper level. If you find yourself dwelling in these diagnostic shadows, please take heart. It simply means that you have the insight to look within yourself and see how you relate to others. This is an excellent start to changing the reality of your life.

* * *

Dr. Bernstein focuses upon five of these disorders by identifying the most destructive personality disorders in terms of the damage they do to our relationships with others. If you have come to a point in your life where you're sick and tired of the way you interact with others, then this section might be your stepping stone toward a new life.

While Dr. Bernstein does not address the concept of good and evil in his work, another professional, M. Scott Peck, M.D., has devoted extensive effort at identifying the field of good and evil. Two of his most outstanding books on this subject are "People of the Lie" and "Glimpses of the Devil." If you are committed to changing your lifestyle, these books will be valuable resources.

Good and evil exist as sure as day and night exist!

Dr. Bernstein chose **Antisocial Personality Disorder (ASP)** for his initial step into the dark world of personality disorders. He calls them "lovable rogues"—though if someone has been stung from encounters with this type of individual, I'm certain that they would not continue to see them in the context of being "loveable." Those who suffer from this disorder use other people shamefully. Both genders can have this type of personality disorder, though it is usually more prevalent among males.

According to Dr. Bernstein, ASP might be of various types—for example, the daredevil, the used car salesman or the bully. Without going into great detail, it is my belief that a true ASP can shift within these behavioral manifestations. To others, this ability to shift between warm and caring then into the coldness of the bully is a frightening experience for others and may cause them to step back from future encounters. ASP sufferers may get what they want, but not without significant cost to others and themselves. ASPs are addicted to excitement.

An individual manifesting ASP can change, but that takes work. Mental health workers often write them off as being un-teachable and manipulative. The only hope of meaningful change is for the person to recognize the behavior pattern and submit to finding a spiritual solution. The focus is on internal beliefs, not on external realities. While the world of mental health care is usually given to writing off this personality type, I want to assure you that meaningful and profound change is possible but it will take hard work and yielding to the spiritual. Curbing the demands of the flesh can be a tremendous—but not impossible—battle.

ASPs are demanding, selfish and insensitive to the needs of others. If this describes you, then let me give you some good news— change starts with the ability to recognize character flaws. It is the first step on the path to freedom. A great way of recognizing this disorder is to check out your personal history of aggression. If in doubt, talk to those who truly love you and let them educate you about what they have seen and experienced in their relationship with you.

The next is **Histrionic Personality Disorder (HPD)**. When you think of this type of personality, remember the term "show business." Dr. Bernstein notes that for these individuals, it is like living out a soap opera in all of their relationships.

HPDs are likely to use whatever opportunities they have to seek out attention and approval. Dr. Bernstein notes that they will sing and dance their way into the hearts of others. They have an ability to make others think they are important, and then they use that skill to prey upon their victims. The end result is a superficial individual who uses others for their own gain.

The key to understanding an HPD is to recognize that they are "always acting" and putting on a masterful performance. This type of individual can be found in both genders, but may be easier to recognize in females. A way to identify individuals who have this disorder is to observe their speech patterns. They use words as manipulation tools to control their own internal needs. They are likely to be unpredictable to others (which is troubling to their victims). The response of others is to move away from relationships with these individuals.

If these individuals get a flash of insight about their own style of interacting with others, they quickly become unsure of themselves. This feeling of insecurity makes them seek reassurance from others. They become all consumed with getting back their sense of internal stability. Seeking attention and needing approval wears others out. The key emotional response to HPD individuals is the feeling of being drained. Change for an HPD individual requires a spiritual understanding that God's grace and mercy is enough.

Another notorious emotional vampire-type is the **Narcissistic Personality Disorder (NPD)**. An encounter with these individuals will always be marked by a "Big Ego," and everything else around them will be unimportant. Their focus is always on ME! They are always the most talented, the brightest, and the "all around best person." These individuals have no concept of modesty or humility, nor would they understand such concepts in others. They drain others through their consistent self-interest and neglect of the needs of those who are unlucky enough to have to share space and time.

Encounters with an NPD will be marked by their insatiable needs. They are special people with special needs. "Little people" would not understand what it is to be such a special individual, so the NPD is indifferent to the needs of others. The picture that comes to my mind is of the individual standing in front of the mirror telling themselves they are beautiful. As others pass them, they are so absorbed preening themselves that they are not even aware of the presence of others!

The greatest fear of an NPD is "being ordinary." Dr. Bernstein describes their needs as "tremendous." He notes that they cannot be connected to anything else but themselves—the world revolves around them, and what they need from others to exist is "worship." These individuals will generally evoke mixed feelings in others. He also goes on to note that they love their "accomplishments, but hate their conceit." In that sentence, Dr. Bernstein describes the internal conflict that rages in the mind of an NPD.

The key word here is "insatiable." An NPD can never be satisfied with anything, and their intense inner needs twist all encounters. Please, though, do not confuse the role of self-esteem with narcissism; they are not related. The behavior of an NPD will always be marked by their indifference to the Golden Rule. Their needs are and will always be superior to the needs of others. Feeding them compliments only feeds the monsters that live inside of them, and they will grow stronger in front of your eyes, when/if you try to appease them with this technique. Spiritually I would guess that they would have a difficult time embracing God as being their Creator. Such a view would violate their belief system that tells them that they are the best in everything.

Next up is the individual who suffers from **Obsessive-Compulsive Personality Disorder (OCPD.)** Dr. Bernstein characterizes these individuals as primarily seeking "too much of a good thing." They are usually angry because they seek perfection in others and in themselves, and that type of standard will drain any kind of relationship. Nothing is ever good enough and their thinking is marked with a one-sided focus on the "product versus process." Can you imagine the struggle of realizing that you yourself are imperfect, but having to deal with a "perfect" OCPD?

There is a difference between **Obsessive-Compulsive Disorder (OCD)** and OCPD. Usually the disorder (OCD) can be managed with the use of medications while the OCPD seems to be rooted in the mental wiring of these unfortunate people. OCD is likely to respond to medication management, but those showing signs of OCPD usually do not seem to have the ability to benefit from the chemical actions of medication. That is why it is described as a personality disorder. These behaviors are an entrenched way of dealing with the world and this personality type sees nothing wrong with having this kind of an orientation. Interestingly, OCPDs may not respond to medications, but often embrace substance abuse as a way of coping with reality.

Inwardly, they see themselves as protecting you from your unacceptable impulses, and in doing so they have no need to look at their own imperfections. Dr. Bernstein describes them as an "Antisocial trying to claw its way out." These individuals will find a sense of peace only when they have made others equally obsessive-compulsive, thus they spread their disorder to others through the use of this behavior. They can excite in others a fear of making even the smallest mistake. I once had a clinical supervisor who embraced this as a form of "management." He was unable to recognize any viewpoint but his own and could see the smallest mistake and would quickly point out his suggestions (mandates) for change. Once I came to the understanding that he had this personality deficiency, I was able to free myself emotionally from his controlling behaviors.

Dr. Bernstein describes the OCPD as seeing that "punishment is equal to justice." The sting of encounters with these individuals will last as long as your own memories. You often come away from this type of interaction with a feeling that nothing will ever be good enough for them, so why keep on trying? When thinking of these individuals you might remember the phrase "this hurts me more than it hurts you." The frightening part of dealing with such individuals is that they actually believe in this idea. The issue is an inability to see his or her own behaviors or the effect that their actions have on others. I guess that my reaction to these meetings can be summed up in the phrase "God grant me the serenity . . ."

Our last personality type is the **Paranoid Personality Disorder (PPD).** Please do not confuse being fearful as a device to guide you in dealing with unfamiliar situations, with being consumed with suspicion and mistrust of others. Dr. Bernstein describes these individuals as people who analyze everything that is said to them. Perhaps the most prominent thought in their minds could be summed up in the question; "I wonder what they meant by that?" The doubts and suspicions about others will dominate all of their relationships. It is impossible to get inside their mind. They keep you at arm's length, but will readily use you to complete their own desires.

Putting it another way for a PPD, 2+2=4, but there is still something about it that seriously disturbs them. Things that occur accidently are likely to set off a firestorm of suspicion and mistrust. And the more you try to point out that an event was accidental, the more the PPD will be suspicious of your intent. A person exhibiting PPD is seeking "disciples" to prove their theories or worldviews. They are consumed with "minimizing their losses" rather than "maximizing their gains." The term "close-minded" may give you a better appreciation of their operating rules.

PPDs view others as a means to an end. This way they can justify using others. In other words, they have the mindset, "I had better do it to you before you do it to me." This results in fragile relationships with others and may cause others to back away from them. Of course this action would only confirm what the PPD already believes about others . . . you can't trust them. Their interactions with others leave their targets with a sense that PPDs are consumed at some deep level with fearfulness that manifests itself as suspicion and mistrust of the motivations of others. I recommend that you follow what you feel inside when dealing with these types and don't try to pacify their doubts—you will only feed the monster within. If you struggle with PPD, recognizing your behaviors and becoming aware of the need to trust in something beyond you is the first step in recovery from this disorder. Let that small window of light illuminate your soul.

PPDs can't tolerate the fact that the actions of others are well intentioned. They must be constantly on their guard in case you're trying to harm them physically, mentally, emotionally, etc. They can change their feelings so they see all sorts of dangers in lowering their guard. They can always figure out how to "teach others" something about how "you don't measure up." The PPD will be willing to use religion as a major weapon, cloaking himself or herself in a sort of false righteousness. Yet their actions will be marked by a dramatic inability to apply these lessons to their own lives. Beware of pointless encounters!

* * *

This chapter has been written to give you some insight into the spectrum of disturbing behaviors that are evidenced by those with personality disorders. Their actions are enduring and seem to resist any efforts at enlightenment or change. Most people respond to these encounters by writing off these individuals as "un-teachable." If others have given up on you again and again there may be something to learn from these rejections. Go back over your history and look for a pattern of responses from those who have shared your journey. You may find some gold nuggets of insight and understanding.

There is a tool that you may use to wrench yourself away from these dilemmas and move you forward into a place where your spirit becomes teachable. That tool starts with hope and the knowledge that whatever you may lack, God's grace is sufficient for your need. You are not in a war by yourself; you have an army of support if you will just take note of the graciousness of God's mercy and grace. You and God make an unstoppable majority.

I recently had the opportunity to attend a workshop on Belief Therapy. At this event, I experienced a "light bulb going off in my head." After 25 years of professional practice, I saw that this information (Belief Therapy) completed all of the knowledge and experience I had previously acquired. I came away *knowing* what is meant by the phrase "My grace is sufficient." If you will just initiate the effort by telling God your situation and asking for the grace to change, He will respond instantly and start the process of healing you from the inside out. It doesn't matter what others think of you or say about you; you are a child of God, and He will never abandon you. Give it all over to Him and watch Him move in your life. Your journey has just started and I hope to meet you on the road we both share.

* * *

God's Grace and Mercy have NO expiration date. His Word has been the same in the past as it is in the present and will be into the future. He is immutable which means that once He has spoken something into existence it is a settled matter. The application to our situations is simple and extraordinary. If we reach out, He will respond. In our brokenness, He will reach out to each of us and make something beautiful of all the rubbish that we have collected in our lives. There is no one that is so far gone that God will not show him mercy and forgiveness. This book is about that reality. I'm not talking about walking across the yard with your Bible tucked under your arm. I'm talking about quietly surrendering to Him. Give Him everything—your treasures and your trash. Give it all up and watch His love start to touch your life. You can be doing life or be waiting for execution; you have nothing to lose. I know what He has done in my life.

* * *

You might wonder about my reliance upon God's word as the main theme in this book. It is based upon my unshakable belief that there is a largely unseen struggle between good and evil going on at all times. Though we are largely unaware of these forces and the influences that they exert upon our lives, this spiritual reality transcends all of life's struggles and reduces these "realities" to the level of child's play. The real battle is a spiritual battle! It will be waged throughout our lives and it ends in our personal appearance before God for our arraignment in the heavenly court of justice.

I KNOW this reality to be the truth. I had my first encounter with evil while serving a term of incarceration at the California Men's Colony from 1979 to 1983. After arriving at CMC-East, I was assigned to become the Catholic chaplain's clerk. Apparently, in accepting this assignment, I became the target of a pattern of intimidation and threatened violence if I did not give up the position in favor of a "lifer" who would use it as a stepping-stone to get a direct favorable recommendation to the state parole board.

My guess now is that the priest was oblivious to the dynamics that were occurring in the chapel. However, it ended with my giving up this job and moving on to doing something else instead—but not without this lifer setting me up to be harmed. Thank God in these encounters I was under His protection. The turmoil the lifer stirred up eventually came to pass with the help of someone who took an interest in finding out the truth.

On a side note, the lifer seeking this position had previously been convicted of first-degree murder. Prior to this conviction, he had worked for a state agency and had been passed over for a promotion which he believed was rightfully his own. When it started to sink in that he was not going to get that job, he resolved to murder his new supervisor—which he did. He was apprehended shortly afterwards and convicted of the crime of murder. So taking that into account, the most remarkable part of this entire experience was the realization that he was engaging in the exact same behaviors that had brought him to prison in the first place. He had not even tried to change his tactics. He just repeated his behaviors boldly in the prison environment; the only changes were his target and the year that this happened.

I didn't give up my religious beliefs and I continued to worship at the Catholic chapel. The individual cited above also served as a Eucharistic minister at the chapel and performed communion services in the absence of the priest. As I went to communion one afternoon, he stood before the altar holding the host and pronouncing the words "The Body of Christ." But this time, as I approached to receive the host he looked at me and smiled with an evil, satanic, cold-blooded garishness that chilled my soul. In that moment I realized that evil could exist anywhere—even in the House of God.

The encounter frightened me deeply. For the first time in my life, I realized that I was in the presence of pure evil. I believe that Satan possessed this individual. Don't misunderstand what I'm saying; he was not intrinsically evil himself, but that his spirit was given over to satanic influences. I'm still not sure if he was even aware of how this influence was expressed on his face.

In that moment, I knew at the deepest level of my soul that evil did exist. I never returned to worship at the Catholic chapel, nor did I discuss that encounter with anyone until long after my release from prison. Eventually this lifer was released from prison on parole and I believe that he re-entered the world worse for his prison experiences.

I started to worship at the protestant chapel and nourish myself on God's Word. It became a period of time in which my spirit grew in knowledge and grace. What this individual had meant for harm, God used for my good.

A while after my release from prison, I had a second encounter with evil. I was having lunch in a Burger King located on Harbor Blvd. in Costa Mesa when an individual walked into the building. As he entered, he looked like the presence of evil itself, which my spirit picked up on. He offered no nod or contact with me, but the actual presence of evil was so strong I had to quickly leave the building and abandon my lunch. I was not just walking away spiritually; I sought to flee this experience. It took my appetite away in the brief moment of spiritual awareness.

Both of these experiences have remained a strong confirmation of the struggle between good and evil. If you have ever been in the presence of true evil, you will understand what these experiences were and how they helped to shape my awakening spirituality. Evil exists and Evil is real. Evil is not some silly encounter; it is a spiteful force that seeks to DESTROY us. Satan hates anything that resembles God's character, and that is the plain and simple truth. This is why the focus of this book is upon God's Mercy, Grace and Forgiveness, and our response in the form of Faith and Hope.

* * *

This book is not about me; it is about the reality that we can ask for God's help at any moment in our lives and He will respond to our cry. WE are all His favorites. Meaningful life changes are one prayer away. Don't take my word for it—ask Him yourself.

* * *

I recently had the privilege of attending a spiritual knowledge workshop in which the Word of God was the central theme. I had an opportunity to see first-hand how spirituality is the essential element of our natures. Further, I came to believe that it all boils down to believing a lie or believing the truth.

The author of this material, Dr. Paul W. Carlin, Sr., and the presenter, David Rodriguez, clarified the issues and presented them in terms of condition versus position. My spirit resonated with this basic truth. Once you experience the truth it will set you free. You will recognize the enemies' lies as they are being spoken.

Lacking clear authority, I have renamed these concepts "situation versus location" to avoid willfully compromising the integrity of their work or using their creative resources without permission. These concepts and their meanings are easily understood. Consider your current situation, which is likely to be the center point of your immediate concerns. It may appear that if you were released from prison tomorrow, all of your problems would be solved. But if you don't understand the difference between situation and location, your problems would be starting all over again as you walked through the gate.

Your situation is not and should not be your primary concern. Believe it or not, God has given you an opportunity to focus on the struggle of situation versus location. If you have accepted the fact that you are a child of God then you are located in His hand. Nothing that you struggle with is foreign to Him. Please remember that He was a prisoner, a condemned prisoner like some of my readers. He knows your struggles, shame, pain, humiliation, fears and feelings of defiance. Unlike worldly supports, He is ready to see you through the rest of your life—one day at a time. You know what your best choices brought about in terms of consequences.

It's not a fun experience to be locked away in a prison far from family and friends. It hurts even worse to think of the mess you left behind for your children, spouse and family members. The hardest thing you will ever struggle with is accepting your own powerlessness. That is just the pre-condition that renders your heart suitable for Him to start working in your life. Once at that point of surrender, a whole spiritual world opens up for you. That world is best described as a walk with Jesus. He will guide every step along the way and make something beautiful of your life. But He requires an ongoing attitude of surrender. We all try to take control over our lives and we make missteps, bad decisions and poor judgments. He has promised to never leave your side no matter how harsh your existence may be at this time.

Think it over and see if your spirit doesn't echo with that basic truth. If you find yourself rejecting this simple premise, maybe you're so caught up in the struggle that you don't even know where you are located on the timeline of your life. Or maybe you feel hopeless; so much so that you have come to believe that you are too far gone to be valued and loved. That is a lie of the devil. If you are a child of God, then you are located in His care.

Do not accept the lie that comes masked as location delusion disorder. Heaven is our home, not this world. If you know the truth, it will set you free in multiple ways. Know *who* you are and *whose* you are. It is the basic building block of recovery and it's your right as a child of God. One of the key symptoms of location delusion disorder is that small inner voice that tells you no one would have you or that you are too far gone—that you are truly without hope. That is the voice of Satan trying to keep you locked into his lies. Remember that he is the father of lies and the prince of darkness. The Word of God is your light source and immediate help, and the light chases the darkness away. Don't be shy to cry out and ask for help; it's your time and help is just that one cry away. It can be as simple as saying, "I don't know what to say or where to start. Please help me Lord Jesus." That's all you need to do to open the door wide to His love. He will initiate the change process within you at that moment of surrender.

There is some important information I need to give you now. These concepts are essential to your spiritual development and they provide a gateway through which Jesus Christ will continue to pour out His mercy and grace in your life.

* * *

During 25 years of professional practice, I've seen evidence of a personal hierarchy of evil. Ranging from the most severe to the less severe, they include:

- Deception
- Distortion
- Distraction

They are equally powerful when used in a direct attack against our spiritual natures. But like any workman would tell you, they are tools and each tool has its own use. You wouldn't use a hammer to do the work of a polishing cloth; likewise, you wouldn't use a polishing cloth to do the work of a hammer. When Satan or his demons use these tools against us, he does so with great skill and care. He desires to cut us off from the Grace of God. Often, he is very successful because we develop a case of spiritual amnesia. The hallmark of Satan's work in our lives is creating a feeling of confusion—primarily about the truth of events, people, places and our relationship with Jesus Christ.

One of the most useful elements from the spiritual knowledge workshop that I attended was the time devoted to recognizing deception in our lives. It is a satanic trick as old as the Garden of Eden. I firmly believe that there is always a lie at the center of his efforts to thwart our relationship with God. If he can't "infect" us with evil, then he has no power to carry out his plans in our lives. If I don't open up the door to his voice, I won't have to wrestle with the consequences. Satan is not a friend, rather he is a fiend determined to wrestle away all control over your life—one decision at a time. He is patient and hates all human beings for a simple reason; we were created in God's image. That's enough of a reason for him to seek our destruction. But just like with Eve, he will never reveal his hand at first.

His initial entry into our lives starts with the remember series:

- Remember when such and such happened to you and how painful it was?
- Remember why this happened and how hurt you were?
- Remember how much anger you have inside of you?

He uses every element of your human nature to conquer your resistance:

- Physical Sensations
- Mental Turmoil
- Emotional Chaos
- Spiritual Uncertainty

He has complete skill at using our human senses to trigger responses targeted at your human nature. He may target one, some or all in his work at oppressing your spirit. Rest assured that when he attacks you, he will aim directly for your weaknesses. He knows all of them and he is familiar with all of your behavioral triggers. This is when prayer becomes you best weapon.

Then the parade of lies will start to pass before you to help energize your slide into sinful behavior.

* * *

The following summary is an adaption of work presented at the Belief Therapy workshop:

- **Constellation Lies**: This is an attack where a number of lies are fused together.

- **Clever Lies**: This is an attack in which original lies (remember series) are changed and reshaped as responses to memory reflections.

- **Custodial Lies**: This attack is focused on preserving the historical basis that will reveal the causes of fear, turmoil, chaos and uncertainty. It is generally fixed on specific memory points to stop your pursuit of the truth.

- **Chipped Lies**: This attack is usually a lie of lesser significance that is discovered after we are able to discover the major lies in our lives.

- **Cosmotic Lies**: This attack is usually oriented around things we study visually or aurally (sight and hearing) and then incorrectly believe.

- **Changed Lies**: This attack focuses upon triggering responses in our human natures to seeming threats that no longer exist.

- **Collateral Lies**: This attack incorporates elements of several forms of lies. These can be bewildering experiences with feelings of being overwhelmed.

In all of these attacks, your principal weapon is prayer!

* * *

Backsliding: This is our response to the influence of Satan's lies. It is always noticeable in our attitudes and behaviors. It's my belief that this process is usually initiated as a reversal of the hierarchy of evil and that it starts as a subtle process (*For a visual presentation of this data see Appendix D and E*). Others can usually perceive it in us faster than we become aware of this insidious process.

In professional practice, I have routinely found that the slide occurs with some injury or perceived injustice that we privately nurse into a grudge. The grudge then takes on a life of its own as we become focused on our wants, needs and rights. Then, while we are consumed with looking inside ourselves, the next step hits. This is the small satanic whisper that "it's not a sin and really it has been such a long time since you let go." Please remember: Spiritual Diversity = Spiritual Danger.

The Essential Response System (ERS) lies in a specific order that shapes us as individuals in terms of cognitions (thoughts), emotions (feelings), and behaviors (actions). Going back to believing the lie triggers the ERS. We all struggle with this process throughout our lives. Remember what Jesus Christ stated, "You will know the truth and the truth will set you free." Please take a moment to consider the reality that everyone in this world struggles with the ERS. It is the basis for our ability to function and to interact with others.

It is essential to become aware of the essence of our humanity. We are:

- Body
- Mind
- Spirit

All elements of our nature are interacting with each other at all times. That is what makes a human being a complex and different creation than a plant or animal.

A plant has a BODY.

An animal has a BODY and MIND.

A human being has BODY, MIND and SPIRIT.

The intent of this book is to offer a practical introduction to Christian Recovery for the Offender. It is not meant to be a complete text on prayer, practice or patience. These are characteristics that you'll develop as you respond to the guidance and instruction of the Holy Spirit.

I would like to offer a way to begin quickly the life transformation process:

- **G**-et right with God. Tell Him all about your mistakes, errors and sins.
- **I**-nvolve yourself in a Christian community and seek their prayer and support.
- **V**-ictims need to have constant prayer to bring about a healing experience.
- **E**-vidence your position as a child of God by making daily connections with others.

The G-I-V-E principle will offer a straightforward way to start the process of change in your life and initiate a deep spiritual healing through God's Mercy.

* * *

I started this chapter with an informational description of the various diagnoses of personality disorders. I acknowledged that these are deep patterns of behavior that control the ways these unfortunate individuals without fail relate to others.

I have seen little evidence of effective long-term change in the literature on psychology and psychiatry regarding personality disorders. In fact, most mental health providers tend to resist long-term therapy with these individuals since the common belief is that they are untreatable and that they drain the emotional and intellectual resources of the clinicians or therapists. There may be some treatments, but usually the assignment of a personality disorder diagnosis sounds the death knell for realistic recovery. This is usually due to the way these individuals go back to their old patterns of behavior when under stress or pressure.

I believe that personality disorders exist, but I also believe that these diagnoses are the scientific communities' attempt to explain the existence of human evil by observing specific behaviors. By and large the mental health industry doesn't want to acknowledge a spiritual side of things to explain bizarre and twisted lives. Instead, they choose medication, therapy, hospitalization or incarceration as a treatment. A pill, therapy, or a hospital or prison stay will NEVER change an individual's spiritual life. They continue to mask, explain, treat (unsuccessfully) or punish the bad behaviors.

Nothing will change until there is a spiritual change!

Having said that, it's time to move onto understanding the spiritual basis for these behaviors, how we become "infected," and how to treat the spiritual infection. Both M. Scott Peck, M.D. and Malachi Martin, Ph.D. observe that there are distinctions between people who frequently exhibit hurtful behaviors toward others and those who do so without giving thought to the harm that they cause others. They define this difference as imperfection possession versus perfect possession. The underlying facts are historically documented and can't be explained away with claims of ignorance or superstition.

Consider the cold reality of the last 100 years. Hundreds of millions of people have been annihilated or have suffered under the hands of various dictators, despots and fanatics. These people have lost their lives due to one inescapable fact and that fact is that EVIL EXISTS in this world and has throughout the history of the world. This is merely a confirmation of God's Word. Read it for yourself and see.

Demonic possession, exorcism, deliverance and redemption are facts, and the Word of God bears witness to these facts. I would like to take time to explore the experiences of a medical doctor-psychiatrist whose spiritual development led him into a series of encounters that deepened his faith and opened the door of understanding the spiritual dynamics that shape our lives. Before I launch into this story, I would like to list the name of four books I have found helpful in developing my understanding of this:

People of the Lie - M. Scott Peck, M.D.

Glimpses of the Devil - M. Scott Peck, M.D.

Hostage to the Devil - Malachi Martin

The Screwtape Letters - C.S. Lewis

This small library will start your journey of self-discovery that will change every part of your life. Taking this journey will be like sweeping from your mind all the ideas you may have had about evil. Be cautious in making the decision to move forward; your personal journey won't be without pain and suffering. But once you've done it, you aren't likely to return to ignorant acceptance. The devil is in the business of lies. That is his primary weapon and it started back in the Garden of Eden. [Note: The word 'devil' means 'liar.'] He re-tools his lies to match the flow of culture and history. A careful study of his attacks on your life and the lives of others back through history is likely to show you how consistent he is in his primary attack. Don't be afraid to approach this subject matter. Ask the Holy Spirit for wisdom and spiritual protection and take the next step forward. It is an eerie journey that you are undertaking; but the truth will set you free.

The spirit of these books is setting the record straight about people who make evil choices as they come into contact with others. This isn't a new problem; it's been identified throughout the ages. Not everyone who is engaged in an evil activity is naturally evil in and of themselves. Sometimes they are being used to do what Satan wants done.

Those who are classified as having personality disorders are not necessarily people who suffer from imperfect or perfect possession (Appendix D). In fact, the authors I have previously cited make reference to the fact that among likely candidates for a diagnosis of demon possession, few actually have the disorder. The majority of these individuals are quirky but not merchants of evil.

As you read about these factual encounters, only you can decide the state of your soul. There are few individuals in this world who have an accurate understanding of possession and exorcism. Many know the value of deliverance. But there is a distinct difference between an exorcism and a deliverance service. It has to do with the how long the evil encounter or possession has existed.

Most individuals experienced in this field consider the fact that one has to give permission to be possessed (a valid understanding). Giving your permission to a demonic or satanic influence can be done unwittingly, since we know that lies, deceptions and falsehoods are part of how the evil one works. However surrendering control to the evil one seems to be how this happens in the first place. It's sort of a pre-condition to possession.

Another fact seems to be the belief that once demonic or satanic powers "possess an individual they fight against giving up their 'home.'" Since these evil creatures are spirit beings, their power comes from the individual's body, mind and spirit. These spirits seem powerless without things that allow them to show off their evil works. Consider the Bible story in Matthew 8:31 in which the demons who had been cast out by Jesus begged Him to send them into the herd of swine on the hillside. It seems consistent with the belief that they have no power without someone or something to possess. Draw your own conclusions.

In their writings, the above referenced authors make note of physical, emotional, mental and spiritual characteristics of those who'd been possessed. It isn't my intention to go through a broad review of the literature on demonic or satanic possession, but I imagine many of my readers will find the topic thought provoking.

I believe with all my heart in the presence of good and evil but I don't view that they occur in a direct line, running from one idea to the next. Rather I'd like to use an illustration in the form of a cross with good represented by the vertical line while the horizontal line represents evil (*see Appendix A*).

I believe that this image better shows how our inner battle of both behaviors happens in our daily lives. Being conscious of God along with an active prayer life are the principle weapons of self defense against the evil one.

This introduction to the spiritual realities of life is not meant to be a complete text on the subject matter; however, I'm thinking it is a useful addition to help those who struggle with a shattered inner life to see their conflict from another direction. It is my belief that the number of individuals struggling with this problem is frightfully large. For all intents and purposes, they are cut off from others in a graphic illustration of Severcide.

I will not open this door and then neglect to give you enough information about the nature of this raging conflict, but first I need to ask your help in developing a clearer picture of demon possession. This book contains an information page containing our ministry name and address and other contact information. I encourage you to use this resource to provide me with feedback about your needs of further understanding and I will respond in future writings. Please remember that it is a journey for me as well.

My father-in law sent me an email today in which he pointed out the obvious. His statement helped me pull together a clearer understanding of the influence of evil in our world. He noted that EVERYONE is under oppression by the evil one. We ALL have struggles in our daily lives, and there is no one without this burden. All struggle with sin and wrongdoing. It is a universal problem that "infects" all human beings. The outcome of this battle doesn't rest on my shoulders or my personal efforts. It has already been decided through the death and resurrection of Jesus Christ. All we need to do is ask for His help. No one will be denied.

I have attempted to provide you with enough information to understand the limits of healthcare or governmental policies. These are worldly tools being used to fight a spiritual war. They will NEVER be effective since they can't make changes in our spirits. But the good news is that you have the tools you need NO MATTER what your situation. God has you covered because you're in the palm of His hand.

I would heartily encourage you to correspond directly with me through the information provided in this book. I invite you to explore this concept of evil—and your understanding of the impact it has had on your life and the lives of others—with me. Let's shed some light on a dark topic.

If you permit me the opportunity to understand your unique experiences I would like to use that for a serious scientific study of demonology and Satanism (with the end result of publishing my findings in a scientific publication, as well as writing a book for the general population). I can't do this on my own. Your experience is critical in making this study a success. Pray about it first, and then follow your heart in responding.

PART FIVE
PERSONAL RESPONSES

CHAPTER 17

CARRYING THROUGH ON YOUR PERSONAL PARDON PLAN

IF SOME MARKETING CONCEPT SPRINGS up in which paid pardons become a part of the societal background and therefore a meaningless reality, that would destroy any integrity in the review process and reduce its value. I am not suggesting the commercial use of the pardon process; I am suggesting an individual meeting within our human spirits that contributes to a true sense of community.

Do you remember the Paris Peace Talks, or the tense interactions, that lead to the Camp David agreement or the Good Friday accords, that largely ended years of death and destruction? These were efforts that were made to end violence and social chaos resulting from various conflicts around the world. Why can't we use the same principles in restoring peace and individual dignity? The one thing we really need for long-term solutions is to come to the peace table as equals. At this time, there is no such mechanism in existence for individuals to formally approach the society in which they live.

You can't hide behind the mask of power and control or the claim that I don't want to play. We must all sit at that table in the future and negotiate (without a power struggle). We must all separate our honest attempts to arrive at a meaningful peace accord. One party can't show up happily saying that they have all of the cards. That would imply that the other party is at their mercy or interpretation of the issues. This would doom the whole process by bitterness and mistrust.

That is why any truly, honorable pardon process must be self-initiated by the estranged individual or group. The intent must be to arrive at some point at which the sins (crimes) are washed away. Society must come to that table and listen to the proposal with a candid and informed realization that no peace can exist between warring parties until they come as equals. There should also be a willingness to understand each other's positions and be prepared to talk openly and meaningfully with each other so everyone can unite.

"Oh," you say, "We can't possibly use that sort of thing to solve the problems of social misfits. That is reserved for diplomats who want to advance the cause of their nations." Why not try it? After all, is the current system able to solve our social ills? Look at the streets of your cities and towns and consider all the budget problems that bleed our economy. Is it really working?

"Impractical," you respond, because you are invested in the belief that there's no other way than the way we do business now (especially with health care, politics and our justice industries). And so we close the door to re-building even when unengaged citizens try to be hopeful. Thus these "citizens" resume their strange experience of Severcide and the nation loses the ability to combine the strengths, skills and abilities of all of its citizens.

The majority finds comfort in the idea that these standards offer the safeguards of security. After all, we all want to be safe in our homes, right? This is a good time to recall the practical effects of Willy Horton's' misdeeds as it cast a pall over the election results of a past presidential election. This was an individual who betrayed the trust that had been placed in him while on a furlough from prison.

One individual's decision to commit a crime (after being given a furlough) became the decision point that angered a nation that feared what could happen at the federal level of government. Wow, Willy was one powerful guy, wasn't he? Instantly, Willy Horton and his actions transformed America's perception of the candidate they would reject. There it was—all the drama—played out in living color in millions of American homes. But, what if Willy had some sort of social conscience and wanted to make things right?

We have traveled light years in terms of moral issues that affected the citizens of the 50s and 60s. We talk about values, morality and the respect for life. Consider two different Governors separated in time by about fifty years. When the execution date for Carl Chessman (convicted kidnaper, rapist and author) drew near, the then-Governor Pat Brown, Sr. of California went deep-sea fishing to avoid the issues and controversy being raised around this execution. Brown lacked the courage to call a halt to an execution of a man who had not taken another life. He didn't want to anger those who approved of capital punishment. In 2011, we had another gubernatorial figure running for nomination in his party's primaries for a presidential election. He stood in part on his record of having authorized the deaths of 235+ (death row) people during his pre-primary tenure. In fact, he seems to be proud of his accomplishments saying that these acts did not bother him (referring to the legality of the process). Some people even cheered at the mention of such a performance record. This was the governor of the State of Texas, Rick Perry.

In that same genre, we have crowds of people cheering the suggestion that those who cannot afford health insurance should be allowed to die. It is a far cry from President Johnson's Great Society. Are we even the same nation? In the 50s and 60s, life held a different value than it does today. There were still abortions, there were still executions, and people committed suicide. But we never cheered at those events; we never demanded a right to kill—even in the name of the law. When it happened, it was something that saddened most of us.

Unfortunately, no such service platform exists to assist self-motivated individuals set right the wrongs of the past. Nor does society establish a forum to discuss the possibilities of understanding one another. Perhaps our leaders secretly feel that doing so would be evidence of personal or governmental weakness. Or they conclude that to recognize the concerns of those suffering from Severcide would result in some sort of official recognition of their claims. It's a brilliant leap into intellectual darkness to reason that the process described above can be used between countries but not between society and individuals. A thoughtful, organized forum would go a long way.

What about individual petitions asking for a remedy to personal grievances? There are few practical solutions offered under the law.

Society holds all the power and their first thought is to ignore these issues. Given the fact that there are few answers for the victims of Severcide, the only practical and spiritual answer would be to design your own pardon plan and to work toward that goal by trying a new behavioral plan.

Why would you want to do that? It would become a spiritual journey between you and God—a step toward real peace and harmony. You may think society will refuse to accept this, but after all, are you doing this for society's approval? It is a purely redemptive act, self-initiated and self-sustained in the face of long-established hostility.

What if society never accepts your hope; will you want to live your life like a condemned prisoner awaiting execution? Or will you reach out and take hold of your life and live it for the good of others on a one-to-one basis? Maybe in time some international rights organization will be willing to tackle this imbalance in powerful national review boards and include recognized leaders to provide direction to this effort.

These international organizations may authorize and fund these boards and focus on individuals seeking a symbolic pardon. After recognizing a commitment to complete an individual's pardon plan, this international body may officially acknowledge that effort through public recognition.

That recognition would be based on evidence that this process works and can then help the individual move along with his or her life, leaving behind any stigma of Severcide. In fact, the certified pardon plan could help an individual eventually seek a legal pardon issued by our government. Why use an international agency to help in this pardon process? Well, the answer is simple; Life, Liberty and

The Pursuit of Happiness are concepts found in the Declaration of Independence, but they are not guaranteed. They were target rights formed by our forefathers' original ideas of freedom. Independent proof may in turn lead to domestic proof or at least support a cause of action. Perhaps the idea of Severcide sums up the need to revisit this theme of freedom and equal justice for all.

These are God-given rights. The government no longer functions as an agency of legal protection. This is shown by the fact that it cannot or will not offer the safeguards of due process and equal protection "rights" to non-citizen citizens. And it fails to show the truth that these non-citizens have the unalienable right to change—granted by God's Word.

Since government only hinders the processes, the only practical remedy for individuals is to openly challenge the applications of the unofficial law of Severcide. The goal to restore human rights requires courage to undertake this process.

This is the spiritual, logical and practical basis for putting together your own personal pardon plan. If you have accepted His offer, God has already forgiven your sins and crimes. But society is another story; they will not be so willing to forgive your sins. So the challenge and success of your plan rests solely with you. It is all on your own shoulders and you can't expect society to stop defining your life by using labels. You can only do this for yourself because you are driven by the fact that it is the right thing to do. You are on your own and you face extreme conditions.

To accomplish this, you have to be the one willing to make this dream a reality—without the hope of any recognition for all you've done. You will need an inner conviction and the same kind of courage displayed by the Bible's Meshach, Shadrach, and Abednego. When these men were threatened with the loss of their lives, they told the king that their God would protect them, and even if He never showed up, they would never bend their knees to worship the king or his god. They were rewarded for their efforts by being cast into the fiery furnace. Up until this time, everything had merely hung on their own verbal expressions of faith. But once they were thrown into the fiery furnace, everyone—including the king—observed four beings walking about in the flames.

The king remarked that he had only thrown in *three* individuals for refusing to worship the way he demanded. But then God showed up big time. He stood in the furnace with His friends and protected them from the flames (to the amazement and consternation of the king). Their bravery and faithfulness to God's Word resulted in the king's acceptance of a Being higher than himself. It had transformed the king's heart.

Now that is what God is going to do for you. If you faithfully step forward into the furnace of society's anger, He will give you the personal power to make changes (in strict association with Him), one person at a time. Your efforts with just one other person, in completing your own pardon plan, will impact thousands of other lives.

Remember the individual stories previously mentioned that showed how a few early experiences with sin would bring untold suffering for many others? The reverse is also true. As you go about your purposeful work, the practical effects of redemption start to appear and your life and the lives of others will start to vibrate with a new awareness. If you have the inner courage to start the process, God will see you through all challenges and experiences. You never have to do this by yourself. Along the way you will meet many others like yourself, those living out the experience of truth and redemption.

Do not worry about going to the store to buy new clothes to get ready. God wants you to start where you are now. Use the sandals you have on your feet, and don't worry about filling your pockets with money or provisions. He will give you everything that you need to complete these journeys. I promise that you will never be alone—from the time you start your journey until you are safely home with your spiritual family. Your victory is assured because you are a precious child of God, and He will not allow harm to come to you or failure to haunt your steps (especially when you are actively blessing His other children).

This journey began when you took those early initial steps to look at all those labels. You looked for guidance from God and for a partner to keep you accountable. Then you continued that steep walk until you recounted that time when you were a loved and loveable child—full of worth and happiness and a joy to behold for those in your life. Those loving and self-loving encounters are earthly expressions of God's love for you. They gave meaning to your early life. Now they help you to get back your worth and an ever-expanding awareness of your future potential. You have left shame and pain for joy and a real future.

So what should a personal pardon plan look like? I developed my own plan largely by default. Unlike my stumbling about for years, I would suggest that you shorten the process by selecting a three-year plan for the misdemeanors of life and a five-year plan for the felonies of life that you have committed against others and yourself.

Stack them all up on the table and start sorting. Remember that you have made a commitment to personal honesty and this is an attempt to restore your own integrity. Sort them fairly into either category (as described later).

Your cleansing won't be complete if you don't honestly complete this task (like the ritual cleansing that completed the healing of the lepers). Having sorted them, you can select a three-year redemptive plan or a five-year exercise in redemptive activities.

Five years sounds like a long time, but is it really? For those who don't have the five years to work with, we'll talk later about other plans you can use. Just know that action is the key, do what you can to start this project now. After selecting a time frame to complete the tasks that lay ahead, you can next select the kinds of redemptive activities you will try. You see, this is a very simple plan; it is self-selected and self-directed.

You know yourself best (including your sins and crimes), so you are the one who knows best what you need to give back to others, whether directly or symbolically. In some cases, it may be impossible to make amends to those you have harmed (this is for you, Kathleen and Kimberly). In that case, reach out to someone else.

Sometimes we are so far removed from obeying the laws of God and man and we have acquired so many labels (societal or self-inflicted), that we can't pick specific individuals to focus on. If that is the case, you may also choose a community to work with.

If you tell someone outside of God and your accountability partner, it does not discharge you from your sin or crime. To tell others what you are doing is to break the silence of your relationship with God and your help-partner. In that event, you will need to randomly choose another individual to help.

You will have to turn your attention early in this plan to developing five essential categories. You can choose for yourself these five categories, but you have to address the seriousness of your offenses. For this to mean anything, you have to concentrate on the feelings of those you offended. Consider their feelings of loss and trauma associated with your past behaviors. What would you want done to help restore your wholeness and personhood? What would it take for you to be able to achieve peace in your own life? That is the measuring stick you have to use in developing your pardon plan.

Again the most constructive part of this integrity-building process is the simple idea of fairness and restoring justice to those you have hurt by your past behaviors. This plan can start while you are incarcerated, but the obvious limitations on movement would seriously limit your ability to find an accountability partner or the completion of your plan. My advice would be to use your prison time to seriously reflect on how you will develop a structural plan, but wait until you are with an accountability partner to work out the actual activities.

I focused on five broad areas to give me the widest possible range of opportunities to reach some levels of success. *I personally resolved first to focus on my relationship with God and my own spirituality.* I sought out information about theology and the world's great religions. I did this to increase my understanding of what everyone was saying about God. I also studied the claims of atheists and agnostics.

Having gained this much knowledge about different theological claims, I started to measure them against my own inner belief system and experiences with God (the Galileo and Columbus system of knowing and experiencing inner truth and peace). After a review of my own belief structure, I deleted those beliefs that couldn't stand up to the information from my personal experiences with God's mercy and grace. I also began an avid search and studied about all the major religions of the world.

My search was extensive. I studied the Torah and started to learn Hebrew with a learned Rabbi (though his untimely death derailed that process). I later extended my studies of the Torah in other venues. I engaged Muslim clerics who voiced an assurance that Mohammed was truthful and Allah is the real god of the universe. And I can attest, yes there are *some* elements of shared truth or similarity in the expression of each religion's dogma and doctrine, but also MAJOR DIFFERENCES.

I undertook studies to grasp the essentials of Buddhism, Hinduism and the thoughts of Confucius. I followed a trail of other Eastern beliefs in attempting to gain some understanding of their principles. Later, I engaged the essential beliefs of the American Indian, as expressed uniquely by each tribal culture.

I also studied the protestors who awakened the Reformation, resulting in the eventual development of streams of Christian beliefs. I took the time to study many of their mainstream beliefs, including the claims made by The Mormons, the Jehovah's Witnesses and the Seventh Day Adventists.

The last step (but not the sole step) on my journey led me to investigate claims of spiritual awareness apart from any organized religions through an understanding of God's Word, the Bible.

Eventually, I arrived at a comfort point, resting on the foundation of the teachings of the Holy Bible and of the Roman Catholic Church (but radically informed by the idea of having a personal relationship with God). After realizing that I intelligently understood this concept, my next step was to approach God directly. I haven't looked back since that day. The first element of my personal pardon plan energized and informed the development of other categories.

The next category was family and that included all known relatives who may have been impacted by my actions. I have an older brother who has been emotionally estranged from all family members since shortly after his marriage in 1959. He is now the patriarch of a sizeable family including children, grandchildren, and the last time that I was informed by someone in "the know", he may have even been expecting the birth of a great grandchild.

I once sent him an earnest email seeking to make amends and restore dialogue. He did not respond, but did change his email address. Though he and I have no direct communications, I maintain a spiritual connection with him and his family members by using my spiritual tools and placing them in God's care. My side of the street has been cleaned and I have peace about letting go of any further attempts to re-connect with him or members of his family. Until we meet again, Brother.

I am glad that I had made an awkward attempt at making amends with him at our mother's funeral. That attempt was brushed off with a disingenuous suggestion that we get together when we both got back to California. Then he left without offering his telephone number. My comfort and closure comes from knowing that I made a sincere effort to heal this long-festering wound. My obligations to my brother and his family were discharged completely by responding to that soft, quiet voice within that was urging action on my part. Other family members expressed varying degrees of surprise and acceptance. Some even offered the warmth of human affections, but those were few in the overall execution of my plan. It did NOT matter what their personal reactions were to my efforts at making amends. All that mattered was that I faithfully discharged these obligations. With each new encounter my inner spirit soared, and I was able to glimpse what lay ahead for me, The Promised Land.

This is a really tough task, and there are few oases on your path. Nevertheless, it is not a lack of nourishment, sleep or acceptance that will determine the eventual outcome. Remember Jesus admonishing His disciples that doing the works of The Father was His meat and drink (John 4:34). This is the stuff of giants. You grow, as you go. You become supercharged with spiritual assurance that you are finally on the right track.

It is not dependent upon individual interactions; it is dependent only upon your spiritual connection with God and another individual within a relationship of accountability. Are you starting to get the picture now that this is a very simple plan to transform your life and the lives of others? As your friends and enemies observe your transformation process, they will eventually seek you out to inquire about the nature of all of the life changes. What a time to step into their gap in understanding and tell them what you have found.

You make this journey of your own choice, hopeful that it will be productive in the lives of others. Be determined to get into peace talks somehow—no matter what it takes. Be determined to sit at the table and recognize the many ways that you have contributed to the problems. Your efforts at the peace table embrace an understanding of what you believe to be the solutions to the problems you have created. They may be actual solutions or symbolic solutions. But attempts on your part are necessary to start the process. Take the Paris Peace talks for example. Someone had to construct an organized plan in order for Ho Chi Minh and Nixon to send representative delegations to the Paris Peace talks. The end of the Vietnam War was a direct result of those early foundational plans. How is your personal pardon plan taking shape?

The next category is yourself! If you are a living saint, then this book will offer you little. But if you are the same as the flesh and blood people that I have encountered out in society, then this book and its suggested activities are for you. You know deep in your heart, if anyone had treated you like you have treated yourself, you might have gotten rid of him or her a long time ago.

In the development of Relational Victimization Theory and a companion presentation on The Psychology of Desperation, I have tried to study the cause and effect of criminal activities on society in the context of modern day systems. I sought to develop an understanding of the effects upon all members of society. But I was not interested in merely constructing a useful explanation. My primary goal was to develop long-term interventions that might prove useful in reducing the number of offenders being incarcerated or being returned to prison for another offense (including violations of parole or probation). Some of these ideas resulted in writing grant applications to various groups (including governmental agencies like the National Institute of Justice). These ideas carried a number of titles like Felons Anonymous and a proposed study that sought to understand the vicarious impact upon non-victims who had firsthand knowledge of a friend suffering from the trauma of rape. You see, these crimes—all crimes—impact those who live and interact with us. Even neighbors, shopkeepers, bus drivers, delivery people and the mail carrier are consciously and unconsciously affected by these tragic events. None of us is immune to tragedy and its consequences.

As a general rule, an incident may be more significant to one person than for another. Recently, I heard the unbelievable allegation that a father had killed his young, disabled son by cutting his head off. That story was very disturbing to my spirit. Given some of the difficulties within my own family, I couldn't understand his actions especially as I thought about the details revealed in the published story.

Why didn't the father give up his parental rights in favor of placing the child in state care or a foster home? I will never begin to understand any of it. What kind of intense hatred and fury drove this father to kill his young son? My thoughts soon turned to the aftermath of this gruesome murder. I realized that I was gripped by what must have happened within this man's psyche and the basic pain and fury that drove him to kill his son.

Will he ever be able to go back in time and find that fury and pain, I don't know. All I know is that his actions triggered some need in me to respond to this and I hunted for a measure of peace by using my spiritual tools: Mercy, Grace, Forgiveness, Faith and Hope. I'm not sure I have any understanding of God's system for evaluating human beings; I only know that He tells us that everyone has worth and dignity, and that we are all His children. It took a long time (I'm not sure that I have yet grasped it) to arrive at any peace with my understanding how these things can ignite such re-morseless fury and anger.

I only know what I'm told within God's Word; He stands ready to forgive this fellow, if only he seeks God's never-ending Mercy and Forgiveness and enters into a personal relationship with His Creator. What an incredible capacity for warmth and acceptance. Only in relationship to His Grace can I approach the Mercy seat and call out to Him from my personal sense of loss. God does not re-quire any explanation for such bizarre behaviors. He already knows where they came from. His Word clearly states that it's not me, but the sin that lives within me.

I realize that I am always engaged in a spiritual battle even when there are brief lulls on the battlefield. So in defining the cause of sin, am I suggesting "the devil made me do it"? No more than pleading insanity when you are sane and rational.

I want to provide you with insight from His Word. This offers me the hope of sorting out all of my self-destructive behaviors and evaluating labels using God's Word as the yardstick. He offers me the chance to make everything right. He will never ask me why I did all of those things; He already knows why. That's not a vain hope—it is a promise, a certainty, and an ever-present help.

* * *

We have come to a split in the road. There are two pathways ahead of us. One pathway seems brightly lit and well constructed. The other pathway seems to be much narrower and dimly lit. Quite a few people are on the brightly lit pathway, and they seem to be enjoy-ing themselves. On the dimly lit path, there are a few individuals try-ing to make their way all alone. What do these pathways represent?

They are symbolic of a choice point. All of the information has been provided for you to choose your future pathway. Will you continue along your present path trying to stay in step with the crowd? Or is it time to go off on your own and use the spiritual tools that you have been given to transform your life?

This is the point where you will decide your future. Will you remain in lockstep with the crowd, even though you struggle to stay up with them in the back of the surging mass of individuals? Or will you go off and embrace the difficulties of making your own way? Unseen to all travelers are those angelic beings assigned to each of us. They are using the resources at their disposal to urge us to choose the narrow, dimly lit path.

For many, even after reading this book, the choice will be a "no-brainer." They will consider the possibility of choosing the dimly lit narrow pathway as a non-choice, but almost in a reflexive instant, will naturally decide to continue their travels on the main road. (See everyone else seems to be walking along that well lit roadway.)

Alongside the main pathway of life is a large crowd of onlookers, also urging us to choose for ourselves the mainstream thoughts and encouraging us to make our own decision to continue with the crowd. It is interesting to consider that you know you will always be at the back and isolated if you make this choice. Nevertheless, the great number of onlookers loudly and publically disputes the wisdom of going off alone on the dimly lit route. Everyone knows that there is safety in numbers, right?

Stop listening to the loud cries from the onlookers and reach deep within yourself. You know that the crowd offers you no security. You are destined to live your own life, one choice at a time.

When you arrive at the end of your life and are facing the sureness of death, will the crowds have made any difference? Will they have added a single moment to your life span? No!

As you launch off into eternity, you will step into the well-lit seat of judgment. This is where you will stand alone to give account of your travels; and the one question that is sure to be asked of you is what did you choose? It will not be about what the crowd decided, but what did YOU do with what you had been given? What individual decisions did you make? Why didn't you accept the alternative route of travel?

This is the endpoint for everyone, whether I choose to believe it or not. Like Galileo and Columbus, the truth will suddenly emerge and I will know once and for all that truth does exist in God's Word. By inference and direct knowledge, I will be forced to accept good and evil as reference points illuminating all of my past choices. Those choices to follow the crowd or listen to society will take on a different meaning. We won't be able to give the excuse, "I was just doing what everyone else was doing." It won't hold water!

I can't use the tools of Mercy, Grace, Forgiveness, Faith and Hope without accepting the reality that good and evil exist apart from ourselves. They are the paths we travel all of our lives. Over the course of time, we first lose interest in making decisions guided by truth. Then we gradually merge ourselves (our choices) with the actions of those around us. Also gradually, I give control of the rudder of my soul to the slightest pressure of society.

In the safety of the crowd, I scarcely glance at the horizon or the sky anymore. I have accepted the belief that sailing on this boat of decision-making by default is the way to go. Later, I'm stunned when

I'm caught up in storms that savage my life. But I'm already on this boat and I seem committed to the voyage now. So we sail on blissfully unaware of the dangers that lie ahead. It never dawns on me to abandon ship into a small lifeboat. After all, the boat I'm in is still floating and it seems sturdy. Why would I risk everything by getting off the boat and rowing to one of the islands I've already passed?

Just like the father that made a choice resulting in the death of his son, uninformed decision-making offers no safety, no matter how large the crowd. This father took his son's life in an incredibly evil act of murder. We say, "But I would never do that myself." Since our lives are constantly influenced for good or influenced for evil, the safety in numbers mentality isn't always true. I may not make the choice to kill, but in the safety of the crowd, I may make equally devastating choices. Those are the unseen currents that guide the boat on its journey. How do you think this father arrived at the choice point to murder his son? The answer is there was evil influencing his thoughts that would even lead him to consider such a choice. The same things happen to each of us. Good and evil are rarely decided on as independent categories that we should consider before we make our choices.

But that is what my conscience is for, right? Our conscience *should* be a trained moral GPS, but the problem for most of us is the fact that our conscience is constantly undergoing a type of social re-programming. This makes our moral GPS useless. It can't tell me my current position or help me to understand attitude, pitch, or yaw that can sway the boat's course. Without all of the technological wonders, I am ultimately responsible for steering the boat.

To be a successful sailor, I need knowledge and experience with these influences, or I won't be able to safely sail the seas. To be successful in using my spiritual tools, my relationships of accountability and the framework offered by KNOWETICS, I must be able to identify life's influences—especially good and evil.

We have established that a lot of people suffer from the consequences of our actions. Remember my reaction to the father who murdered his disabled child? I experienced inner turmoil and conflict. This kind of gut level reaction can be compared with the actions of Hitler's "government" which had rippling effects throughout the world. His decisions—and the decisions of those around him—still impact people today. Few would deny that these decisions typify evil, but let's attach this understanding to our own decision-making. Actions have consequences. This gives us the opportunity to segue back to the preparation of a personal pardon plan.

The next category is the community.

We don't live in a vacuum. Like billiard balls, our actions cause reactions with others. All of our behaviors influence those who live close to us. We may be aware of this influence or we may be so busy with the issues of our own life that we can't understand the influence.

If I am consumed and burdened by the events of my life, I may fail to see the influence that is spreading like ripples on a pond. Once the ripples have begun, I can't control their flow. This is true for all but especially for the violent alcoholic, drug addicted, emotionally homeless or morally lacking members of the community. A label is attached (to describe their value) and they are affected socially by limiting the resources that support their community lives.

Oftentimes, this is where the process ends with an individual living out their limited potential as defined by their particular label.

Like the ripples in the pond, the energy transferred by throwing a small stone and disturbing the water's surface has consequences and creates ripples I cannot personally control. That is not an invitation to abandon our responsibility to set in motion counter-ripples. That's right: counter-ripples. Just remember, your worth is not defined by your labels; your worth is defined by God's love for you.

I seek out discreet (non-public) opportunities to create counter-ripples every day. I don't do this to alter your perception of me. I do this because I choose to see the value of each human being—no matter how far down the scale of life they may have fallen. I choose to see them through the value scale that God has attached to their lives. He calls them His precious children!

It is only in recognizing the value of others, that I can understand my own value as a human being. Then as part of my personal pardon plan, I start to develop a consciousness of opportunity, seeking small daily encounters with nameless others. Each opportunity offers me a possible engagement within community life to reach out and affirm the worth of others. Why would I abandon my own misery in favor of touching other lives? I do so because each individual I encounter has indescribable worth in God's eyes.

In recognizing and affirming that worth, I begin to walk along the pathway of restoring to others what I have carelessly and recklessly taken from those I have offended. In restoring to others their dignity and worth by recognizing their inherent value to God, I set in motion a new series of ripples. Watch and see how they spread across the surface of the water (community life), and you will be amazed at the unexpected consequences of your new actions.

The two key elements of this part of your personal pardon plan are the quiet acceptance of responsibility for your prior behaviors and a willingness to embrace the radical belief that from now on all of your choices will count. You see, each choice we make has the effect of setting those ripples in motion—consciously and unconsciously. Do I dismiss you as a crank and unreasonable person? Or do I make that inner effort to reach out and connect with you?

No matter how unreasonable or cranky you appear to be, no one in your community should ever know of your inner resolve. This transformation of relationships—one person at a time—is strictly between you and God. So what would this look like in terms of personal behaviors? These counter ripples are all started in the choices I make from this point on in my life, though they are very, very small choices usually unseen by others. Some examples include holding the door open for another individual, smiling at the clerk who offers no willingness to think beyond policy issues, or simply recognizing the small people of life (those cast aside by the labels of society and of course the precious children who live amongst us). A good rule of thumb is to treat everyone shorter than you with a special kindness and warmth. Not only are they precious to God, but also in a few short years they will be running the world in which you live.

I particularly like to look over at cars traveling beside me and smile at some child who is strapped into a child safety seat. I am making a quick connection that shows warmth and feeling for the child's individual worth. No one but you and that child will ever know that you had this brief contact, but hopefully it will add meaning to their future lives.

Can you imagine what it would be like if everyone you encountered in your daily life offered you a warm smile or even a pleasant greeting? Maybe that small child is just at the point of disconnecting, and is moving away from the belief that they are a lovable person. In an instant, you can transform someone's reality. You re-engage their experience of inner worth. We tend to be willing to smile readily at the pretty people of life, but hesitate with the less attractive. A recent social study confirmed what we already knew; attractive people make more money in their lifetime than those labeled as ugly. With each new encounter I can confirm that study or I can reach out and smile at the less valued.

Here is another example on how to create a counter ripple. Recently, a neighbor was suffering through a period of unemployment. Leaving his home one evening, he mentioned that he was on the way to his mother's home to "borrow" milk for his little boy. There was a clear opportunity to reach out to that family by buying a gallon of milk during the next shopping trip and leaving it anonymously on their doorstep. What a boost to their worth! It doesn't matter much whether his employment situation changed. What matters is the here and now experience of affirming worth and dignity.

Personally I like to sit in the back of the church when I worship and look at all of those who are sitting in front of me. I enjoy having time to pray for the families sitting together in those pews. It creates a special warm feeling of "family" by embracing each of these individuals in God's love. I then move my eyes among my fellow worshippers to those who are handicapped or disabled. I let my eyes wander, looking for opportunities to bless others with my silent prayers.

At my church, several individuals come for worship in wheel chairs. There is one man in particular who has impacted my life by the example he quietly sets. I have been informed that he previously worked as an airline pilot. Apparently, a driver struck him as he was out on a morning run and the result of that accident transformed his life. He moved at that moment from the label of being healthy and productive to being unofficially labeled as paralyzed and unproductive.

But to me, he is a hero and always will be. He didn't necessarily do anything to suggest that he has heroic potential. He shows up each week and worships with his wife or members of his family. He comes dressed well and ready to engage in worship. But through his courageous example, he has touched my life. He didn't take to his bed and withdraw from life. Instead, he took that tragedy and he re-shaped his reality. He stands tall in my estimation.

Another worshipper extends his hand to the willing in an embrace of love and affection. As worshippers make their way toward communion, he reaches out his hand and extends his hand of friendship to those who are willing. In that brief encounter of a handshake, he is transforming others one handshake at a time. He does so by the simple act of offering his hand to others.

Both of these individual's touch the lives of those who encounter them in a community setting. Neither man is likely to catch anyone's attention at Wal-Mart or at a community function; but in their small acts of courage and acceptance, they are transforming their community and letting their lights shine brightly. God must smile broadly upon these individual acts of value. Each new church service or handshake offers a brief glimpse at God's power to transform our lives, no matter what our personal circumstances.

Out of this new context of attempting to engage others by seeing their individual worth and dignity, my life has been radically changed into an endless stream of encounters in which God's love has become visible. The process of accepting His love in my life transforms my own life. In the brightness of His love for us, the judgments and labels of society become insignificant and powerless.

So one day at a time—one person at a time—my life at the community level becomes an endless series of opportunities to bless others. It takes no special talent or time commitment to shape these encounters into a reflection of God's love for me. Reach out; find out the practical effects of letting others enter your life in a procession of living experiences. You will soon find your personal comfort level in extending yourself to others. Simply starting down this pathway will open you up to a radically transforming experience. Soon you will be reaching beyond your comfort level and grasping new opportunities.

Does this mean that I am able to recognize all of these potential encounters or that I must embrace each offered opportunity? Not at all! I am just like you. I am limited by my own stuff. I miss a lot of these potential encounters with others. But I have chosen to express myself by consciously committing to this process at least 3-5 times a day. In making individual decisions throughout my day, I am also engaging in individual acts of symbolically restoring to the community what I have taken from the lives of others in the communities in which I have lived. Each of these events becomes very private encounters with the lives of nameless individuals. To me, they are like those children in the passing cars, each hopeful of some small expression of individual warmth and acceptance.

Thus we are able to make a community peace plan without going to all the trouble of a formal meeting with officials. It doesn't cost me anything to engage in these small private acts of kindness, but it really transforms my experience of living. Loving acts of kindness, by those identified in this book, have given me the unique perspective of seeing beyond the moment and into the future. Just like those who have made individual decisions to define and reinforce my individual worth. So the practical implication is that we can change our community one small act at a time.

Having started a process that is only limited by my creativity, I have put into motion a community strategy that supports all of my choices. Without complicating my life or the lives of others, the most remarkable thing about this process is the gradual increase of my own personal value while I work to benefit others. This knowledge shapes my experience with life. Now I can seek out fresh encounters as I begin to grasp a sure knowledge of individual worth (including my own).

Others close to you will be the first to recognize these subtle changes as you accept the challenges of developing and using your personal pardon plan. Please remember that your plan is your own plan and doesn't depend on the acceptance of others. Making these small personal efforts may not be recognized by most of society. You also don't make these choices as a peace offering with God.

They are entirely made by your own need to restore a sense of community one small private act at a time. The outcomes are reflected in your growing awareness of your own individual worth and dignity. The growing inner knowledge emerges from the richness of your private encounters with others. Every new act of recognizing individual worth and dignity in others changes your own awareness of your own personal worth and dignity. And so, it becomes a cycle of reinforcing your new inner vision and your interactions with others.

A word about how this process relates to individual spirituality. My plans have no value on their own. It's like owning stock in a defunct corporation; it has no value to others or myself until I begin to make these experiences real. I must act on my inner beliefs and use the tools of spirituality in dealing with others. I offer the harvest reaped from these small, basic, yet valuable encounters as small symbolic gifts back to God for His continuing to confirm my worth in His eyes.

I'm now able to use the tools (ingredients) of spirituality to work with others engaging them as we come into contact with each other. These are all "here and now" experiences. They have no value when you review them in terms of the past or the future. They are the promise of a sweet-smelling and rich-tasting fresh fruit experience (definitely not a Dorian experience). One encounter at a time, I warmly apply the concepts of Mercy, Grace, Forgiveness, Faith and Hope as I plant these awesome seeds in the lives others.

I start off on the journey that can change community life—just like counter ripples working across the pond. The reward isn't in watching those ripples, but in tossing the pebbles (ingredients) that begin the rippling process. My spirit becomes energized as I slowly become aware of these ripples in the lives of others. It is a selfless act. I do not do this for God's forgiveness; He has already forgiven me.

These acts have no value to others or myself until I apply them to those in the pond. But out of each new choice, I slowly recognize that these choices are impacting my own life. I have become re-engaged in community life. I no longer need outward signs showing my value. I begin to know and experience God's view and His simple system of valuation. I am a precious child of God, as are others. We all have the same value and that is expressed in God's love for me and my actions toward others.

This is one way to organize the community portion of our personal pardon plan. I don't need to find the cure for cancer or find the solution to the problems of crime to keep me aware of my personal worth. This whole process is an inner experience of living life in these brief "here and now" encounters. Nothing dramatic is expected as the center point of my actions. Each small seemingly insignificant act alters my life. What society thinks of me (by way of all the labels) loses all ability to inflict pain in my life. Remember that hurting people hurt others. Since my personal pain has lessened, I'm free to reach out with small loving acts of kindness within my community.

The next category is the international community.

I think I can read your thoughts at this point. "How can I—just one person—take on the woes of the world?" I'm not asking you to shoulder the pain of all the people in the world. Just open yourself to the possibilities. Is there one small thing you could do to turn a wrong into a right? I think so! This could give you the opportunity to help people of different time zones, social status, education, levels of personal finance, skin color, parentage, ethnicity or differences in religion. The sole limitation to this exercise is that

I must choose others far away from me and I must choose others who couldn't possibly return my act of charity.

This offers a perfect vehicle to put my plans into action. Yes, we as individuals—small, unknown and similarly rejected individuals—can reach into the lives of others. I can reach across oceans, mountains, hemispheric obstacles and the endlessness of political differences by a small act of personal and community kindness. In doing so, I offer unseen and nameless others the hope of discovering their own inner sense of worth and dignity. After all, each person is my global neighbor.

Some of the past projects Quinta and I have undertaken include partial funding to equip a home church in Siberia and partial funds to help a small community in the Dominican Republic acquire water storage facilities. Later partial funding was given to help this village to get electrical services. Prior to their receiving the necessary funds, when the local utility provider experienced production downtime (brownout), thieves would climb the utility poles, cut the existing electrical wires and sell the wire for the value of its copper. Now the village has a continuous link to electricity and life at the community level has changed for the better.

Other efforts include providing on-site services at an HIV/AIDS clinic in Thailand and professional consultation and scientific updates with staff members at another facility in Indonesia. Quinta's personal favorite was working with the railway children in Jakarta. Long before she came into my life, she would regularly reach out to these children who were living in a shantytown. In addition to her weekly visits, twice a year she put together special outreach programs to touch their young lives. These outreaches included swimming trips to a local pool during the hot and steamy Jakarta summers and Christmas parties and small gifts for the children (while the sounds of speeding trains were not more than 10 feet away). The trains were *so* close; I was always amazed that relatively few individuals were killed crossing the railroad tracks. There were lots of times throughout the years helping these children sort out their experiences with the harsh realities of poverty and social injustice. To many others they were just street children, but to us they are the promise and hope of tomorrow. I do not know about the interests of the World Bank or IMF, but I have had the personal experience of watching a child's delight at receiving a hamburger.

Other opportunities resulted from joining with various organizations having special interests in the location or targeted beneficiary programs like water wells for Africa. Sometimes opportunities arose to fund a student's tuition for a year or to support a camp meeting at some remote location. An opportunity also arose to equip local missionaries with satellite phones, which helped them reach out to natives in formerly inaccessible jungles of New Guinea. The phones were used to quickly identify the needs of remotely located groups and to acquire needed resources to help these isolated people.

Every year, we make a choice to fund at least one international need at whatever level of contribution that our finances will allow. Few of these projects are completely funded through our outreach, but to a greater or lesser extent we have been able to connect with others each year through these outreaches. We always experience a feeling of joy when these small gifts help to transform the lives of others.

International travel, customs regulations, language barriers and time zone differences don't get in our way when making these inspirations come alive. With each passing year, we can add a flag to our symbolic map of the world. In addition to these unique efforts, we continue to provide funds directly to several organizations whose mission coincides with our outreach interests.

It does not take some giant corporate structure to offer changes for unseen others. My international travels have taught me about the richness and luxury of living in a first world nation. With access to such a privilege comes the responsibility to care for others.

Labels have many levels. Understanding labels offers a chance to understand the needs of others domestically and internationally. Use these opportunities to build bridges of knowledge and empathy. Through these small anonymous gifts we all have the opportunity to transform the lives of others in some meaningful way. What outreach will you consider?

These suggested ideas are important to your personal pardon plan. You may question, "Why go to all of this effort when I already know that I'm an okay person?" The labels of life represent the restrictions and confinement of life. They may be accurate in terms of describing prior behaviors or they may have been assigned in an attempt to help better understand society's role in your life.

Either way, it is essential to undertake the work of looking at each of those labels, and pull out an understanding of what they tell about past personal behaviors. Now that you have this gold nugget of truth, it's time to lose those labels to that black trash bag and set about changing your now and your future with the new things you've learned. With each effort, a new pathway opens until you can look back to that point in time when you were a loved child: a precious child of God.

You will be left with what remains of the errors of your life—a distilled knowledge of your personal meeting with truth shown by your history of behavioral choices. How do you deal with the leftover issues? The answer is simple. Set about the task of making your wrongs, right! Go into your inner workshop—the change factory—and work at your workbench crafting a personal pardon plan. Create a plan that offers others your personal best in all of your current and future undertakings.

* * *

Mental health therapies may not offer much help. Psychology, which has lots of tools for processing these events, is focused on the past and its effects upon my current life. It suggests that there is an orderly process for doing this work, and that process is called Cognitive Behavioral Therapy. A major premise of this school of thought is that we all have developed "schemas" or plans that inform our life choices. The psychologist tells us that it all starts with our thoughts that then trigger our emotions. Then with the emergence of an emotional response, we act. We display a behavioral response that is based upon what we told ourselves about our situation. In the context of a therapy relationship—(remember the power differential between doctor and patient)—we make personal changes by challenging our "self-talk." We do this one faulty thought at a time.

Quinta is a far better psychologist that I am. At one point, I was attempting to explain this theoretical construct and its application to KNOWETICS. After considering my thoughts, she slept on this information and earnestly sought God's direction via prayer.

Something that I had said while describing this process had troubled her. Wisely she offered no objection at that moment, but took her time to work with the concept, using her personal spirituality as a guide. The next morning she asked me to listen to her understanding of the problem. Remarkably she told me that it was her belief that "actions dictate feelings." In this simple offering she urged me to consider that actions trump (are more important than) emotions.

With this small but essential revelation, Quinta was able to provide the locking pin linking the work of KNOWETICS together. You see, to God it doesn't matter what we have done in our lives. He is always ready to forgive us and help us to move on. He graciously extends His love to us constantly. Just like the sun is always shining as the earth rotates, His healing love is always available to us. The process of creating a KNOWETICS reality is to understand the constant expression of His forgiving love for us and to accept that forgiveness and move on in a fresh experience of living.

Through the knowledge of that constant love and acceptance, recognizing my personal defeats and failures and discarding my labels, I come to a point in my thinking where I want to set wrongs right. I want to reach out to others in love and friendship. I don't need to act this way to secure God's love, or put together some elegant plan before asking for His pardon. He has done so already. I know that at the deepest level of my being, I want to reach out to others and touch their lives for good. I organize these efforts by developing a personal pardon plan that guides all of my actions.

I want to make a difference in the lives of others. I'm driven to seek out opportunities to change the daily experiences of my life. I want to reshape and remold my character out of the EXPERIENCE of knowing that I am a precious child of God (and so is everyone else). I'm no longer motivated by selfishness. I construct my personal pardon plan, not because I am seeking society's approval or a governmental pardon, but I make my plan and I start to apply it to everything I do because it brings me joy—plain and simple joy. I don't make these choices to impress others; I do so because it feeds my soul. It takes me back to that point in my life when love was unconditional.

Only now, it's not about me receiving a steady flow of unconditional love. My life now hinges on my ability to give others a steady stream of unconditional love by working my personal pardon plan and doing it largely anonymously and without any expectations. Just small gifts of love and understanding toward those I encounter. I right the wrongs that I have committed to the best of my ability, but I go further beyond that notion. I now create a new way of interacting with others: one person at a time.

Something magical starts to happen within us as we go about our daily tasks while looking for opportunities to connect with others and blessing them with our small acts of love. We unconsciously start to toss all of those labels to the compost heap of forgetfulness. As others try to bring out the skeletons of our past, we recognize that they are talking about someone else. Their attempts to wound us or assign us to some category of worthlessness have no impact on our lives. We recognize that we have been healed and we are unmoved by their actions. We can understand their motives and we can look beyond their behaviors and see the fear that drives their actions. Love and fear cannot co-exist. You have made a choice to love and reinforced that decision by your actions toward yourself and others. You don't need to defend yourself; you know that you are a changed person and NO ONE can shake your belief in yourself.

You will start to experience the warmth and love of others as they reach out to you. Do you remember the story of the Prodigal Son? A careful reading will show that his father had a story also, and his story is simple and easy to understand. He didn't label his son's behaviors or malign his character by reminding him of his foolish choices. He simply loved him. The son had a personal pardon plan ready to unfold before his father. It contained the provision that he would serve as his father's servant.

Among his other transgressions, he had dishonored his father by demanding his inheritance before his father's death. In doing so, he culturally inflicted a grievous wound upon his father. Instead of responding with justifiable wrath, the father tenderly embraced his lost son, reaffirmed his personal worth and welcomed him home. What love! He applied the teachings of Jesus Christ to his own situation without even being aware that he was doing so. In that brief moment in time, both of their wounds were healed and each of them became free to love again.

* * *

Modern literature gives us many secular examples of individuals overcoming their inner conflicts and experiencing a sense of personal redemption. A few examples are:

Catcher in the Rye (J.D. Salinger)

Tom Sawyer (Mark Twain), and

A Lesson Before Dying (Ernest Gaines).

History has many examples of missed opportunities. Consider:

The Spanish Armada (misinformed, poor planning and perhaps overly confident)

The Wreck of The Edmund Fitzgerald (circumstances and location), or

The Titanic (lost through the arrogance of cost saving design errors and a blind flight into harm's way in order to set a transatlantic ocean speed record).

The record of man's past reveals that man's thoughts contributed to every disaster. A close review of that same record reveals that man's inner processes can guide him through all hurdles.

An understanding of these disasters will reveal man's reckless and arrogant willingness to put himself and others in danger. A review of literature will show man's ability to rise above the challenges of life. The former process is guided by greed and pride. The later process is guided by love and compassion for self and others.

Your personal pardon plan becomes a roadmap to guide you through all challenges and difficulties of life. It becomes the center point of your life. It is not a vain attempt to win favor with others, but a practical approach to make peace with God, family, friends, yourself, the community, society and your global neighbors.

You know what you already have in life. A personal pardon plan becomes a way to shape the rest of your life and add true meaning to every one of your future choices. It takes thought, effort and lots of sacrifices, but it restores you to that point of unconditional love that you last experienced as a child. By unconditionally loving others, you remake your world, one person at a time. Change is an inside job.

CHAPTER 18

AN INVITATION TO DIALOGUE: DISCUSSING THE BURDENS OF MAINTAINING A SECRET LIFE

THIS MAY BE THE MOST important chapter in this book. The picture has been painted in the previous seventeen chapters. We know how it works; we've seen the evidence of secret lives all around us and the destructive ways they shape our own lives. I'm convinced that no one takes that first drink determined to become an alcoholic. Neither does the person who experiments with pornography or alternative lifestyles prepare for a divorce or possible social disapproval. It's all done one small step at a time. We play a shell game with ourselves believing that these are all very private activities that others don't know about us. The myth of privacy is a pleasant fantasy in which we all indulge.

The reality is that most of our behaviors are readily observable to others and certainly, in the current world of security-consciousness, even the smallest acts may draw notice by others. That is when labels start to be applied to our persons and our activities and the unmasking starts to happen. While we dwell in our fantasy world and think that others have no knowledge of our true lives, consider that they are also busy engaging in the same process. They can easily recognize deception because at some level they are busy living out their own similar life experiences. Each of us struggles to some extent with the deceptions we embrace. It's a good time to go back to the seven deadly sins. None of us are immune; the problem underlying all of this is our human nature.

That's not an excuse to avoid cleaning up our lives. One way or the other, we all play out the hands that we've been dealt. Transparency is a virtue that we haven't spoken about previously. How sweet it would be to go back to that point in our lives when we didn't weigh ourselves down with the problems we have now. The fact is that we can do exactly that by making a decision to abandon secrecy as a way of life. Just like this entire process started with the small acts of lying, stealing, and cheating and so on, we start the healing process the same exact way—one small act at a time. Our spirituality is the guide joining the tools of Mercy, Grace, Forgiveness, Faith and Hope as they are used in our own lives. But starting a relationship of accountability is the framework in which we conduct our activities.

But you say, "I could never tell anyone some of the things that I have done. I'm too ashamed." There is a saying that "we are only as sick as our secrets." Don't make a leap in your thinking that destroys all of the work that you've done up until this point. Don't jump backwards in fear. You've allowed yourself to hold onto the warmth and hope of a different life, a purposeful life. You're so close to your goal. Don't let the shadows frighten you. They are only shadows;

they have no power of their own to harm you. Let's shine some light on the pathway. Freedom is not very far away.

It is never easy to look back and reflect on our misdeeds and the harm done to others. But what you need to recognize is that we're not just looking backwards, we're looking ahead to a meaningful life. Aren't you tired of ringing that leper's bell everywhere you go and shouting out "leper, leper"? It's time to remember that Jesus Christ reminded us "the truth will set us free." Truth is a precious, soothing ointment that heals our wounds. The truth is that no one in the world is without worth to God. Even the worst among us have value in God's eyes.

We all need to share with someone else; we weren't meant to live our lives in isolation. Do you remember the lesson from Genesis 2:18 that says it is not good for man to be alone? Life is a gift, not a burden. So let's start the renewal process. It's time to start house-cleaning. Having discarded the labels of life, we figured out which personal behaviors gave us those labels and we want to set things right, if it's possible. It starts with that inner resolve—a commitment to yourself and God.

* * *

In our lives, we make an unknown number of decisions and the end result is the people we become. We're the product of our thoughts and choices. That is the nature of our lives. Recently I was watching *East of Eden* (John Steinbeck) and his work clearly reflects this process in the lives of his characters. It might be worth going to your local library and checking out a copy for yourself. Consider it homework. The story unfolds about the lives of several individuals from childhood onward. Those early decisions mark their lives in predictable ways. Once you've seen the movie, you might better be able to apply these ideas to your own life. How is the fruit of the tree of your life, bitter or sweet?

A friend from California used to talk about his addiction to morphine and the many things he had done to acquire a regular supply of this drug for his daily needs (such as buying it on the street or using a variety of substitutes). He had lived a secret life out of shame and fear of condemnation. These unknown actions had become part of his "take-it-to-the-grave secrets" and he could not bear to let anyone close to this pain, so while he wanted to change, he sadly continued on the pathway of addiction.

Over the years, he continued to wrestle with his choices. These periods were mixed with brief attempts at sobriety, but they never lasted. You see when he was clean and sober; he was left alone to deal with the horrible decisions of his life. He couldn't bear to dump the contents of this sack and examine the contents in the light of God's love. He was truly alone, and even when he was not using drugs, he was in constant emotional pain. In our work together, he eventually was able to come to a point where he became willing to grapple with his history.

The courage he found to clean house had little to do with our relationship. Rather, it sprung directly from his discovery of the spiritual tools of life. He didn't become a seasoned Christian, moving to the front of the altar; instead, he started with a small budding awareness that grew on its own. His life was transformed as he recognized the truth and started to use his spiritual tools to reshape his life. The secret that gave him a lifetime of pain was later revealed. As his mother lay dying with Stage IV cancer, he would steal her pain medication. She knew exactly what he was doing, but never complained or spoke of it to anyone else, and she suffered great pain as a result of his actions. What haunted him most was the look of love in her eyes.

When he was finally able to open up and tell his story without being judged, he was set free. At our last contact, he hadn't gone back to his prior addiction. He not only made peace with his mother and himself, but also was able to take the shame and pain of that experience and reach out to others who were suffering from similar addictions. His last known employment was working as an orderly in a hospital. He had specifically requested to work on the oncology unit. He wanted to help ease the sufferings of others through daily acts of kindness.

Society—had they known his actions toward his mother—would have hated the thought of such a person working around terminally ill patients. There would have been no forgiveness, nor would he have ever officially been given the opportunity to repair and restore the harm he had once committed. He would have been beyond personal redemption. Consider the fact that hundreds of doctors and nurses have had the same experience of stealing medications from needy patients to feed his or her addictions. Most have come to terms with their behaviors (either after they were caught or when the burden became so heavy that they could no longer shoulder it).

Consider next the twenty-some-year-old woman whose husband has been sent to prison for several years. She has a young baby. This particular woman was estranged from her parents, family, and few friends and she was desperately lonely. During her husband's imprisonment, she had a single encounter with another man. She later regretted her actions and wished with all of her heart that she could wipe the slate clean. After her husband's release, she confessed her single indiscretion to him and sought his forgiveness. He repaid her confidence by seducing her best friend. Shattered by his betrayal and hateful actions, the marriage soon ended in a bitter, hateful divorce.

Take-it-to-the-grave secrets must to be handled with care. They are like unexploded bombs that can go off at any time. But that isn't a reason to bury them even further in our memories or attempt to justify our actions. That's why we use our spiritual tools in combination with relationships of accountability. I was sober fifteen years and had not revealed my most shameful act to anyone. I carried that burden with me everywhere I went. My shame kept reminding me that NO ONE would ever accept this past conduct and I also realized that I had no reason to offer it. I had no logic to support my horrible decision, so I suffered in silence. I'd committed this dastardly act and had to live with the horror every day. That mindset set me apart from others, always reminding me that I was unforgiveable and beyond redemption.

During a health related stay out west, I was finally in enough pain from the secret and decided that I had to get rid of it. I selected a man that I had met only a few times who seemed to be friendly and open and I asked to go outside with him and talk. My true fear was that if I talked about my prior behaviors inside the building, they would somehow be captured and forever linked with my name. My actions weren't criminal in nature, just not what I would have expected of myself. Moving far away from the building to abate my growing anxiety and paranoia, I bound my new friend to the 4th and 5th steps of Alcoholics Anonymous and blurted out my offense.

Later, he told me that he hadn't committed anything similar, but he calmly reassured me that what I'd done was within the range of human activity. In other words, he clearly understood that my prior behaviors were regrettable and painful expressions of personal depravity. His kind words and thoughtful acceptance set me free, and I haven't looked back since. I found the strength to forgive myself and move on. In that moment of acceptance, the self-imposed mark of Cain was lifted and I was free to live my life. What an incredible gift from a stranger. It transformed my thinking and shaped my focus to helping others, so they in turn become free of their "take-it-to-the-grave" secrets. That moment was the foundation for writing this book nineteen years later.

We really are only as sick as our secrets. You may live with constant fear of exposure and possible punishment, but you must realize that such thinking traps you and keeps you in constant pain. Out of the billions of people on this planet, there is someone out there who will hear your story and accept you as you are, without adding to your pain and isolation, or acting as if they are shocked by what you've said. That's the reason this book was written, to help to set you free. Free from your personal pain and the burdens of carrying endless labels. IT DOESN'T MATTER WHAT YOU HAVE DONE, you are a precious child of God and NOTHING can block you from your birthright or your inheritance.

Does anybody really know you? Have you ever shared your take-it-to-the-grave secrets with someone else? Don't be reckless when you do; it needs serious thought. Take, for instance, the young man who (after getting sober) wrote a letter to a woman he had raped years before. He was genuinely seeking to make amends. She hadn't even known that she had been raped. Apparently, he had slipped something into her drink and had then taken advantage of the fact she was unconscious and he raped her. After learning what had happened, she filed a police report and he was arrested, convicted and sentenced to prison.

While his confession cost him dearly, I bet he is the type of person who couldn't live without clearing his conscious. And if the price for that is suffering, at least he is now free of this horrible burden he's been carrying around with him. Do you remember the wisdom of Nikki, the server, who stated, "You would have to tell someone or it will eat you up?" She was right. Though he decided to rape an unconscious woman, I applaud his actions in coming clean and doing the best that he could to right this wrong.

Start this process of personal revelation by looking at the legality of your actions. If you live in fear of discovery and possible prosecution or sanctions from others, then it is time that you start to put your spiritual tools to work. If you don't see a way to reveal yourself without causing more harm, I suggest that the first step be prayer and an attitude of honesty and willingness, and be open if God provides the opportunity. The desire to be set free will become your guiding light. It is no accident that you are experiencing a surge away from bondage and toward real freedom.

Having had years of experience in shaping these opportunities for others, I am willing to work with the unique factors that keep a person chained to the past. There is no need to jump into specifics immediately if you are truly willing to be set free. Together we have many ways to cut those chains without endangering you or others. When you experience that moment of true freedom from your past, you will know that it has changed your life forever.

As a trainee therapist, I once held a workshop for similar souls. The goal of the workshop was to tell your take-it-to-the-grave secret to others in a group of twenty individuals. The secret was not to be verbalized in the group. Each member was to decide the best format for revealing their misery and then on a selected Saturday, we would all come together and throw our slips of paper into a box outside the door. Some individuals would type out their secrets on nondescript pieces of paper. Other would cut words out of a newspaper or magazine and paste them to other pieces of paper. No one wrote out anything by hand, and of course, there were no identifying marks on any of these pages. Each page contained the horror story of that person's life—the previously undisclosed event that kept them chained to the past.

After verifying that we had a page for everyone to read, I went around and asked the participants to pull out one folded sheet (it could not be their own story). We proceeded to read these secrets out loud to the group one at a time and to discuss what it must be like to carry around that personal pain, and reflect upon how it might affect the life of the sufferer. Each person's story was discussed and members of the group offered the anonymous author compassionate understanding and acceptance. No one raised a word of judgment or tried to diminish their own failures by comparing their actions to the actions of others. Each participant reflected upon his or her own struggles and how alike everyone was based on the pain each experienced. There was no room for a rating system based on what it was the person had done. The members had secretly offered past behaviors ranging from participation in a kidnapping, theft, and child abuse, to many sexual indiscretions including sexual assault on a child.

When the group at last closed its final session, each member had come to terms with the sad reality that we were all co-sufferers. While we had victimized others, we had also victimized ourselves. Each member gained a new perspective on personal pain. This was an early effort showing how take-it-to-the-grave secrets affect our lives. It also became useful in later developing Relational Victimization Theory.

I don't believe that a single member of that group left the final session unchanged. Each of them had developed empathy toward one another. Another example of their humanity had blossomed. They were free to see others without the air of judgment that seeped into our families, communities and society. Each member gave the gift of self to all of the others. They left that session freer than they had been before attending that workshop.

All of us are knowable within the context of love and compassion. I don't have to embrace the choices of others, but in order to live in peace, I need to be able to recognize their personal burdens and not add to their pain by placing labels upon them. KNOWETICS is not about spreading pain to others, it is about helping others heal and how that response supports our own healing process. I think that Father Charles was right when he told the various prison gang members that they had all better learn how to get along since they were going to be neighbors in heaven for all eternity!

As a professional, I have had an interest in the psychology behind critical incidents and their aftermath. My interests have also included the belief that individuals may create their own post-traumatic stress disorders, given the incredible harm which we are capable of doing to each other. In a conversation with two young psychiatrists, I raised this point, but they quickly dismissed it. Later in a different context, I again raised this question with a seasoned psychiatrist who voiced her support for this idea. The difference between these professionals was the fact that the first two doctors had little practical experience along with their education. The latter doctor had enough experience under her belt to recognize what it means to inflict pain on others.

My purpose in writing about this isn't to create a new category of mental health care needs or to offer an excuse to others. It's to remind ourselves that all actions have consequences, including the unintended actions in raising others, punishing offenders and participating in approved acts that inflict violence upon others. These unintended consequences are reflected in the stories we read or hear in the daily media. Little effort is spent on understanding how these encounters shape our lives and our interactions with others.

I also strongly believe in the concept of institutionally induced Post Traumatic Stress Disorder. Consider the lives of children who are abused and unwanted and are left to be raised in state care facilities. Or consider state and federal prisoners or members of the military who may live with the fear that their lives are in danger. Since no one wants to appear weak in these situations, the problems that shape the lives of these individuals are rarely addressed. You don't have to be a prisoner of war to be subject to life-transforming pain.

During an earlier phase of my work, I had the privilege of working with law enforcement officers throughout the state of Louisiana. In conjunction with others, I had an opportunity to apply for a demonstration grant from the National Institute of Justice that focused on the effects of stress on law enforcement families. The grant was to be used to develop helpful interventions for the benefit of officers and their families. It was intended to help them adjust to the traumas that they regularly encountered through their work.

Two cases stand out in my mind as I think back to those situations. In the first case, three police officers attempted to defuse a situation in which a man with a knife was threatening them. All of the officers had their weapons out. Each was reluctant to hurt or fatally wound the individual holding the knife. They were in a no-win situation. The man started to charge at them, so one of the officers fired a single shot that killed the individual. Later in a private small session, this officer sobbed over having taken a life. He also voiced his concerns that he was now "lost" and going to hell because of his actions. That man was continuing to face life-transforming trauma.

Another incident involved two police officers who responded to a call of a man with a gun barricaded in his manufactured home. They entered the house with weapons drawn and spotted the individual walking from the bedroom toward the living room with a rifle—the rifle as being held upward against his shoulder, like you might see in a movie of soldiers marching in step with their rifles.

As he approached the living room, the officers attempted to disarm him and take him into custody. During this scuffle, this individual reached for one of the officer's weapons, so the officer shot the individual. As he was falling to the floor, he looked at them and said, "You just killed me." When I met with these officers, they gave no evidence of being emotionally disturbed by this situation.

Instead, they seemed able to support each other and justify their actions, almost unfazed by this encounter.

Each officer had been exposed to a horrible situation. They made split-second decisions while feeling their lives were in danger. No one can second-guess those decisions (especially those that have never had that experience). Each of those men will have to live with their decisions all the days of their lives. No one can tell how those thoughts will come out in dreams, depression, divorce or self-destructive actions (such as suicide or divorce) in the future. Once an individual is no longer in the middle of the situation, it's almost impossible for another person to understand how these events will play out later in their lives.

Another example of the aftereffects of trauma is a young man in Southern California who had recently been released from prison. He was driving down a city street when he was stopped by a police officer for a minor traffic violation. When he was asked for his driver's license and vehicle registration, he was unable to supply one of the documents. The police officer noticed his prison tattoos and decided to take him into custody. When the officer tried to make the arrest, the young man pulled out a gun and shot the officer to death. Another officer responding at the scene became engaged in a gun battle with the young man and fatally wounded him. This second officer was also wounded in the exchange of gunfire.

I later heard people comment on this young man's foolishness. Some stated that he'd learned nothing from his stay in prison. I disagreed. I believe that he learned something essential to living the prison experience. What he learned was that he never wanted to go back to prison again. He would rather die than go through that

experience again. The officer who stopped him for the traffic violation had no way of knowing that he'd just stopped a dangerous man
that was prepared to die rather than lose his freedom again.

It doesn't have to be incidents that take place right in front of us.
Sometimes the effects of an incident don't appear for years; instead
they creep up on us without any evidence of a prior connection.
Consider the soldier who served in Bosnia during the Bosnian conflict. The conflict had been a study in genocidal fury. This solider
was serving as a member of the occupation force-dividing combat-
ants. He never fired his weapon beyond the training fields of the
U.S. Army; he was merely in Bosnia as a peacekeeper.

His unit regularly patrolled several small nearby towns. They
drove through each of the towns making sure that members of the
community were being protected from violence. His assignment
was to ride in the back of a Humvee and use his presence to help
stabilize the country's mixed ethnic factions. Several times a day
they completed a circuit traveling through these towns.

One evening they completed their circuit and returned to base
with no indications that anything was amiss. He reported that the
next morning as they were making their first circuit of the day, their
vehicle turned a corner and there, between two houses, was a pile of
dead bodies. On top of the pile of bodies, was the lifeless corpse of
a six-year-old boy face up with a bullet wound to the forehead. The
child's sightless eyes were open as though he was staring into eternity.

Our soldier observed the scene, and after dispatching others
to care for the dead, his team of peacekeepers again moved onto
its established route. He noted that at that exact moment, the scene
didn't bother him. The military team moved on about its business

and eventually he was rotated out of that unit and returned stateside. His life returned to normal. He eventually married and had several children of his own. Life moved on and Bosnia faded from his immediate memory.

At least, his life appeared to return to normal. As his children grew, he started to use alcohol more frequently and became more withdrawn and isolated. His military commitment required that he continue to participate in various deployments and other activities. During these years, he and his wife became distant though neither of them actually fought with each other. It was a sort of co-existence without agitation or controversy. They may have lived together, but somehow they no longer nurtured each other.

His son approached the age of six and this soldier slipped into a working state of depression. He didn't notice it himself. He just managed to push through his days, get home, eat and go to bed. He would wake up the following day and push through that one also. He eventually was sent on another deployment. During this time, his wife found a boyfriend and became pregnant by her new lover. When her husband returned home, she was very much pregnant and was determined to have the child. You see, she'd gotten involved with the boyfriend because she had spent years without the comfort of her husband. She was angry and felt that her actions were justified because he didn't care enough for her.

Neither of these people realized that an unnamed dead little boy in Bosnia a decade before had touched their lives. Or, that a brief moment of exposure to trauma resulted in a divorce and new pain for all concerned. This story didn't come from months of intensive therapy or the soothing effects of some psychoactive medication.

His story came as a result of his personal work in a relationship of accountability. There are few resources available to help those dealing with the effects of post-traumatic stress experiences. If you are going to deconstruct the harmful effects of past experiences, the burden will fall to you and you alone to make the effort.

KNOWETICS offers one avenue to purge yourself of the disabling aftereffects connected with your past behaviors and/or exposure to events beyond your control. It doesn't require special knowledge or training. All of the knowledge and experience you need come from your spirituality so now you have all the resources that you need to set yourself free. The one thing I can't provide to you is the courage and inner strength to take this information and apply it to your own life.

This book isn't about wishing and dreaming of a new life. This book is about working hard at creating that new life right now. You have everything that you need to be successful. The road ahead isn't easy, but it is a simple journey. From today on, it doesn't matter what others think of you; all that matters is what God thinks of you. You are His precious child and nothing else matters.

Please don't think for a moment that this is an invitation to hide from your responsibilities or to magically deny the harm that you have done to others and yourself. Nor is it an attempt to minimize the harm that others have done to you. It's a practical step—a first step—to reduce harm and then later to eliminate harm. It comes from an awareness that your life isn't over; you haven't completed your journey. Today marks the start of the rest of your life.

There ARE some things we can *never* undo. The abortions that I personally triggered by my selfish actions, the virginity of others taken in a spirit of youthful conquest, the dollars stolen from nameless and faceless people, and the joy of living which I stole from others as a result of my former behaviors can't be undone. I can't restore these lost treasures to those who deserve direct compensation.

The people of my youth who have transitioned to eternity and those whose love and sacrifice were repaid with acts of betrayal can't benefit from my awareness and transformation. Many just don't want any further contact with someone who caused them so much pain. One of my first girlfriends feels this way. After coming to the realization of the pain that I had inflicted upon her, I attempted to locate her and make amends. I went so far as to hire a private investigator to find her. The investigator was successful in the search and spoke with her and told her of my motivation and even spoke of my current professional efforts. My past girlfriend laughed bitterly at the notion that I could make any meaningful change in my life. She then asked that the investigator not give her contact information to me.

It was a sad reality to understand that there are those that we can never reach, but that's the price we pay for the pain we inflicted upon others. I now know that people who *live* in pain *inflict* pain on others. They thrash their way through life and often live this way until the end of their days. And it continues to happen until we have a spiritual awakening. This girlfriend is beyond my hope of reaching, and so are my middle daughter and oldest brother. Those who have already died are also beyond my hopes of righting my wrongs and restoring what I have taken.

That is why a personal pardon plan is so important. There are a number of actions that I cannot undo, but there are billions of opportunities that await my new decisions and choices. Each future encounter becomes an opportunity to touch others for good and to set unseen wrongs, right. By shouldering the burdens of someone else, I renew my commitment to make every day count, applying *carpe diem* to each new activity.

The book has used the term KNOWETICS to remove it from the fields of science and religion. Neither of these domains can lay exclusive claim to its statements on application of the truth to our lives. It exists because I accidently discovered that those in the past have given great thought to the harm that we have inflicted upon ourselves (and others) through our sinful activities. This book has also included an understanding of the harm which crime inflicts upon ourselves, others, the community and society as a whole. For me, both of these ideas come under the category of crimes against God.

My primary objective is to examine my life in the context of my relationship with God. All other relationships flow from this primary relationship; nothing else really matters. All crime is against God. All sin is ultimately against God. It is my acts of rebellion against my Creator. Therefore, all efforts to right the wrongs of my past life must stem from my willingness to restore a right relationship with my God and nothing else matters. This is the stem from where my hope and strength flows. All healing comes from that sole pursuit, and nothing can replace the experience of knowing that I'm in right standing with my Creator.

I said before that this is not a book about science or religion and these statements don't change that. I'm not talking about embracing a religious or scientific viewpoint. I'm talking about a relationship. This is a concept that stands on its own merit and has no attachments to either point of view. This relationship is based on individual worth and dignity as expressed in our own unique spirituality.

Arguments that try to say this book and its contents seem ridiculous are fruitless, since each individual has some type of spirituality. The fact that this book was written by someone who holds a leper's role in society proves that spirituality exists within all of us. No one can lay claim to having more or less spirituality than another. No one can claim they understand another's spirituality. And no human government, organization or force can deny the existence of spirituality within each of us.

Consider the strange life of Ted Bundy, executed in 1989 for his many crimes. The day before his execution and on the morning of his last day on earth, he spent his time with James Dobson making a video for others that might offer some insight into his life choices. I've heard others claim that the making of this video was self-serving, and they dismissed any possible benefits that might come from this effort. In that video, Bundy stated that pornography—especially violent pornography—helped shape his ideas on acts of rape and murder.

Those of us who have worked in the field of mental health are well acquainted with the legacy of pain and destruction connected with an addiction to pornography. There was truth in his last words. He may have been everything that others claimed him to be, but in the final analysis, I believe that he tried to make some small attempt to rectify the harm that he had done by warning others of the dangers, which lay ahead of them if they indulged in similar activities.

* * *

Each individual has had encounters with others that left them wounded or uncomfortable. This seems to be the nature of life itself. While most of us have never gone to the point of murder, we've all failed to show Christian love or compassion for others. What we do with this information will shape and influence all of our future relationships. Think of it as putting on a pair of blue-tinted sunglasses. When we first look through those lenses, we'll notice everything looks darker and seems to have a blue tint. As time goes on, we get used to the effect of the blue tint and hardly notice it. Our brains just accept the tint as the "norm".

The same thing is true of our interactions with others, what we think about others, and the methods that we develop to process and dismiss those ugly moments of our daily lives. We generally give those moments little time for reflection. We attach a label and move on to the next project. And over a period of time we "effectively" learn how to handle people who challenge our coping abilities and our spiritual resources. If you stop to think about it for a moment, those are exactly the kind of people who constantly asked Jesus Christ for help on His journeys. He referred to them as His sheep.

Now, sheep are easily startled and that is why they seek protection amongst the herd. I have also heard it said that sheep are "stupid" animals. I once heard someone describe an encounter with a single sheep that had come to the edge of an embankment. After realizing the land was falling off in front of it, the sheep became frightened; however, it just stood in that same spot, looking ahead and bleating in fear. The shepherd found the sheep, lifted it up and physically turned it around and it quickly scooted back to the safety of the herd.

That's the way we can be at times. So transfixed by the events of the moment, we lose sight of all practical alternatives. Society expects that we know better. So does our family and friends. But we stand there trapped by our fears, unable to see the alternatives. In our lifetime, we'll meet lots of people who may want to take care of the sheep. Most of them are sheepherders. Their role is to round up the sheep and keep them in a herd. Few of us encounter true shepherds in our lives. These are people who understand our unique circumstances and use their knowledge and skills to "physically" lift us up and turn us in another direction.

In my life, I've had the privilege of meeting a few shepherds. They are generally extraordinary people. Rather than becoming exasperated with others, they seem to have an endless capacity for loving and caring for others. The sheepherder wonders why the sheep are so stupid; the shepherd recognizes its plight and provides a loving assist. Both deal with sheep, but the difference between them is dramatic. Jesus told us that His sheep know His voice and that they trust Him. The difference between the sheepherder and the true shepherd is love.

We are all sheep and have had the experiences of just being tolerated or truly being loved. We can easily recognize the differences. Those of us who have had a shepherd don't fear the rod or the staff. We know that the rod and staff are used lovingly for our protection and not to beat us. Unlike sheep, we are all born with free will. That means that we can choose any path that seems right to us. The efforts of science over the last 150 years have pointed us to the belief that everything has some cause and is usually not chosen. According to this belief, our choices are limited and our futures play out without the freedom to change the course of lives. What a grim view of life.

From page one of the Bible, we learn that God's plan for our lives has always focused upon free will and the freedom of choice. We learn of the sins of disobedience and murder, which led to our fall from grace. But we also learn that even in the presence of such great sin, God made provision for each of us and did not leave us standing at the edge of life crying out in fear. Adam, Eve and Cain were allowed to live out their lives productively, but they rejected the splendor God had chosen for them. Instead, they chose the lowest kind of life. God respected their individual choices.

Cain, the world's first murderer, was not struck down by God's righteous fury; instead, he was sent off with his wife. They settled near the area of Nod, bore children, made a life for themselves and they even built a city. Clearly God still saw value in the lives He had created. Their sins and acts of rebellion did not cut them off from a future that might bring good things out of new choices. He did not see them as worthless and dead because of their transgressions and sins.

This book has been written with this lesson in mind. The past is the past. The future lies ahead; it is an unwritten page in the book of our future lives. If you've really made a mess of things up until now, there's still time to turn to a new page and be creative in what you write down for the future. Create something beautiful. Study the responsibilities that go along with being a shepherd. Look for the lost sheep. Listen for their cries. They're all around us.

Everything that has happened in your life has great meaning, and it can be used to help others. Nothing is ever wasted in God's economy. The value is not to be found in listing your defeats or failures, the true value is found in what you do with them from here on out. This is why it is so important to be honest with yourself. Look deep inside and identify the secret life that you've hidden so well. By being honest with yourself, you'll finally see that God still wants to make your life beautiful, if you let Him. Out of that wretched tapestry, He will create a treasure. It's never too late to start.

I began this book with a bold statement. I said that the right to change is a God-given inalienable right not subject to denial or modification by any government or civil authority. This book is dedicated to that basic principle. Now it's your turn to make it a reality. This is the ultimate proof that you have free will. You can change directions at any time. There is a New Testament verse that speaks about the one who steals. It tells the thief to stop stealing, get a job and help others (Ephesians: 4:28 NIV). This is another endorsement of the hope for changed lives and is a mandate for you and me.

There is no life so dark, bleak and hopeless that it is beyond God's ability to use for His honor and glory. It all begins with a decision, but He is the one who does the work in our lives. To some degree or other, we all have elements of spirituality within us and all transformation stems from this spirituality.

There are those who will read this book and still remain convinced that they are beyond hope because of the choices that they made earlier in life. There may be relatively few murderers living amongst us, but by examining your own actions, you may come to the realization that even though you've never physically taken someone's life, how many of us have killed someone's spirit? How many of us, by judging actions, have taken from others their good name and hopes for the future? How many of us have allowed lies to roll off our tongues on a daily basis? How many of us steal from others each day with our eyes and hearts?

These are tough economic times for everybody. The job market continues to shrink. Money is tight and it seems that prices are constantly rising. Do we realize we're all struggling in this environment? If you're behind the curve because of baggage from the past, it's like running a race with a giant ball and chain attached to your leg. All of your actions are hampered by the effort of having to pick up the ball and run with it. Those are social, not spiritual burdens. There are NO spiritual balls and chains if you use what you already have available.

I'm not suggesting that we break the law. The law can only condemn, it can never distinguish the state of our hearts. Only God—our ultimate Judge—knows the state of our hearts. While I live with the knowledge of my errors, failures and defeats, they no longer shape my daily life. They're in the past and what we've learned from those past events provides a sound basis for making choices today. I'm more than my behaviors. That's the heart of God's life within me.

More than anything, the most important bit of knowledge is that I'm a spiritual person capable of making new choices at any time. Nothing is ever lost or without meaning, if I accept the fact that I'm learning how my actions affect others. When I'm low and downcast, I refuel my hopes and dreams by remembering that there is meaning in every one of my actions. I may be in one of life's storms now, but I have the ability to move beyond the storm.

How easy it is to forget that I have a choice and choices serve as the rudder of life. That is the rudder of my life. Simple things like opening a soft drink instead of a can of beer, going out and filing a job application, holding a door open for someone else, or just being kind to someone in need of a smile or encouragement have dramatic effects in our lives. Nothing happens by accident. Coincidence is how God remains anonymous in the events of our lives. Nevertheless, He is always there with us. Maybe it is time to step out of the boat and walk on water!

Do you remember Peter's short excursion of walking on water? He asked Jesus to bid him come and walk on the water. Only, he lost sight of his purpose and became distracted by the wind. It was only by his faith that he could do the same thing as His master. We are made in God's image. That is our authority to live as children of God. It doesn't matter what others think of us or how they view our actions. I'm not here to answer the expectation of others; I'm here to live out my life according to His plans for my life. He will never abandon me. He will never fail me when I call out like Peter did with Jesus. I am His and so all things have eternal meaning and the smallest act doesn't go unnoticed.

In John Steinbeck's work, *East of Eden*, he draws on the lessons of Cain's life to bring a special meaning to the actions of his characters. The meaning of the Hebrew word *TIMSHEL* is explored since it refers to the way that God dispatches Cain after the killing of Abel. Eventually those discussing its meaning are informed that learned Rabbis had come to interpret it as "Thou Mayest," not "Thou Shalt or "Thou Will". (The distinction lies in being given permission rather than being *required* to do something.) *TIMSHEL* has equally great meaning in our own lives.

You see the word *TIMSHEL* was used AFTER Cain killed Abel. In the context in which Steinbeck uses the word, he points out that "thou mayest overcome evil" means future evil, not just past evil. It is the road ahead that leads to redemption; the past only points to our need for redemption and nothing more. Since redemption is a matter between you and God, society has no say in the process. It is strictly a personal encounter like Peter walking on water. What the other disciples thought of those steps made no difference to the reality of that experience.

It is time to step out of the boat and take your first tentative steps. You can't do this simply for the applause of your family or friends; this has to be an entirely personal matter between you and God. Like a proud parent, He will be watching your every step. He is always there to catch you. But like a parent who is teaching a child to ride a two wheel bike, it is necessary that He let go of the back of your bicycle seat and allow you to learn on your own.

The crashes into the fence or bushes and the small bruises to skin and ego are stepping-stones to the freedom of riding that bike with the wind blowing through your hair. What a sense of accomplishment! Merging your past defeats and failures are the same thing. Get back up on the bike and try again. There is no sin or crime that He can't or will not forgive. He is only waiting for you to stand back up and try again. He will create the situations that lay ahead of you, and He will tailor those circumstances to strengthen you.

Do you think that Peter was the same man when he returned to the safety of the boat? His life had changed forever. He had a moment like Galileo and Columbus. For a brief moment, reality was suspended. He had no words to describe His encounter with Jesus

Christ out on the water. The disciples had witnessed the event, but Peter had no way to describe his own experience. That's what we are being invited to have today, an experience so unique that we have no words to describe it to others. Scientists would call it a myth or a fairytale and dismiss it accordingly. But Peter knew what that experience was like—he had just lived it.

There is something to be said for timing. As I read the stories in the Bible, I was struck by the fact that all of these encounters between God and man have an element of timing about them. Please remember that Peter had just walked on water. He had a peak personal experience with Jesus Christ Himself, not just a miracle that he had watched Jesus perform.

Peter was the go-to guy among the disciples. He knew Jesus personally and he followed Him for three years. He saw the sick healed, the mentally ill restored to health, and he even witnessed Jesus raising people from the dead. He was a hand-selected disciple, but apparently, like the rest of us, he was a little slow on the uptake. Just look at some of the questions that he and the other disciples asked of Jesus. They were trying to understand a pattern beyond their understanding. All they had to guide them was their faith in Jesus alone.

Even that was shaken at the time of Jesus Christ's trial. Do you remember how Peter denied Him three times? This was after he had witnessed all of the events that occurred during the three years of discipleship. It seems to me that hanging out with Jesus was a fulltime event. You wouldn't have wanted to miss a moment since you never knew what might happen next. What an exciting time for Peter and the disciples. Yet at the moment of His trial, judgment, crucifixion, death and burial, they were traumatized to such an extent that they fled. Only one stood below the cross. I'm sure that more than one member of the Sanhedrin smugly thought they had put the fear of God into this rabble and would hear no more from them, but God had other plans.

It seems to me that when you fail God, you have made the biggest failure of all. But that's not how God see things. He still had plans—mighty plans—for these men who were busy hiding themselves from the authorities. Have you ever felt like that before? Hiding and shaking, waiting for the crisis to pass, and wondering *will* it ever pass? Fear binds people together. Remember the days immediately following 9/11? People were talking to each other: Talking with people they'd never spoken to before that event. Others filled churches looking for spiritual consolation, trying to get their questions answered and their fears abated.

Things were no different in Jerusalem when the upper room was buzzing with conversation, unanswered questions and visible expressions of fear. Don't open that door; we don't know who is on the other side. Even when the women returned from the grave early on Easter morning, their shouts of joy were answered by disbelief and dismissal.

It was just too incredible to believe that He really kept His Word. After all, they saw Him die, they saw Him buried, and they grieved His loss together. Now it was time to get back to work, to get on with the real business of life and take care of their responsibilities. They had already wasted too much time on this foolishness.

But, He did rise from the dead and soon there He was standing in the middle of them. "I am not a ghost," He stated. He knew their innermost pain. He knew the sense of shame that they were all feeling about not believing in His Word. He knew it all. He is one with us. He wasn't offended by their humanness. He understood fear perfectly, that's why the Bible tells us that where fear exists love cannot exist. Jesus, the embodiment of love itself, came and stood among them and welcomed each of them as His friend. In that moment, fear was cast aside and the disciple's lives were changed forever. Their whole paradigm, or pattern of life, changed in an instant.

Well you say, "That was then and this is now. That doesn't relate to me or my situation." Let's return to one of our earliest moments together. Truth has always been truth and it will always be truth. It doesn't change with time, location or circumstances; it is constant! What is your truth? Is your paradigm starting to shift? Are you starting to see the big picture clearer now? Your future is unwritten. Those pages don't have any marks on them. What you write on those pages is what will come to be. The future is yours alone: to do whatever you wish with it.

The disciple's lives were radically transformed in that upper room. Not in the years before His crucifixion, but in that moment when He stood in their midst. All the while He had told them the truth; He showed them the evidence of it in His daily actions. But it wasn't until He stood in their midst that they KNEW the truth.

All those moments leading up to this point were preparation time. In that moment of His appearance and His reality in that room, they were transformed forever. The evidence of that transformation is to be found in the history of time. The subsequent actions of the disciples transformed the world. Life in the twenty-first century is clear evidence of that remarkable encounter. The evidence of the truth is all around us. That capacity for radical transformations lies within all of us.

* * *

Have you had the experience of seeing Les Misérables and absorbing its storyline? Its protagonist is assailed by the endless attempts of another individual (antagonist) to track him down and unmask him as a criminal and fugitive. In doing so, the antagonist vindicates himself and his methods and it appears that the "law" will triumph in this relentless battle. This story highlights the limitations of the law. By its nature, the law can only be used to identify the guilty. The innocent, the uncaught and those who wear their masks tightly affixed to their faces always stand in danger of being unmasked for there are truly none innocent amongst us. There are just human beings mostly doing the best they can at the moment.

Therein lies the difference between law and grace. We've all become offenders and outside of mercy and forgiveness, we're without hope. Grace is the substance that carries us ahead in spite of the failures and defeats in our lives. It's God's hand on the back of the bicycle seat helping us to remain moving forward. We may not feel its presence. We are given to flights of fancy thinking that we're something special. We're making it all happen on our own. In our arrogance, we assume that we've done something to earn the blessings of our lives, while others have done things to earn the curses of life.

That's where the problems of good and evil enter the mix. They are external influences. They can't be seen directly, but we can assume their existence from the actions of others and ourselves. Paul stated, "It is not me, but the sin within me" (Romans 7:17 NIV) to help us realize that we're struck daily with a variety of opportunities for good and evil. If I know that I'm going out into stormy weather, I dress accordingly. But with matters of good and evil, I assume that I'm in control and can make appropriate choices. Therefore I launch off in my small boat daily and ignore the warning clouds on the horizon. After all, I'm the captain of my own ship, right?

If you haven't read *Silas Marner* (by Mary Anne Evans, also known as George Eliot) it might be useful to do so just to reinforce the concept of good and evil. A victim of injustice, Silas goes off and creates a new beginning. The labels of his society have marked his life, so he sets about creating a life apart from everyone with only the most essential interactions with others. Life then deals him an unexpected hand and he has the courage to play the hand that he has just been given. That decision transforms his life and the lives of others. It's great literature, but more importantly, it's a simple story that shows us how spirituality molds our lives. Rather than losing hope, becoming bitter and casting away a supposed burden, he assumes the burden and his life becomes an example for all to see.

That same opportunity exists for each of us today, but it comes masked as a burden. It's not a delightful, sweet-smelling package containing some beautiful trinket to delight us. More often, it comes wrapped in handcuffs, bills, divorce papers, health problems, bankruptcy, homelessness or hunger. Each of these dreaded encounters hold the potential for personal redemption. Every time that one of our masks slip off of our face and our true personality is uncovered, it becomes another opportunity. Not a mark of shame, but a hope of future glory in His company.

Only you know what corruption is in your soul. You're the only one who knows how far down the scale of life you've slid. Only you know the despair and sadness of your life. No one can ride that downhill slide with you; it's your personal burden. It's your own creation. But it hasn't been a wasted journey if you can find meaning in these events. Not only will this re-start your life, but it will also help you reach out to others with similar experiences. The whole world is hurting and waiting for someone to acknowledge their pain and shame, but most of all to acknowledge and re-affirm their individual personhood.

Until the death certificate has been signed for you and me, we still have purpose in our lives. Just glance around you and that will confirm what I'm saying. We don't need to go to the next town or cross an ocean to accomplish good for others and ourselves; we can do so at our front door. Sometimes we want anonymity, but we must never hide from the challenges we face in our lives. When I'm busy doing this work, what society thinks of my efforts or me has no bearing on my life; it's all between God and me. As I go about my life's work, those labels have a strange way of fading into the background. My soul starts to hear a new song of hope. It doesn't matter much what the law says since I'm living under grace.

God's Word tells me, "If anyone lives in Christ, he is a new creation" (2 Corinthians 5:17 NIV). There is no evading these words. They are clear and direct; "a new creation"—*not* a remake, remodel, or refurbished unit. We'll be a brand new man or woman, one of God's own creations. That's where my hope flows from, His Word, the Bible. He tells the Truth; He is Truth. You already know exactly what you have in life. Take a moment and look at the cards in your hand. Do you still want to play that same old tired losing hand? Or are you ready for God to deal you a brand new hand?

There is no one so far gone that he's beyond hope. That's even true for the man about to be put to death. God has been and always will be true to His word. My primary connection with Him is my inner sense of spirituality. From this point on in your life, your spirituality will be your personal safety line. It's not promised that we will be free of future storms. Just remember that it's God who has the other end of our line.

So why do all of this work if it has no direct impact upon society's view of us? It's a fair question. Do you remember in the prologue when I discussed that time in life when we were loved for who we were? It was unconditional love. We didn't have to do anything to deserve it. The things we did were out of our love for others. That small picture we had drawn (that may still hang on your mother's refrigerator) was an expression of your love for her. I make these life changes, not in hopes of some future reward, but as small acts of love for my God.

He has loved me unconditionally. He at anytime could have smitten me while I pursued my lawless and reckless behaviors. But in His mercy and by grace, he preserved me through all of the burdens I brought upon others and myself. Having recognized that great love, I now want to bless and honor His name in my daily choices. I often fail, but sometimes I succeed. Like that awkward picture hanging on the refrigerator, I offer those small acts as love offerings to my Creator. They in themselves will never redeem me from the consequences of my life choices. Jesus did that for me on Calvary.

It's out of the love I have received that I seek those opportunities to make wrongs, right—nothing more and nothing less: just small acts of love.

Do these offerings always have the desired effect on others? Not really. People are busy going about their own lives trying to figure out the paradigm. But they are just as precious to God as I am. So, it's my rightful duty to extend my hand to others no matter how they take what I offer. My only obligation is to throw a lifeline to others who come into my life.

There have been times when that intent was misconstrued, especially when dealing in the matters behind the mask. But I have no regrets, because I'm at a point in time where I can see that God uses all outcomes for His own honor and glory. My job is to merely throw out the lifeline and then stand ready to help haul my brother or sister toward the shallow waters. In the final analysis, it's not what man has to say about me that will be important; only what God has to say about me will stand for eternity.

This isn't my exclusive task. It's a task that we all share equally. If the twelve disciples transformed the world in their lifetimes, what could six billion of us do in a year—especially those most wretched among us. You see, we have had the privilege of seeing the world from a different viewpoint. We look up, not down on others. Use that viewpoint to shape the world of your neighborhood. Take a step today that you have never taken before. Do something remarkable today, something small for an easy start.

These are merely words on a page. In themselves, they have no meaning. They hold no inherent value. Perhaps they will ultimately wind up among the millions of other pages held in libraries, databases and computers all over the world. If that is their end, then it is a sad end indeed. These words were written to inspire and challenge the least of us. In spite of the comments of previous publishers who said offenders and their family members "don't bother to read," I'm betting my life's work that there are others out there who have had the experience of being lost and alone; that there are millions of others who have been labeled and continue to suffer the consequences of those actions.

It's not about a battle, but rather it's our hope of which I speak. It's time to walk away from the war mentality and to make peace with those around us, one person at a time. After all, they'll be our neighbors for eternity. No one has ever made friends with me by fighting with me. Those who have loved me have learned how to disarm me quite effectively. That's one thing that makes the marriage between Quinta and myself such a remarkable happening. It's just more evidence that God has a plan for our lives: If He has done this for us, what is He willing to do for you?

* * *

A word to the wise: any attempt to manipulate this suggested program of action won't succeed. It won't succeed if you're only looking for personal benefit. Everything that has been written in this book relates to others and the way that we interact with them. It is not a book about self; rather it is about others and the way we influence their lives. If you set out to use this book to create a new life for yourself as the main beneficiary, then you'll fail. Those who benefit will be people in your life. No one will ever stand up and commend you for your actions. It's entirely an inside job.

If you seek acclaim or acknowledgement, then save your time and look elsewhere: This book is about love and service and nothing else! But in those acts of love and service you'll catch glimpses of how your own life has changed as a result. You'll even see brief shadows of God at work in your life and the lives of others. That is a promise.

That is your sole reward; nothing more. Your personal pardon plan will never earn respect or admiration. But it will ease the lives of others and bring a smile to God's face. Remember He is a personal God, not a remote spiritual figure, who is always looking on you with a scowl or frown. It's never too late to say, "I'm sorry I really blew it." It's never too late to ask for help. He's not just the God of your past. He's the God of your future.

* * *

In attempting to put my thoughts into a useful format, I've gone back over some of the private notes that I kept over the years. There have been times when things happened, either publically or privately, and the only relief I could obtain at those moments was to write something about what had just happened. Those writings provided a cathartic or therapeutic release and allowed me to move on emotionally to other challenges.

Many of my patients have touched me profoundly with their stories and the courage that they have displayed in the face of stiff opposition. They have been among those I call remarkable people. They have all added something special to my life. My life would certainly have been drab and guarded without the freshness of human spirit found from our sessions. I have received far more in return than I could ever have given to others.

My own spirituality has grown and become renewed as I tried to understand my patients and to seek God's direction for them while in my care. A few left after several sessions to strike out in another direction. Some left with referrals in hand when it became clear that we weren't moving along the same track. But none left because they felt abandoned or because of personal conflicts of interests. All patients had been offered the best that I could provide. The standard of practice used in my assessment and treatment of patients was a spiritual standard. I'm accountable to my God first, then others. No regrets here!

I have a passion to reach others who suffer in silent pain, and to seek out those whose lives are textbook examples of the practices of alienation and Severcide. Like Nikki said, "You have to get it out or it will eat you up." There aren't a lot of safe places to get those deeply personal things out and to get help in healing those wounds. For some, reporting those long buried secrets would resort in arrest, conviction and imprisonment.

I'm reminded of a news story that I followed many years ago. In a western state a medical doctor married a woman with a twelve-year-old stepdaughter. I have no idea how the practice began, but at some point he started to give his stepdaughter weekly physical exams. He quickly realized that he was in emotional trouble and sought out a psychiatrist for consultation. After learning the facts of the case, the psychiatrist sent reports to Child Protective Services and law enforcement.

The doctor was promptly arrested. His medical license was immediately suspended and later revoked. His stepdaughter was immediately taken from the home and subjected to numerous interviews, usually without the benefit of a familiar face. She became surrounded by well-meaning individuals determined to get the facts and set the matter right.

The young woman kept to herself and resisted the efforts to make her talk about what had happened. When the stepfather's trial came before the courts, the girl refused to testify against him. It's my understanding that she was placed in juvenile hall and was told that she would not be released until she testified in the criminal proceedings.

I seem to remember that she was held for an extended period and then finally released when it became apparent that she would not testify. The criminal charges were dropped against the stepfather and after his release from the county jail, the girl's biological father beat him up. I don't remember hearing anything else about that case.

I was struck by the obvious lesson to others in similar situations: "Don't ask for help. If you do, you'll wind up facing criminal prosecution." Of course, the laws are there to keep children and others from being victimized. But it appeared to me that the one who was truly victimized was the young girl whose loyalty to her family exceeded the personal threats of justice. Everyone lost: there were no winners in this matter. Society was not served by these events.

There has to be a place for people to get the story out so they can attempt to start a new life, and that is partly what this book is all about. Licensed professionals, clergy and educators are among those who are charged with mandatory reporting requirements. But, not everyone in your life must report this information. There are many individuals who would be willing to share your burden and show you light and grace. Consider the service members who participated in atrocities during their tours of duty abroad. I don't need to cite the record; it's available at your local library. Who do these individuals talk with in *their* suffering moments? Up until recently the response was "suck it up."

There's a way back from the pit of hell. This book breaks the silence on secret lives and points a way out of the trap. No topics are taboo. All cards are on the table. Play out the hand that has been given to you, but do so with care. Not everyone who calls themselves a friend is a friend. There is always one friend who will never betray you, Jesus Christ. He is totally committed to helping you wipe the slate clean. It's time to move forward and free yourself from those chains. The first step in this process is going back through all of the old labels and finding that time when you were loved unconditionally.

If no such time exists in your memory, then rely on the knowledge that you were carried in someone's womb until the moment of birth. God's Word says that He knew you before you were knit together in your mother's womb (Psalms 139:19 NIV). Let that awareness of His perfect love for you carry you through this transformation project.

Sort through all of the labels of your life, and make a special list of those in which you can see truth. Then, discard the labels forever. They have no further use in your life. Examine your individual behaviors and acknowledge to yourself, to an accountability partner and to God the nature of those wrongs. You don't have to discuss specific actions to clear the books on these sins or crimes. There are no cold case detectives working in heaven.

If you can't find a suitable person to help make a connection, contact me directly and we'll work out the challenges that are limiting you. As a retired, unlicensed psychologist, I'm not seeking to do therapy with you. My only goal is to help you get past the secret life and move into the realm of mercy, grace, forgiveness, faith and hope. There are no laws against this. In fact, God, in His Word, wants this to happen.

The most important thing to remember is that you haven't committed any act that hasn't previously been committed by others. Remember the words of Solomon, "There is nothing new under the sun" (Ecclesiastes: 1:9 NIV). These steps aren't meaningless. They are essential to the process of inner restoration and peace. No one is too far gone. I would travel to any state, federal or international environment to help you right the wrongs! God is my Provider; He knows best exactly where I'm needed. More importantly, He knows exactly what *you* need.

In the beginning of this book, I mentioned the right to change. If you're weary of the burdens you carry, reach out and allow someone to shoulder that burden with you. This book discusses what God has done in my life. Go beyond your fears and isolation and together make a beginning. I don't expect you to do this alone. I'm certain that the strong voice of fear will seek to stir you to do nothing and to remain silent. If God already knows everything about you, what is there to fear?

Recognize that voice, and remember it. That's the voice of your enemy and my enemy whose primary weapons are fear and hatred. Inaction is his best recommendation to those thinking about a new life. *"Yes of course, I want you to change, but let's do it tomorrow. Then we'll get a fresh start on this plan of yours."* If you only know how many interruptions and distractions I have experienced since I started to write this book. You would understand his harmful influence. Remember what Jesus Christ called him, "The Father of Lies" (John 8:44 NIV).

I've said my peace. I've offered you an open hand. I've sketched out for you the journey ahead and I've offered to travel that pathway with you. Listen to that sweet, soft voice within that calls you

His precious child. Don't take my word for anything. Take nothing at face value. Test all things that I have written in this book. Get on your knees and ask God if it's true and if it's something that He wants you to do. That's the ultimate reality test for all of us.

My dear wife Quinta knew we would have a considerable amount of time apart while she completed the International Dental Studies program at the University of Colorado (in Aurora). In her wisdom, she wrote a prayer to help me to start my day. That prayer, and our morning and evening prayers via telephone, kept us strong and committed. He will do the same for you and your family. I would like to share that prayer to help guide you on your journey. You'll note that in the sections marked 1–26, these are some of the issues I have experienced in the lives of others as they sought to be released from the burdens of their secret lives. These may or may not reflect your own issues. Use this model to reveal the most secret shame and humiliation to Him who is able to do all things.

MORNING PRAYER

DEAR HEAVENLY FATHER,

I ACKNOWLEDGE YOU AS MY sovereign King. You are in control in all things of my life. I thank You that You are always with me and will never leave me nor forsake me. I ask you to fill me with the Holy Spirit so that I may say no to sin and yes to You. I ask the Lord Jesus to heal me if there is any bitterness from any bad things that have happened in the past.

I now take my stand against Satan. I plead to use the authority of Your holy name. In the name of Jesus, I cast the spirit of: (sample list of sins):

1. Adultery, Anger, Arson, Abuse, Addictions

2. Blasphemy, Brutality, Blaming, Broken Vows

3. Condemnation, Cursing, Controlling

4. Damning, Destruction, Delight in Harming Others

5. Exorbitance, Exhibitionism, Envy
6. Fornication, False Testimony, Failure to Help Others
7. Godlessness, Gossip, Greed
8. Heretical Beliefs, Homosexuality, Homicide
9. Idolatry, Ingratitude, Instigation
10. Jezebel, Jealousy
11. Killing, Kidnapping
12. Lewdness, Lesbianism, Lying, Lust
13. Murder, Mayhem, Mutilation, Masochism
14. Neglect
15. Oppression
16. Pride, Passion, Persecution, Promiscuity
17. Quarreling, Quenching, Quibbling
18. Robbery, Rape, Ransom
19. Sexual Sins, Suicide, Self-Mutilation, Slavery, Sadism, Satan-Worship, Selfishness
20. Trauma, Torture
21. Usury, Unbelief, Unreasonableness
22. Violations, Victimization
23. War, Wounding, Waste
24. Xenophobia
25. Yelling
26. Zoophilia

to depart from me. Cleanse me from all iniquities. I choose to put on the full armor of God, so that I may be able to stand firm against all of the devil's schemes.

Instead, I want every good spirit of you Lord. Please give me the spirit of:

- Obedience
- Purity in Thoughts
- Humbleness
- Self-Control
- Your Wisdom that will guide me all through the day.

I submit my body as a living and holy sacrifice to God and I choose to renew my mind by the living Word of God. And let me be spiritually bound to Jesus alone. I pray that the Holy Spirit will renew my spirit, in order that I will be spiritually healed. I ask that an angel of Jesus be my guard and in the name of Jesus, cast away any angel of darkness that had been oppressing my spirit in the past.

PLEASE BE WITH ME AND my family all through the day. I want this day to be a glorifying day for my King and Savior, AMEN.

CHAPTER 19

GRATITUDE

IT'S NATURAL THAT GRATITUDE WOULD be one of the final words in this book. You see, I'm personally grateful for the incredible opportunities that have been given to me throughout my life. Through it all, God's loving hand has been guiding my life even though I've often done my best to shake off that loving influence. Now I have arrived at a place where I have a much better view of life and it's clear that God has always intended to bless me. The ultimate blessing has been living life and turning toward the Son.

For one who has experienced deep valleys and high mountaintops, I have no need to impress others with the significance of my spiritual experience. I know the truth and it truly has set me free. Those who share this reality with me need no convincing. They have had their own experience with His truth, and those who have not found this freedom may be encouraged by the ideas expressed in this book.

If your spirit is visited with a passion of thinking in terms of possibilities, then grasp the gift that's been offered and hold onto it like a lifeline. It truly is a lifeline, crafted just for you. Hold firm and it will take you to places you've never dreamt about. Labels have a shelf life. They expire as soon as you decide to abandon them in favor of new life experiences. Believe me, there won't be anyone in heaven that will say, "Do you see that addict over there?" or "I can't believe that tramp actually made it here."

It is the mercy, grace and forgiveness of God that ensures our presence in His kingdom. We contribute nothing to this process. We're His guests because of the work of Our Savior, Jesus Christ. It's all a gift. We may offer our imperfect gifts of faith and hope, but they have no meaning if they are not linked to the reality of His gift of salvation. Someone very close to me read sections of this book and quickly identified it as a book about theology.

I have no skills or talents in the domain of theology, but I do know about gratitude. I've been the recipient of God's perfect grace. My spirit knows the gifts of mercy and forgiveness. My heart speaks with gratitude about My Savior's love for me. I don't speak from any other reference point. This book has only been authored to glorify God. There's no hidden agenda, just the burden to tell others what He's done for me. Out of that telling, my hope is that others will be blessed with the same hope I've been given to live out these experiences.

It's my belief that faith grows out of having understood the majesty of His plan of salvation for our lives. That plan is NOT just for eternity. It's a here and now plan. It's freely available to each of us like a dependable personal lifeline. Here I am again, confronted with the problem of describing vanilla ice cream to those who have never had that experience. Such personal help as described in this book is available to each of us. We're His children and nothing we can do will cause Him to disown us *IF* we're willing to accept His offer of loving direction.

When I was a defiant and rebellious adolescent, nothing my parents offered me or did for me was enough to change my life course. Though they earnestly sought to bless me and bestow good things upon me, they were unable to do so. My attitude and actions upset their best efforts. Well, it's the same thing in our relationship with God. He loves us so much that He has given each of us the freedom to choose to either do what we want or to accept His help in our daily lives. This is the essence of the gift of free will. God will never force His plan for our lives upon us.

God is the ultimate gentleman. He loves us without needing anything from us. Consider the fact that a gift is not a gift until it has been accepted. Being in the Dominican Republic at the time of this writing, it's easy for me to imagine someone stumbling out of the jungle mad with hunger. If I were the one driven by famine, my sole focus would be getting something to eat: anything that would sustain my life. Before accepting the free gifts of God, I WAS that stumbling man blind, deaf, hungry, and desperate.

So what actually happened that made it all different? I made the discovery that my life was NOT made up of a random series of events. Little by little, I realized that all of these events were playing out on a stage where I wasn't the principal actor; instead I had a brief walk-on part in the great drama of life. The actual play was about the ongoing struggles in the battle between good and evil which are being played out on a daily basis in our individual lives.

We are nothing more than bit part actors making choices that reflect God's love for us or the evil Satan has urged upon us. We aren't major actors and we have relatively few lines in our entire appearance. But we do have the POWER OF CHOICE. We ultimately make the decision where we spend eternity. We make that decision—one choice at a time. It's NEVER too late to make a new choice, even as you draw your last breath. That's the compassion God has for His creation. He desires that none of us would be lost (2 Peter 3:9 NIV).

As the reality of these promises starts to penetrate your consciousness, you come to realize that all things are possible with God (Matt 19:26 NIV). Everything we do counts in some way. No effort, no prayer, and no act of kindness is ever wasted. Each of our choices has cosmic (beyond our personal awareness) consequences. We're not individual or isolated human machines operating on a need and want basis. We're God's loving creation. It's never too late to put our hands out and ask for His help! He is always ready to turn trash into treasure.

As I sit here trying to convey the potential that awaits you, I turn back to the ice cream problem. My words are awkward, confining and severely limiting. Would that I could, I would sit with you and explain the incredible promises of God's love for you and me. I can assure you that if your spirit is stirred by what you have read, Satan will hasten to try and steal away God's promises and your joy. The battle is waged within you.

My faith in the truthfulness of God's word has led to the development of hope in His promises made to each of us. God's word isn't only for the saved; more importantly, it's for the most miserable living among us. It's like the key to your individual cell. God sends His word to truly set us free. The flow of gratitude comes out of understanding this truth. In my life, gratitude has flowed from the two springs of faith and hope. In turn, it has fueled a sense of personal joy.

Happiness is a quality that comes and goes. It doesn't seem to be anchored to anything in my life. It is unstable and unpredictable.

It seems to be dependent on how satisfied I am with my personal wants and desires. So it's temporary. Yesterday, I wanted a cold soft drink; today, I want a quiet environment so I can complete this chapter. And who knows what I'll want tomorrow. I'm aware that my desires can quickly turn into demands for satisfaction.

My personal unseen struggles have taught me the meaning of disciplining my desires and re-defining those things I've come to see as needs. It's been a lifetime process getting to this point of understanding. It has ONLY happened because God's word has become a light to my path (Psalm 119:105 NIV).

This is another aspect of God's promises becoming obvious in my life. Let's compare His promises to facets of a precious gem, making this ongoing experience easier to understand. My life is marked by these events of self-discovery, and like the joy of a child presented with a piece of chocolate, my life is enhanced by the discovery of these ever unfolding treasures.

I've tried to convey my experiences in this book. I'm not saying that I understand the personal nature of your sufferings and trials. But I know that God's word tells me His Son experienced all trials common to man and He did so without sinning. That reality is why we call Him the spotless Lamb who was sacrificed for us. He was sacrificed to pay the price for ALL of our sins. Only a spotless sin offering could satisfy the demands of a Just and Righteous God.

Back to the analogy I provided earlier in this chapter. The starving man stumbles out of the jungle into a beautiful garden. There he sees a feast in front of him with every imaginable kind of food. He circles the table and is awe-struck by the elegant offerings in front of him. Even though he's dying of starvation, he keeps stumbling around the table looking at the food laid out before him. It's all been prepared expressly for him. This feast will not only fill him with life-saving food, it will meet all of his needs including the need for joy and happiness!

His Host knows our friend intimately. He knows his every want and desire. Most of all He knows all of his needs, and nothing is hidden from Him. Our friend would be crazy to continue walking around the feast table growing weaker by the moment while the Host continues to urge him to eat and enjoy the banquet that's been prepared for him. Just reach out and start to feed yourself, it'll save your life. But our friend continues to circle the table mad with hunger, and when the Host encourages him to eat, he murmurs something about doing it tomorrow.

Can you see yourself in this picture? The Host isn't denying our friend anything. In fact, He's urging him to make a life-affirming decision. What the Host *can't* do is force him to make the choice to reach out and TAKE the gift freely offered. Remember, it doesn't become a gift until it's been accepted. And so our troubled friend eventually starves to death just inches from the table that bears the nourishing feast prepared just for him. Our friend would have to be crazy to forgo life itself when all he had to do was reach out and accept the freely offered gift.

Do you see the role of free will in our decision-making and how it can be used to destroy ourselves? God will never go against our free will. We have to make the choice to accept His freely offered gifts. You may still have a tomorrow, but would you be willing to bet YOUR life on the hope you'll wake up tomorrow morning? I want you to understand that the choice is solely yours! It's not God doing it to you. Just like our starving friend with the feast, NOT MAKING A CHOICE *IS* A CHOICE!

Science and some of our friends will hastily attempt to reassure us that all will be well. After all, whose life is it? If God were really a loving Being, wouldn't He save us in spite of ourselves? I don't think so! The feast is prepared today for us. It's fresh and ready to eat, but won't help our tired and weary bodies until we reach out and put the food in our mouths. God doesn't make that choice for us. He respects our ability to make that fateful choice. He respects our individual dignity and worth, since we are made in His image.

My parents couldn't force me to make the wise choices that they urged on me. Ultimately, they had to let me go about life as I wished to experience it. Those choices, which looked so attractive at the moment, led to incredible pain and suffering for others and myself. But they were MY choices. Now I have lived a life that has led me back to God's word. I can't afford to fool myself with self-destructive whispers that promise rewards for lies, stealing, gossip, and promiscuous behaviors (along with any other sinful choices).

In this book, I've wanted to avoid labeling anyone else's behavior as "sinful." I only know that so many of the choices I've made in life were sinful choices. My experience with God's mercy, grace and forgiveness has given me the assurance of His love for me in spite of my sinfulness. More importantly, it's provided me with the experience of personal freedom. It's given me freedom from oppression, want and impulse. I know that those who have struck out toward me were probably driven by their own destructive whispers.

Once understood, it becomes easier to let go of hatred, pride, arrogance and a desire for revenge. I firmly believe that NO ONE is going to get away with anything. If you have been wronged, then quickly offer the gift of forgiveness. If you have wronged others, quickly seek forgiveness from those individuals and always from God. One of the areas I struggled with as a young man was the sheer number of people I harmed along the way (some maliciously). It was a burden I carried with me and couldn't shake loose. It made me certain that I was lost, without hope, and with no way back!

My faith has led me to understand that all have sinned (Romans 3:23 NIV); we just vary in types and frequency. No one can stand before a Righteous God in sin (Romans 10:3 NIV). God's sinless state cannot allow sin in His presence. Just like the fact that light and dark cannot co-exist in the same place at the same moment. Either I'm covered by the Blood of Jesus, or I'm making the CHOICE personally to pay the penalty for my actions.

Like the starving man, I don't need to know how the food was grown and harvested or how it was cooked or seasoned to benefit from its nutritional value. All I need to do is reach out and enjoy the feast. Likewise, I don't have to have a perfect knowledge of how Jesus Christ walked on water to benefit from His sacrifice; I merely have to accept the gift He has freely made available to all of us. It's that simple. No wonder gratitude is one of the closing subjects of this book; it is the stuff that will carry you forward successfully.

I don't need to understand great philosophical or theological constructs to experience the love of God. All I need to do is to reach out for that love and assurance of salvation. Nothing more! I'm a child of God and nothing will ever undo that truth. So those who judge us and rush to cast stones at us are like children without any comprehension other than self-interests. They're only acting on impulse. It's a form of ignorance.

God doesn't want us to be ignorant of His will for our lives. I believe with all of my heart that if you take your daily struggles to Him in prayer, He hears you and will guide your decision-making with the practical assistance needed to live through each day. Knowetics is about coming to that level of understanding. It's about knowing that you are finally free and not subject to the surges and struggles of life. It's about that special Father-child relationship which overshadows all of the conflicts of life.

Like the vanilla ice cream problem, you may "know" about vanilla ice cream without ever having tasted it. If in the course of my life, I miss the experience of tasting ice cream, I haven't lost anything essential. On the other hand, if you're waiting in a cell for a judge to schedule your execution date, or you're wasting away because of a dreaded disease, then you are faced with an essential choice. Do you show up in God's presence and try to plead your cause, or do you cover yourself in the Blood of Jesus Christ? It's your choice exclusively!

If I were allowed the privilege of spending a complete day with you, I would tell you my story. I wouldn't leave out the alcohol or drug addictions, the arrests, trials, convictions and imprisonment that followed my misadventures. Then I'd get down to the incredibly painful and lonely life of living for myself alone. I'd share the burden of constantly being in conflict with God's word. Together we could talk about always missing the mark. I'd share with you my deepest pain and sorrow, and I would hold nothing back.

Then I would lift my head and tell you about my deep sense of gratitude that all of these events had occurred in my life. Yes, I said the word "gratitude" in the same context as describing my sufferings. You see, that's what it took to open my eyes to God's promises and blessings. That's also why I'm so certain today of the reality of spirituality in our lives. It's probably the most under-used asset we have in life; yet its harnessed power makes the power of nuclear energy seem like child's play. We're talking about the glue that holds the universe together and moves it forward according to God's plan.

Please don't take my word for it. Just like ice cream, it needs to be experienced to understand its true nature. Knowetics is about the power of God in your life, but it goes beyond anything that you've experienced religiously or theologically. That's why it's been presented to you outside of the domain of religion. It stands apart and it stands alone. It is totality independent of any other aspect of life. It's the nature of your relationship with God. I wrote these words for you, because if you are like me, you need to truly experience this reality.

I can't make the choice for you. It's absolutely your own choice. No one will force you to accept the free gifts of God. But if you deny them, then let me tell you that you are missing the essence of life itself. Even now it's not too late to ask Him if what I've written here is accurate. I know my Father; He won't withhold any good thing from you. If you sincerely seek the truth He will show you and also confirm it to you.

As a Christian, it has been my experience that when God shows me something important, He always confirms that experience through someone else. It is like the quiet assurance my spirit craves to know that I can step out and trust His word in any situation or problem.

You see my friend, I'm convinced that He never intended for me to make this journey alone. Close your eyes for a moment and consider where you are in your life. Do you want to continue on alone, or could you use some company?

If you have no conception of how God wants to interact with you, or if you have no capacity to believe what I have expressed to you in this book, then use the next best thing available; hang onto my faith, my belief and my hope. I will gladly share it with you. Sit down and while your struggles are fresh, write to me. Tell me about those struggles. I'll reach out my hand to you in love and support like so many others have reached out their hands to me.

While I've often chosen a lonely and isolated pathway for myself, there's no requirement that you need do so. Suffering and loneliness are optional from this point onward. One of my great discoveries in dealing with my alcohol addiction was the reality that I was not alone. In twelve-step meetings, I discovered that there was virtually millions of people just like me. I was not a freak of nature or a hopelessly lost individual. Later I moved on to the experience of discovering that my sinful condition was not unique to me.

Suffering is still optional when the grace of God is there to help you through every trial of your life. The incredibly good news is that we are ALL the same. Some of us have acted openly and time after time have demonstrated sinful choices. Others have harbored those choices secretly within their spirits. Either way, we are all guilty before God. Do you remember the standard set by Jesus Christ? There is no difference between committing the act of adultery physically or in our minds; we are all equally guilty (James 2:10 NIV).

The good news is that you don't have to hang your head like a public sinner. Look up and see what the Son has done for you and me. Today we are free. That's His great gift to us at the cost of His life. NO

ONE ELSE IS FIT TO JUDGE YOU! He has paid the complete price for our freedom. Now live like the free person you are and let the spirit of gratitude flow into your life and all of your interactions with others. They will notice the difference and you'll become a shining light to them. Jesus Christ will use you right where you are; this is a faithful saying. Do not take my word for it. Ask Him right now!

What He has done in your life will be multiplied in the lives of others. They will start to receive the blessings given freely to you because you are now living them in your daily choices and actions. One day at a time your spirit will be transformed and renewed. Until you act upon these words, they remain words on a page. Stop and envision the governor or president signing a full and complete pardon with your name on it. Would you resist that gift? If you were suffering from a terrible, terminal illness and your doctor hastily came to visit you with news of a drug which might reverse the course of your disease, would you argue with him or her over this gift of life? Not likely!

All at once, where despair and anguish ruled your days and nights, you would now feel the stirrings of hope deep inside your heart. Out of that experience would grow the tender shoots of faith in a different outcome and the hope that it was true. Later a profound sense of gratitude that you had survived the pending death would emerge. Your spirit would give off the glow of those lost and then found in the eternal realms.

Nothing I said or did would shake your belief that your experience was real. Gradually, your gratitude would take on a quality of personal transformation, like a badge of honor that you proudly displayed to everyone around you. In that way, gratitude becomes the hallmark of the process that has occurred in your life. They might not know the specifics of your encounter with God, but they can observe the difference it has made in your life. Nothing could get you to deny your experience.

It's fitting that gratitude is so close to the end of this book because it's the evidence of your healing for all to see. Do you remember how Jesus reached out and touched the lepers and healed them of their disease? We know that one of the ten returned to worship Him for His great gift. That former leper was grateful for what God had done for him PERSONALLY. God is about people—not institutions or governments—but that doesn't mean we should continue to live in strife with any elements of society.

I'm quite sure that after the leper was healed, he took a bath and put on clean clothing. He had been given a brand new life. He had changed on the inside, so he made sure everyone could see that Jesus had given him this gift. As he told others of his experience as a former leper, you can be sure that a lot of people didn't believe that Jesus Christ had miraculously healed him. After all, there were many people who denied Christ's divinity and classified Him as a magician.

Who do *you* say He is?

To me He is Lord! He is my healer! He is the restorer of my life? I have no desire to return to a time before when I'd been so selfish in my life. That infection of selfishness, like leprosy, shows itself off in all kinds of sinful behaviors. Today I stand before you and freely tell you about my leprosy. I don't want to diminish the repulsiveness of my disease. In fact, I gladly embrace my history as it serves me with the opportunity to reach out to others who are just like me.

WE are not alone. WE are empowered by the gifts of God. WE are new creations. WE are His righteous and His goodwill ambassadors in all things. WE have a reason to help others now that we have been set free. Fear is just an illusion; it has no power on its own. Please remember that Jesus was and IS human and divine. My spirit knows that He experienced all of the human feelings right up and through His death. Even while still on the cross, He asked His Father to forgive us since we did not know what we were doing.

Let's do an inventory now and see what we possess that we can freely give away to others. How can we support, educate, and bless others as we emerge from the long night of sin in our lives? We *all* have talents and abilities that can be useful to others. Until WE give them away, they are merely the potential for good. Take stock of your situation and decide on one thing that you can change today. Then do it. Sometimes a smile or cheerful nod can be more meaningful than a check for a hundred thousand dollars.

None of us are so poor or so deprived that we do not have some small gift to offer to others. There is no one trapped in a death cell or a dying body who doesn't possess the potential to bless others. The question becomes, do you give it away freely or do you keep it to yourself? Only you can decide and only you and God will know your decision. Please join me and let's make a new start today, just like the leper in the Bible story. All it takes is making the choice to act WITH the grace of God.

Ten lepers were healed. Only one returned and gave thanks (sounds very believable in terms of modern society). For years, every time I got myself into a difficult situation, hastily I would try to make a deal with God. *If He would just rescue me one more time . . .*

Today, I know that everything that has happened in my life was purposeful and that all of these events have served God's purposes in some way. I also know that no matter what I experienced, I was never alone. God's grace was always with me. Today I can express my gratitude for the substance of my life since God has used it to serve His divine purpose and to glorify His holy name.

If you are a "leper" or can relate to the experience of exclusion, please contact me directly and I will be happy to share the path and the promise of personal redemption.

THE FOLLOWING CHAPTER WAS WRITTEN by the author and is based upon years of correspondence with a friend serving life in prison. Every element in this story was revealed in the letters the offender has shared with the author. All facts are true and relate directly to his life. The emotions expressed are his emotions. The thoughts expressed are his thoughts. The author's only contribution to this work was to organize the material and bring the offender's words alive for the reader. Hidden by years of invisibility, the offender refused to allow the author to use his name. His request for anonymity has been honored. He is currently serving his fortieth year of incarceration.

Chapter 20

A KILLING AND THREE DEATHS

AT THE END OF THE day, I'm confounded with multiple thoughts, a whirlwind of emotions, regrets, grief and a profound awareness that somehow I am less human. You see, I took a life in a moment of miscalculated intensity and misguided strength fueled by the need for my dominant demands to be met. My estimation of life was wrong, and it resulted in the death of another human being.

I have no way to convey the horror of that personal experience, nor could words describe the fear that shook my frame as I slowly became aware of what I'd done. The hardest moment of all was that instant when I realized that nothing I could do would restore the life of my victim. Up until that moment, I scarcely recognized this person as a victim, but an absence of life, due to my actions, soon produced this shattering reality.

While this moment in time drove me to control my reckless behaviors, the chase was on and it was only a matter of time before I was captured and jailed for my offense. Once publicly identified, I was confronted with the evidence of my wrongdoing. There was no place to hide, least of all deep inside my consciousness. My name was known and associated with my actions. There is nothing to be gained by a public review of the facts.

Almost four decades after my crime, the only meaningful reflection that I have is to write down these thoughts for you to read. My momentary lack of control has put me through a lifetime of bodily and spiritual incarceration. During this time, I've had to acknowledge and manage the fallout from my choices and accept the person I had become.

These ideas aren't offered as compensation to the society I've damaged. There's no way to repair the tear in the fabric of the community I have offended. Neither is this an attempt to re-invent myself during the great amount of time that has gone by since this crime. No, my words are nothing more than an expression of the life path that I have experienced. That path has led me to the reality that my actions have produced a responsibility that can't be lessened with the passage of time.

You see, it doesn't matter whether the parole board declares that my prison journey has ended or whether I become dust in an early grave. Neither of these are remedies for the harm I committed in my youth. I am also reconciled to the belief that my place in eternity will bear the marks of my behaviors. I'm certain that the mark of Cain associated with my name will yield to the promise of a quiet cleansing and the welcome embrace of a gracious Father.

I'm not trying to excuse the horror of my actions. What I'd rather point out is that even the most reprehensible crimes can make a person choose spirituality. These people face a lifetime in prison or the end of life itself in the form of the death penalty. But these are human attempts to define and respond to the ill-fated passions of offenders. They are temporary physical solutions to spiritual problems. Limited as they are, they appear to satisfy the demands of the moment.

Then the problem goes away and we settle in with the thought that everything's been resolved. The trouble starts when we decide that invisibility and exclusion or execution are the only solutions to the problem. Remarkably, the dying continues to go on, though largely unseen by the public. Rather in the aftermath, the public's resources must now be used to clean up an accumulation of broken relationships. This is the fall-out that winds up as news and justifies hurried attempts to restore a façade of peace and tranquility in the name of law and order.

"Everything is okay now," we're reassured. "It's all over. Go on home folks," the community leaders urge those who assemble and try to make sense of the latest act of violence. It's an elegant masquerade offering the hope that they have everything under control, so there will be a restored sense of peace and community. Even as the people return to their homes, they're troubled with fears and suspicions about all the others who live in the community. The reassurance is unsettling and makes us more cautious about the faces behind the masks of courtesy. That's a death occurring at the community level, and it's a direct result of the loss of another's life. And so slowly the ripples in the pond begin to spread beyond our comprehension or ability to absorb their meaning as the consequences of tragic and senseless violent acts emerge.

The community was the first to suffer when the news got out that yet another killing had taken place in the crime-riddled city. There was nothing about this event that offered any light or sense of purpose; it was just another senseless crime. As the news spread throughout the community, people were impacted beyond what I could understand. It wasn't a celebrity crime or an event of any notoriety or fame, but it did cast a pall of shared pain over the community.

My act furthered the death of trust, love and hope at the community level. In its wake, people withdrew into their protective shells and guarded their homes with a restless, irritable and distrusting view of others. This spread quickly, like a terrible unseen virus. The shock of the community was a part of the process of events that had come from my own actions. While I was still in the midst of the community, I watched what this tragedy was doing to those with whom I lived.

While I hadn't been discovered yet, I had a hard time ignoring the cries of my conscience. My actions had brought about horrific consequences beyond anything I could imagine. The throb of conscious pain was intensified by my knowledge that I hadn't intended this death of another human being, but my actions brought about that reality. It's relatively easy to numb the senses and drug the brain into a minimal state of function, but no one can escape the truth. Indifference is a mask to hide behind—a way to shield yourself from shame and humiliation—while you sort through the millions of thoughts running through your mind.

Indifference was merely an act, covering up what I'd initiated. No matter where I looked for physical, mental, emotional or spiritual refuge there wasn't a place to hide. My arrest brought with it a great surge of fear, but also a calming sense of relief. My future was out of my hands. My arrest brought an end to my denial. During my trial, I may have sat silent (and to some, stony-faced), but inside

I couldn't resist hearing my conscience. I had witnessed how devastating my actions were to the community and I couldn't make amends to anyone because the tragedy was too great.

This dying process was soon followed by another death of a more personal nature. The family and friends of my victim (who loved her dearly) were soon informed of the circumstances of her death. As I've realized over the years, it wasn't just a physical or emotional loss, but rather a series of deaths that affected these innocent people.

With the news, their lives were pitched into darkness and pain. I can only imagine the questions that flooded their minds as they tried to find some kind of peace and understanding. Eventually they had to experience the death of her constant love and presence in their lives. Another death took place as they surrendered their hopes for the future, releasing all claims to the next generation. Maybe the most devastating part for her family was their anguish that they had failed to protect her. This death also took with it any sense of comfort they could have had as her parents.

The facts of the crime added to their pain when viewed through a long lens. It had been a senseless and brutal crime—a crime of passion—made worse by my years of hiding. You see, if I had been arrested immediately, these people would have begun the process of healing long before my actual capture. So my actions prolonged their agony and uncertainty.

In spite of my desire not to inflict any more pain on others, the fact that I was able to live on a daily life was an overwhelming reality. You can never run very far from yourself. No matter where you go, there you are! My arrest and conviction may have eventually brought these quiet people some closure, but it would never replace their loss.

The third death took place over a prolonged period of time. This death went unnoticed and rightfully so. It was a death unseen and unacknowledged in traditional form. Some may argue that it was a direct consequence of my actions, a point well taken. After my arrest, my wife initiated divorce proceedings to formally sever the contact between us.

I had always assumed, as though in a fantasy, that the marriage would continue onward effortlessly. But the divorce actions brought the starkness of my situation into sharp focus. My wife rightfully made provisions for herself and our son to transition through the events that were thrust upon them. Her reasoned response and graciousness are clear indicators of the personal dignity that she had always possessed.

The coldness of my loss was discernible in the death of the marriage, though if I were truthful with myself, I'd already failed my marital responsibilities long before the events that led to the divorce. Being capable and ambitious, I had always reckoned that I would be able to "fix" any situation that arose in my marriage. But now there was no way to undo the harm I had created.

Sitting in county jail awaiting trial, I had the experience of daily revisiting my choices. Perhaps this amount of time in the process is a good thing since it's useful to stop and consider reality, real reality. Another useful aspect of this time is the realization that only personal accountability offers any hope of closure or future healing.

Letting go of the marriage was a death of its own, and I recognized the true loss. I had brought this on by my own actions and I couldn't run away from that fact. All I could do was find neutral ground. The burden was mine and I was the only one to carry it.

The death of the marriage gave way to another death: the hope of the marriage that was the birth of a son (a child that I loved to the best of my limited abilities).

As time slowly crept by, I harbored the hope of a continuous loving relationship with my son. I thought the earthquake effect of my crime, that had shattered my marriage, might mercifully have left me with a son. This was a promise for the future and a hope I could use to keep going day by day. But over time the relationship proved to be no match for the pain, uncertainty, shame and fear brought on by my actions.

That relationship eventually gave way to brutal reality. In time, the only thing I could do was to let go of this dream and watch the next death play itself out before my eyes. My son's choice was to sever contact with me. I knew the reason for this: my prior actions. The view from a prison cell is clear and direct. It extends beyond time, space or distance, and that view is always a painful reminder of what I left behind because of my arrogant choices. And so another death brought with it dark days of sorrow and regret.

Even as I recognized the justice involved, I found myself reeling from its effects. I found limited comfort on the prison yard, doing what I could to maintain my body with weight training. It offered a small distraction and a purpose to focus on. It also helped me through the challenges of prison life. Without that sense of direction, life itself would have spun down to nothingness.

As I refocused my view of life, shifting from the hopefulness of lost joys to the starkness of my present reality, the prison environment gave me the most personal of deaths. Losing the connections to life were deaths in their own right, but the most painful of deaths was about to occur, just beyond my field of vision. This death caused the spark of life to withdraw completely and what was left was an animated corpse.

Slowly I was overtaken by the loss of self, the hope of being a productive citizen, and a member of society with all the rights and responsibilities involved. Inside I was reduced to the status of a shadow, like an unheard whisper, an unseen wisp of nothingness, a bloom that never blossomed. There was no appeal from this life sentence because it happened inside of me. It was a purely interior reality that was beyond description. It was my burden and mine alone to shoulder. It was the ultimate punishment, truly a living death.

As the reality of these deaths sunk into both my consciousness and unconsciousness, I found myself wrapped in an extended period of mourning that went beyond selfishness or self-interest. These deaths brought the full meaning of my actions into harsh relief that contrasted sharply with my understanding of the meaning of life. They slowly brought me to the truth and an emerging sense of direction. This was my lot in life.

Somewhere I've heard that it's the purpose of a seed to fall into the soil and die so it can produce more seeds. This was how my dying followed my long fall from grace and purpose. Dying is a quiet time: a time when the celebration of life fades into the background. The life behind and the life ahead both come into view. For just a moment in time, we stand in the quiet of eternity before we surrender ourselves to history.

These deaths that I've written about are nothing more than spiritual rehearsals for the future. Out of the mulch of my past life, I was slowly starting to experience a budding of hopefulness. I didn't know what was fueling this. I returned to my bed each evening waiting for my physical death; I would have gladly welcomed it.

In spite of my personal darkness and despair and in spite of my willingness to peacefully blend into quiet nothingness, my body carried me forward with its basic demands for food and rest. My days switched daily from meals to sleep. I did this while I waited for my consciousness to end. I was ready for the relief that death would finally bring.

Life then made unique unexpected demands on my person. While I'd surrendered to a non-future, life-giving awareness started to fill my very being. This occurred because of an infusion of love from my family members. They wouldn't allow me to withdraw from their affection and attention. This transfusion of love was at the core of my spirit and while I hadn't reached out for this comfort, it became life sustaining. This love was the source of a new vitality and awareness regarding the meaning of life.

And while I tried to take hold of this concept, there was another reality emerging just outside my view. Out of all the destruction that I'd done, the parents of my victim extended a helping hand. While I was waiting to fade away and die, they established a link with me that was life giving. Their spirit of love and concern became a driving force that ultimately led them into a prison chapel for a day of reconciliation and forgiveness.

These two life-giving transfusions brought me out of my prison stupor and unsettled my plan to seek death as an escape from life. My days became purposeful as I lifted my head off my pillow each day to confront a new sense of myself. This was a slowly emerging reality. It started with the germ of hope. That seed of hope eventually became a visible thread that I've been able to build on. The thread eventually became a branch that I've been able to build into a meaningful life. I know that it will sustain me through all future challenges.

While it took time and purpose, eventually meaning and personal peace have now become my legacy. No longer is my life plagued by the surges of politics, economics or the response of people to perceived criminal activity and the endless cries to "lock 'em up and throw away the key." That reality has arrived and it has not diminished the rampant fears of the public. Sitting inside of a prison, one develops a keen insight into the endless cycle of whipping the public into a frenzy by continually igniting battles better suited to the land of Don Quixote and his endless charging at windmills. Well-stoked fears always yield economic windfalls for those who seek power and control.

Entering my fortieth year in prison, I'm no longer concerned with the end of my life. You see, whether I continue on into eternity haunting the cells of this prison, or my bones finally come to rest in some shady place, I know that there has been a remarkable purpose to my life. Perhaps I would never have risen to a place of meaningful consequence in my prior life because of my own moral decay. But my actions have given way to reflection and reflection has paved the path to purposeful living.

My purpose is contained in these pages. You see, my senseless past has given me the awareness that nothing we do during the course of life is wasted time or energy. Even the worst of wicked behaviors eventually produce a rich soil of hope and promise. The most diseased portions of our lives can yield to a quiet awareness and transformation; it happens if we let it happen.

For those who follow me behind these walls into a darkened place of grief, sorrow and regret, I hope my words can offer some light to their pathway. For those who breathe the air of freedom on a daily basis, my hope is that they would seek meaning and consequence rather than give way to their passions and pursuits. Even now, they may turn around and find a new life.

Inside or out, we've all been created for some purpose. The adventure of living is a solely individual experience. If your purpose has been colored by want, greed, lust, revenge or just plain anger, then create new choices for yourselves and your loved ones. It's never too late to turn away from the arrogance, ignorance or misguided pride and fear.

Unfortunately, many will ride their choices right on into oblivion, while others will suffer the painful consequences of their actions. My words can't create a new spirit within you. I'm not capable of doing that. But there is One who is willing to shoulder any burden or offense you bring to His care. I can assure you that it will be just like the welcome of a prodigal son or daughter—never the cold shoulder of contempt and judgment.

This reality exists beyond most of our vision. It seems that only crises and tragedies bring this into sharp and immediate focus. Before the disaster or after the storm, each position offers its own relief from painful encounters with ourselves. The restlessness of profound regret and shameful behaviors will give way to peace and personal acceptance if you are prepared to make the journey.

Within the United States, I'm one of two million individuals who are incarcerated for a crime. My identity—what my prison number is and even who I am—is unimportant. I'm one with you and at the deepest level, I can relate to your pain and regret. Now a new paradigm, a new model is unfolding before us. Please join me in living out the remainder of your lives in a fellowship of men and women committed to renewal and hope. WE can do this one day at a time as brothers and sisters living each day to the fullest.

This story ends on a positive note, but not as the result of lengthy incarceration or any judicial process. Falling well outside of the magical influences of a pardon or parole, events have brought together forces that have changed my life in the midst of prison life. Redemption and reconciliation have forged a powerful union of events and realizations that have given me a new life: a meaningful life, a life worth living. This has fueled my life over the last forty plus years.

This process shaped my soul far from the view of the public or prison officials. My story is only one of two million stories waiting to be shared. These are the stories that will bring new life to communities, families and individuals. My seed will die and fall into the unplanted ground, but my hope is that while I'm a single tree in a dense forest of prisoners, my seed will produce seedlings that will grow into a small patch of hope for the future. Be Blessed.

PERSONAL STORY

THERE ARE FEW THINGS MORE intimidating or challenging than writing about one's own true nature. Most of us make assumptions about the character of various people we know based on how we see them behave and how they interact while in our company. Our pre-conceptions are often shattered when we are given some behavioral report that does not match our own personal observation.

Herein lies the problem with trying to understand human nature. We often harbor conflicted feelings that are driven by our memories, thoughts and the unconscious that push through our psyche toward the daylight of behavioral expression. In such moments, it is rather easy to talk around the subject of one's intentions. It is a much more difficult process to look inside and recognize the swamp that sucks our defeats, failures, sins, guilt and crimes under the surface of the water. But we are always aware that the surface tension of the water is easily stirred.

I can't write a book about the pain and suffering found in the families of offenders or how to begin dealing with it in a helpful creative fashion without first meeting a pre-condition that is not yours, but mine alone. I must offer you the truth about what it is like to live as an offender. Then I may use my redemption experience to offer a new understanding of faith and hope for all who suffer through this insidious, intergenerational cycle of hopelessness and destruction.

Even now, thirty-five years after the change process started, it is difficult to think about and much harder to acknowledge in writing. But such is the stuff of meaningful change. One must be willing to document the entire process in order to reach out to others. I will not glamorize my sins or crimes (as they need no illumination to those who know me well). Nor would it serve any useful purpose to inscribe the list in this book. Those who don't know me have no need to be burdened by my prior actions.

I have attempted to focus on the aberrations of character that I displayed during this period of my life, not the events or people who unwittingly provided me an opportunity to vent my rebelliousness and anger. Therefore I have restricted this statement to major turning points, rather than focusing upon a life littered with the debris of my sinful life choices.

What I hope to offer you is a shared journey about the way it felt to live inside of me through all of those years. Only then will you be able to develop insight into the processes that mark an offender's life and all who come into contact with them. My writings are guided by a close family member who has assured me that this is an essential part of this book. My hope is that the Holy Spirit will help me remember the essential recollections that will make this effort useful to others.

I came on the first wave of post-World War II babies (1945) and arrived in a strict Irish-Catholic home. My arrival, though not unexpected, added another dimension to the shape of the family. While my birth was greeted with anticipation and pleasure, I am sure that my later life choices left bitter regrets in the lives of those who loved me.

As a young child, there were times of great joy and great fear. Family members seemed to embrace a sense of kinship and caring, but at times there were gaps in my understanding. That is when the fear crept into my life: a great fear that things would spin out of control. I was overwhelmed as I tried to encircle these surges with an understanding beyond my years.

Family members brought joy and pain: a very conflicting predicament for a young child. One seemed distant and unpredictable: using alcohol on a binge basis, quite possibly to cope with the stresses of life and a houseful of children (each with their own special needs). It was a time when hand-me-downs were fashionable and obedience to one's parents was akin to the rule of God.

Another family member demonstrated unpredictably in terms of emotional behaviors, and constantly slid along the continuum from stable to unstable and back. As the years went by these swings would become more pronounced. Sometime beyond six years of age, I became aware of a growing competitiveness among the children in our family. The goal was that one sibling would not be outdone by another sibling (though this was often used as a whipping tool). It was difficult, upon reflection, to get a true sense of where I started and ended as a person.

One sibling had the amazing power to manage and divert the ever-lurking tension and potential domestic violence. I remember how my feelings of fear would soar whenever this sibling left the home. Why did they have to go out and leave me alone to cope with problems that might emerge within our family? At about this time, another child was born who shook up the order of attention. This child required care, love and attention beyond my understanding, but the worst part of the new arrival was the requirement that I share in the responsibility for the baby's care. It seemed an awful burden at the time and I did not understand the nature of family love since at times it felt like every man for himself. It was a chaotic environment and a dreadful place in which to instill a sense of responsibility.

As I mentioned earlier, I had been raised in a strict Irish-Catholic home. Church attendance was not at ones discretion. The nuns who taught at the parochial school I attended were exceptionally focused upon teaching us the law of God and the reality that violating it would lead to eternal damnation. They were also adept at teaching us an excellent basic elementary education. I am more and more impressed at the value of this endeavor. It became a foundation for subsequent educational endeavors after hitting several road bumps.

With the full fury of God hanging over my head (conscience), it became difficult to contain my resentment about being shoved into an emotional corner (or so it seemed at the time). As my "rebellion" started to emerge in behavioral terms (lying, stealing, being sulky and generally unhelpful), I started to be the target of criticism on the part of friends of the family. I deeply resented that I had no privacy and that my activities were not shielded from others. At a deeper level, I responded to these perceived attacks by shielding myself through distancing myself from others.

My bicycle became my tool of exploration and an expression of freedom. I wonder now if I simply used that mechanism to "run away from home" with each new adventure. Unfortunately, I had to return to the reality of living at home. On one such exploration trip, I went further from home than ever before and had a collision with a bus and ended up in the hospital for, I believe, three months. The outcome was surgery for a depressed fractured skull and an extended period of recovery. I apparently scared my family out of their wits (I was expected to die) with this antic and I subsequently lost a full semester of school that meant that I would not be promoted onto the next grade.

It seemed that not only was I lonely, distant and rebellious, but now I had evidence of being stupid. It appeared that my situation was getting worse, not better, and the worst part was that no one could "fix me" no matter how many people were encouraged to "talk to me." Attempts were made to invoke God's wrath by telling me that perhaps the angels would come and take away someone I loved and feared while I was at school.

Now, I know that it made the task of learning an impossible experience. My mind was consumed with real fears over which I was helpless. Confusion swept over me like a hurricane. I could not pay attention to what I was being taught. Rather, I became the "class clown" and suffered for my actions by becoming the target of extraordinary efforts to discipline me into a state of compliance. That strategy backfired and I became angry and sullen in most environments: *except* when I was outside the house and free to roam.

That period of time also introduced professionals coming into the picture. Perhaps I was acting the way I was due to residual aftereffects from my accident and subsequent surgery. The struggles intensified until I felt that I was living under a microscope, and my only escape was when I was outside of the house roaming. I know that if you roam long enough you are going to become exposed to some unsavory characters; but at the time, I did not think it could get worse. In fact, I wondered if I wasn't just an evil child.

No matter what my intention, each new encounter brought more pain and shame to my family members and I seemed helpless to overcome my knack for getting into trouble. I did not know of anyone I could really talk with at that time. Looking back, I'm not sure if I was even aware of what was going on inside of me so that I *could* talk it over. The pain of being completely out of relationship with God added to my burden and for the life of me, though I had intentions to the contrary, I ALWAYS seemed to make the wrong choices.

In adolescence, I was introduced to sexuality by a neighbor child who assured me that it was all quite okay to indulge one another and ourselves in such pleasurable activities. Earlier in elementary school, I had engaged in a "you show me yours and I will show you mine" adventure with another child in the grade below me. Obviously, we had been observed because the matter was quickly reported to the school principal (who determined that I was the primary culprit). Actually, I had only joined in at the urging of my younger friend, but I was to bear the added shame through the label of being damaged.

There was no inherent pleasure in that moment of curiosity, but there was a lot of consequential pain afterwards. Quickly I put together the facts that there must be something wrong with this type of curiosity and thus a lifetime of struggles were born in the aftermath of this event. I still lacked any knowledge of sexuality and was rather innocent at that time in spite of my anger and rebelliousness.

Later I saw no reason to resist pleasure when it was available at a moment's notice. Besides, inside I felt hopeless in the spiritual battle that was raging within. I started to give up hope of moving past this focus and engaged in a number of exploratory activities that added to my carnal knowledge and increased the potential for frequent random encounters. From my initial introduction until manhood, I would become involved in an ever-deepening struggle that was rooted around sexual behaviors. Later that focus would include extensive use of pornography. All of which convinced me that I was a lost cause.

At the same time that I was surrendering my soul to this course of action, I also became quite pleased with myself as demonstrating sexual proficiency that drew others into an ever-widening network of partnerships. Oddly it seemed common and something good. It felt like when our clothes came off, so did all the pretenses. They were just like me. So onwards I traveled, encountering few barriers. On one occasion, a priest told me in confession that he would not continue to give me absolution if I did not intend to change my behaviors. But I was already lost, wasn't I?

Hopelessly lost in the dark reality of selfishness and now comfortable with demanding sexual activity as the price of a relationship, I soon reckoned that if you wouldn't indulge me in sexual activities then there was no use wasting my time with you any further. This became predominate in my thinking: people were there to be used and they could use me for their own pleasure likewise. I came to believe that I was doing an affectionate service for all of my partners. That's love, isn't it?

There had been many uncomfortable touch-and-go moments, but by this time, I was an active alcoholic entering the world of drug exploration. These seemingly harmless, mind-altering chemicals would soon begin to inhibit any conscious self-restraint and when I encountered a partner who seemed reluctant to engage in sexual activity, I would use verbal skills or even physical pressure to help them relax and enjoy the "gift" I was giving them. Many did relax, enjoy and got actively involved, but others did not. Given this slide into the depths of depravity, I can now see that all personal boundaries as individuals ceased to exist when I wanted sexual activity.

Marriage and the birth of three children (two by my first marriage and one from an extended encounter while I was in the U.S. Army) did nothing to deter my activities: either sexual or my ever-increasing passion for chemical relief. Clearly I can see now that as my choices continued to degrade into perversion, I had to use a variety of chemicals in order to live inside of myself. I was medicating the reality of my choices away so that the pain would barely be noticeable to me (though others had the insight to see into my hidden agenda).

Many tried to warn me and my response was to escalate my behaviors to the point where I finally prevailed upon my partner to engage in swinging activities. After all, we were young adults with a zest for fast living. It seemed a natural road to end the personal turmoil that raged within me. The only problem with this set up was that my partner, who initially was reluctant to engage in this conduct, discovered how pleasurable it could be and eventually embraced it as passionately as me.

The handwriting was on the wall; it was only a matter of time until the marriage self-destructed (either over sexual activity without boundary or my full-blown chemical addiction). But I had an answer to that problem, and I taught my partner the value of drugs: particularly marijuana and pills (uppers). We engaged in therapy as a last ditch effort to avert the obvious, but I think now that it only hastened the downward slide into oblivion.

Once it became apparent that the end was in sight, at a deep inner place, I saw everything sliding away. I gave away our dog without ever telling the children of my actions and fled to the state of Alabama where I stayed with swinger friends. Later I went to stay with family in New York City, but I could not stand the reality that I was back where I started as an abject failure, so I bought bus tickets for the children and myself and we wandered for some time before eventually returning to California.

After staying in an empty church bus, I finally conned a church member into taking us into her home she shared with her three children. She was a resentful individual, so we were well paired. I could never muster the desire to engage in sexual activity with her, but I readily exploited her credit cards and financial standing. There was no thought at that time over the subsequent impact these actions would have on her own children or mine. I was completely oblivious to the needs of others and was still in hot pursuit of booze, drugs and sex.

Eventually I managed to get my own apartment for myself and my two children (from marriage), but I continued to hide from my former partner until I was stopped for a traffic infraction and jailed for failure to follow court orders. It seemed that my partner had gotten a custody order and that it had been escalated to the attention of law enforcement given my quirky behaviors during this time period.

Later I succeeded at regaining formal custody, largely due to my ex-partner's living arrangements. By this time, I had the children in Catholic school and was seeing a Newport Beach therapist weekly for family therapy. Shortly after I prevailed in court, I was feeling on top of the world; it seemed that I had been vindicated and affirmed in the same process. One would think that this would be a major turning point in my life, and in fact it was; I became worse than before with booze, drugs and sex. I was taking risks with others that could have landed me in jail. Eventually it did when I came home and proceeded to have a sexual relationship with the babysitter while her cousin slept in the children's bedroom. It was a new low in the dimension of perversity. But curiously I was not sorry for the behavior, only for getting caught.

I was arrested later that day and subsequently charged with nine felonies, which were later reduced to four felony charges. My children were placed in state care and I remained in jail until a month or so later when the woman I had previously financially used arranged my bail and retained an attorney on my behalf by using the equity in her home. I had a great sense of relief emerging from jail, but quickly had an experience that literally was the beginning of change in my life. I had lost everything through my own choices. This had nothing to do with others; it was all my own doing.

Through the Grace of God, I experienced a spiritual awakening when I visited my attorney's office to review the police reports and witness statements. He was not there. He and his family were away in Europe, so I sat in his chair reading all about my behaviors, searching in vain for a way to explain it all away. When I got to the back of the file, there was a copy of my FBI "rap" sheet summarizing all of my prior encounters with police in various jurisdictions.

While the children were still under the custody of the state, they would be returned to me shortly pending the outcome of my trial. It was a temptation to blow it all off and go get loaded and celebrate being out of jail, but this time it was different. I knew I was in deep trouble. I had no one I could open up to within my family, especially given the charges and the shameful behaviors I had displayed. Boy, I suddenly realized that I NEEDED a drink to soothe my pain and fear.

Finally, after years of people telling me, the light finally came on and I understood what they had been trying to say. As I reviewed the rap sheet, I became aware of the unwritten facts clustered between the list of criminal activities in which I had engaged: the divorce, the bankruptcy, the loss of family and friends and the incredible number of jobs from which I had been dismissed. The only ones who were dependent upon me were my children: whom I later learned loved and feared me, much the same as it was in my childhood home. They were in a desperate situation with nowhere to hide.

At that moment, I felt physically ill as I saw my life laid out in the attorney's paperwork. I did not just need a drink at that point; I WANTED several drinks to ease the pain and feelings of shame. In a moment of clarity and spiritual urgency, I reached for the phone and called Alcoholics Anonymous. They directed me to a local Alano Club in Garden Grove, California. Even after having made the phone call, I still played a little game for myself as I left the building. If I turned right I would go have those drinks I desired; if I turned left I would drive to the Alano Club and turn myself in.

I turned left, reflecting with extraordinary thankfulness (probably with the help of Jesus Christ and my guardian angel) that the battle was about to end. While I stopped using alcohol fairly fast after my initial encounter with A.A., I continued to smoke marijuana for another month, not quitting all chemical addictions until September 20, 1977. The healing had finally begun.

The arrest had happened on July 9, 1977. I fought the criminal charges: using three separate lawyers during the course of prosecution. In May 1979, I lost my father and returned home for the funeral. During that time I disclosed my arrest and the pending charges to a family member.

As was common as a child, my shame was exposed to other family members with the excuse that the burden was too heavy to bear alone. I returned to California and shortly thereafter went on trial in May/June 1979. My attempts to defend my actions failed and I was found guilty on all charges. I was subsequently sentenced to six years and four months in state prison.

While being transported to the prison I remember thinking, "I don't belong here!" But the reality was that, in fact, I *did* belong among those other prisoners because of my sinful actions against others. There was no place to hide from this reality. I was totally stunned that it had ended this way. For several months I was horribly confused by this turn of events.

What followed was a definite period of disillusionment with God. I had gotten sober and clean, but He did not seem to be doing His part. I tuned my attention to things I could accomplish in a powerless environment. God did not let me walk out of that prison until I paid my debt to society in full, but he opened the door for therapy, education and He continued my spiritual awakening in the prison setting. I have written elsewhere about the nature of living with evil over that period of four years, but He always protected me and even sent a Christian guard to witness to me personally and through varied spiritual reading materials.

I was incarcerated four years and one day. During my four years in custody, I managed to write down an amends list, which I later initiated as a free man. The first item on the list was to find my daughter (born of the military relationship) and make amends to her directly, owning the responsibility for my actions. After the initial contact with her, it took ten years to cement a friendship: a remarkable blessing. I also left prison with an Associate of Science degree from Cuesta College and a Bachelor of Arts degree in Psychology from Antioch University.

God had used my four years in prison as a time of healing and restoration. My mind, emotions and intellect were nurtured in the heart of a prison. I was also released having six years of sobriety from all chemical addictions. It was a period of constant and intensive healing, a true turning point in my life. The gains were consolidated after my release, as I was able to find housing, employment and social support from various individuals. I applied for admission to Pepperdine University and completed the requirements for a Master of Arts degree in 1986. That degree was in the field of Counseling Psychology.

I am mystified by my slide into degradation and confused that I had actively pursued that pathway consciously. I am sure that part of the educational process was an attempt to put the pieces of my life together and also perhaps understand the lives of others who had been in prison with me.

I worked for a period of 18-24 months and was disappointed to realize that my graduate education did not put sufficient teeth into my intellectual skills. While I maintained an ongoing—albeit confusing— connection with Christianity, I was more of a marginal believer, putting greater stock in applying for admission to a doctoral program. God was very patient with me. At this point, I was re-introduced to a relationship with my two children. I also was successful at starting a small business to help sustain all of my other efforts financially.

I was finally accepted into the General Psychology program and later transferred to the Clinical Psychology program at United States International University. Thanks to the grace of God, I graduated in 1996 with a doctorate in Clinical Psychology. Throughout the course of my education (Master's and Doctoral levels), I had the opportunity to travel extensively (both domestically and internationally). Therefore my education now encompassed a cultural awareness of many of the world's geopolitical entities and a growing realization of my responsibility to reach out to others who lived lives of pain and shame.

Applying for a Marriage, Family and Child Internship credential, I checked the back of the application in the box that asked if I had been convicted of a crime. Several years later someone reviewed the application when I filed a request to sit for the licensing exam. That triggered a response from the Attorney General of the State of California in which my licensure application was denied by the MFCC board.

I appealed their decision and after an extended hearing the administrative law judge recommended that I be allowed to move forward toward licensure. The MFCC Board overruled his recommendation and issued a final denial. At about the same time, I was permitted to argue aspects of my original appeal before the Ninth Circuit Court of Appeal. While they acknowledged the legal issued which I raised on appeal, they found that the case was then moot since I had already been released from incarceration and had completed the parole requirements. It was a time of incredible highs and devastating lows.

The pathway from doctoral academics eventually led to an invitation to complete my internship requirements at a University Medical Center within the Department of Psychiatry. It was a year of passionate learning: one of the most intense learning experiences of my life. But having been through the experience with the MFCC Board in California, I was highly resistant to full disclosure on applications or licensing statements. I did make a full disclosure to one of my internship supervisors who courageously urged me onward. This supervisor became a mentor helping to smooth the rough patches that I seemed to encounter.

It was not all smooth-sailing, but I eventually applied for licensure in Mississippi. I did not acknowledge my past unlawful behaviors out of fear and past experiences. I took the exam, completed my oral boards and was issued a license as a clinical psychologist on September 19, 1997. It was twenty years *to the day* that I had my last chemical adventure. Coincidence, I think not! The learning curve steepened as I realized that enormous effort that would now be required to competently apply the theory and skills I had been taught.

Later, I found myself looking deeply into literature and researching gaps that I had discovered in the science. Little did I realize but

God was leading me back to my Christian roots and revealing truths that seemed to conflict with my educational values. I spent the next years in practice—often resistant—to the barest suggestion that there was an alternate way to evaluate patients. I did eventually take to reading a number of spiritual books that also challenged many of my pre-conceptions.

In 2008, I retired from a state job and accepted a position working for the U.S. Navy as a civilian contractor. This time I made a full disclosure to the agency recruiter and completed the National Security Agency background questionnaire truthfully. I put myself into God's care and hoped for the best. Twice a special security agent interviewed me about my responses on this disclosure form, and I gave complete and truthful responses to all questions.

During the three years of my employment as a Navy Psychologist, I came into contact with clinical presentations that re-ignited my interest in the connections between psychology, psychopathology and theology. This triggered an intensive period of introspection in which I looked at my own character formation critically and took note of the life discrepancies that marked my life's journey. This period was filled with endless personal questions and formulations about the basis for deviant responses and where they all started in terms of development.

I later was able to draft an inquiry template, which I started to use with both genders, as well as supportive reading materials that were distributed at no cost to the client or the Navy. These questions were listed for your own information. They were asked in a specific order intended to help the patients start the process of stripping away the masks (pretenses) that they used to hide behind. To refresh your recall the questions are:

1. Can you remember a time when you told a lie and got away with it? Afterwards, you might have felt bad about telling a lie, but you never made any attempt to come clean with anyone afterwards, probably out of fear of potential censure and discipline.

2. Can you remember a time when you stole something that did not belong to you? This was one of those "must-have-it" objects. Later, after you got home, you might have felt ashamed of your behavior, but did not make any attempt to return it since you had already committed an act of theft. You may even have thrown it away or put it into a junk box from which it never again saw the light of day.

3. Can you remember a time when you cheated on an exam, a financial agreement, or even a relationship? Can you remember the awkwardness that you might have felt in response to your actions? Did you ever discuss this matter with anyone of significance in your life? Did you just push the conflict away and avoid further internal confrontation?

4. Can you remember a time when you were engaged in a sexual activity with another person? As the act continued, you may have become aware that you no longer wanted to finish this activity, but you lacked the inner courage to tell your partner. You allowed yourself to engage in this act and later beat yourself up for not having the fortitude to speak up.

The questions are focused upon revealing a pattern of behaviors, which if allowed to continue, may be the start of the soul-killing process. In each question, the theme of regret and denial are critical to that process of learning to live at peace with one's self. These are not trick questions; in fact, they have often been impasse breakers. Hopefully in the short number of sessions that we had together, these questions would encourage the process of self-examination. In my opinion, any intervention that assists the patient looking within himself or herself is a useful intervention and a potential turning point.

I started to routinely use these questions whenever sessions lagged or started becoming stagnant. From January through mid-March 2011, I was referred a number of patients suffering from Borderline Personality Disorder. As was my professional practice, each was given a series of personality and functional assessments. If I encountered substantive resistance, they were offered a referral to the other psychologist or our visiting psychiatrists.

My enthusiasm for trying to identify a starting point in their personality disorders resulted in lowering my guard and ignoring caution flags as I engaged them in questions designed to help me understand the nature of their individual psychologies. The list was very similar to the questions listed above, but also contained questions about their current activities and was targeted to revealing those behaviors that brought them feelings of discomfort.

My efforts yielded several complaints and triggered a background investigation as the matter was referred to Naval Criminal Investigative Services (NCIS) for further investigation. The lead investigator pursued a background check that revealed the previously disclosed information. I was summarily removed from my position and arrested on three criminal charges in three separate jurisdictions.

Those charges (two misdemeanors and a felony count) were either dismissed in court by the reviewing judge or in the case of the felony it was never filed for prosecution by the district attorney. Each location had relevance: one location was in the jurisdiction of the naval base, another was within the jurisdiction of my practice, and the last was within the jurisdiction of my home. These actions were accompanied by an NCIS disclosure to the Psychology Board of the State of Mississippi, leading to the revocation of my professional license based upon the non-disclosure of my prior criminal history (even though it had ended 34 years before the facts were revealed).

Overall, it was a devastating experience professionally, financially, socially, personally and health-wise. But like the prison experience, God had a plan. Over the twelve months that followed these actions, I was led to write three books (of which this is the third), and to abandon all efforts at protecting "my image."

The end result has been the birthing of a ministry for offenders and their families. While the project started with writing a handbook for mental health professionals, it has quickly grown in scope and extent. The navy affair was only a "setback" as my mother would say.

My intention in revealing the current events in some detail is not a vindication of my decisions, nor is it a vindictive indictment of others involved in the administrative processes of government. I have tried to walk a thin line, erring on the side of ownership rather than casting a long view on these events. No matter what the individual intentions of those involved in the process, I find that we were all serving the purposes of God in performing our roles. Therefore I have no regrets, nor do I harbor ill feelings toward those who acted, based upon their legitimate concerns. Somewhere I have read that God uses all of our intentions and actions to bring about the fulfillment of His Will.

I am sure at this point in time that evil actually exists. I had my own dealings with this dimension of life. I recognize its presence in society and perhaps embarrassingly in the actions of others (even those who masquerade under the pretense of caring for others). It is pervasive in our culture and this book is a partial endeavor to document my journey back from the edge of perdition. I offer this life summary to provide insight into the emotional journey that has been my lot (all my own choices). Nothing in this book should be construed as blaming others; my journey is the result of my choices.

God always has a plan for our lives. He alone knows the highest good which can be revealed in a surrendered spirit. This book has tackled the issues of living through a prison experience. Now, arm yourself with the knowledge that you are not alone.

Various chapters in this book focused upon a sure solution to all of our failures. If I can offer help or encouragement, contact me directly and I will do my best to provide you with assistance in finding your footing and moving on toward living the life God has given to you.

* * *

VISUAL DATA SUMMARY

Ages: 7-8 to 31:

A Path of Personal Degradation

Fear and Confusion

32 to 64:

A Path of Personal Recovery

Faith and Hope

65 to ?:

A Path of Personal Ministry

Service to Others

KEVIN J. MCCARTHY
POST OFFICE BOX 1484
SLIDELL, LOUISIANA 70459
MAY 13, 2012

SCRIPTURAL REFERENCES

THERE ARE BROAD REFERENCES TO scripture inserted throughout this book. They are there to guide you in your journey forward. Do not just take my word for it; take the time to look them up with a Bible and a concordance. Those words are written specifically for you. Those containing both chapter and verse are provided to assist your search. Understanding these verses will be a light for the path that you are walking. I hope to meet you on your journey, but surely at the Wedding Feast of the Lamb.

THE EXTRAORDINARY PRISONER

IN ALL ASPECTS OF APPEARANCE He seemed to be unremarkable, a solitary testament to the indifference of nature: yet his very presence drew crowds of other isolated individuals. It was as if he was the embodiment of hope. His words floated gently across crowds of seekers touching a wide assortment of people. For some his very presence stirred their anger and a desire for vengeance, while others found that his words touched their lives in some magnificent way. He was truly a man of the people, without peer. He dwelled among those most lost in the rush of the day. From an aged widow to a hated tax collector, he had the ability to center in on the most intimate struggles of their lives.

Today we often attempt to bridle those who become too open, by telling them that it is simply too much information. *Let's keep this superficial, that way I do not really need to get to know you or understand the essential struggles of your life. We can keep this all very distant, that way perhaps I can avoid dealing with the intensity of your life or the demands of shared spirituality. We can do this all very informally.*

To have His attention was the ultimate moment of respect and joy. To have Him rest His gaze upon your weary stooped shoulders was the essence of meaningfulness in drab unwanted lives. It was the essential validation of worth, yet some hated Him for freely extending this gift to others. There are those today who live within our communities whose lives lack any evidence of compassion. Rather their lives are seared with bitterness and vengeance, consumed with unreasonable fears and unbridled hatred for others. They are pools of polluted water seeing themselves as sparkling springs.

Like those who gathered to hear His healing words we all have the opportunity to reflect on the legacy that He bequeathed to us. We have His words and His spirit on a daily basis, but many somehow manage to fool themselves into believing that His message is dated and inapplicable to twenty-first century life. Oh how narrow-minded we have become in our worldview when we fail to see that man only communicates and travels faster than before He walked on earth. Our personalities remain unchanged as we selfishly grasp at things we believe will make us happy.

He never looked for personal happiness but was filled with joy when He recognized what made for a happy spiritual life in another. His days were filled with reaching out and blessing others, urging them to continue on the Kingdom pathway. His needs were few and rarely met, yet He had time to meet the needs of others. He was keenly aware of the issues of His day, the problems surrounding social justice, yet He encouraged us to keep our eyes on the goal. He claimed no victory for Himself, but offered all praise and glory to His Father.

He made no claim on anyone else's time or resources. He simply invited others to reach out in faith and hope. Then He blessed them when they responded to His call. He held nothing precious except His service to do the will of His Father. In following this call of living service, He made sure we knew we were all precious in His sight. He took joy in children and old people. He saw the reverence some held for His father and with sadness and tears He also saw man's rebellious and sinful nature throughout time. Yet we often live today as though He was just a kindly loving historical relic.

A modest man with a conscious love for His own family and the family of man, His manner was mild and soothing. Yet He had a capacity for righteous indignation when others abused His Father's house and tried to isolate and abuse others in the name of the law. For Him the law was not a weapon to be used for beating others into submission, but rather a Godly provision to help us recognize our human limitations. He knew our frailty and the struggles each person faced as they made their way through life. Humble and faithful to His Father's call, He walked amongst us as a King and Savior.

He *is* the living example that proves we are all created in the image and likeness of God. How could one man walk amongst us and have such an impact upon lives down through history? His gentleness and acceptance of others are the very hallmarks of His ministry. Yet it was these aspects of His word that eventually would lead Him to be condemned to a felon's death upon a cruel cross in Jerusalem. His love for us assured His death. He was hated for the promise of His Father's love to all who accepted Him. Was there ever a greater legal travesty than His trial and crucifixion?

The time came when others could not stomach His message of love and acceptance any longer. Consumed with hatred and bitterness they schemed to put an end to this Man and His ministry. They waited for a moment when they could act without incurring the wrath of the crowds. They were cowards, like those of us who intimately know Him today and refuse to share His message with others. All the time He was keenly aware of the hardness in their hearts, but He chose to use His time and ministry to reflect the love of the Father. He put aside His own life for our lives.

The day finally came when the rage of the religious leaders ignited and gave way to a plan to remove Him from their presence. "Better one man should die than the whole nation," was the words of one of the leaders. Today we recognize that the words of Jesus Christ are both salt and light to troubled lives, but not just those struggling with the issues of life. Those words contained meaning for all of us, since they are words of life itself. Yet they are also inconvenient words that make us aware of the gift of our lives and the responsibility we all shoulder.

Like modern-day prisoners, He was accused of crimes and isolated. But in His case He never committed any offense against man or against His Father. He honored His mission and the love of His Father. I have often wondered about His thoughts, His hopes and His dreams as he sat there in some cell below Pilate's mansion. He knew what was coming and yet never defended Himself against the lies thrown upon Him by the religious leaders and His own people. What a magnificent Man; what a gracious God. Will we continue to abide in silence as we approach our own deaths, or can we muster the courage to tell others about Him—to face the abuse and rejection that will surely come upon all who stand up in His name? Will you join me today in standing up and proclaiming His promise joyously? Life is but a brief moment in time, we are here and then we are gone. Let's pull together and lift up every fallen brother and sister, especially prisoners in His name.

CONCLUSION

WHILE THIS BOOK COMES TO an end with the conclusion, there is no ending associated with the hope and promise of God's word. He keeps His promises. Even the most wicked, perverse and depraved individuals can seek His forgiveness through a relationship with His Son, Jesus Christ. If you are like me then perhaps you will draw comfort from the words that a friend shared with me recently. He said, "You are just like me, you want to finish the race well!" Please join me and those who love you at the finish line—we will all be waiting for you.

APPENDIX A

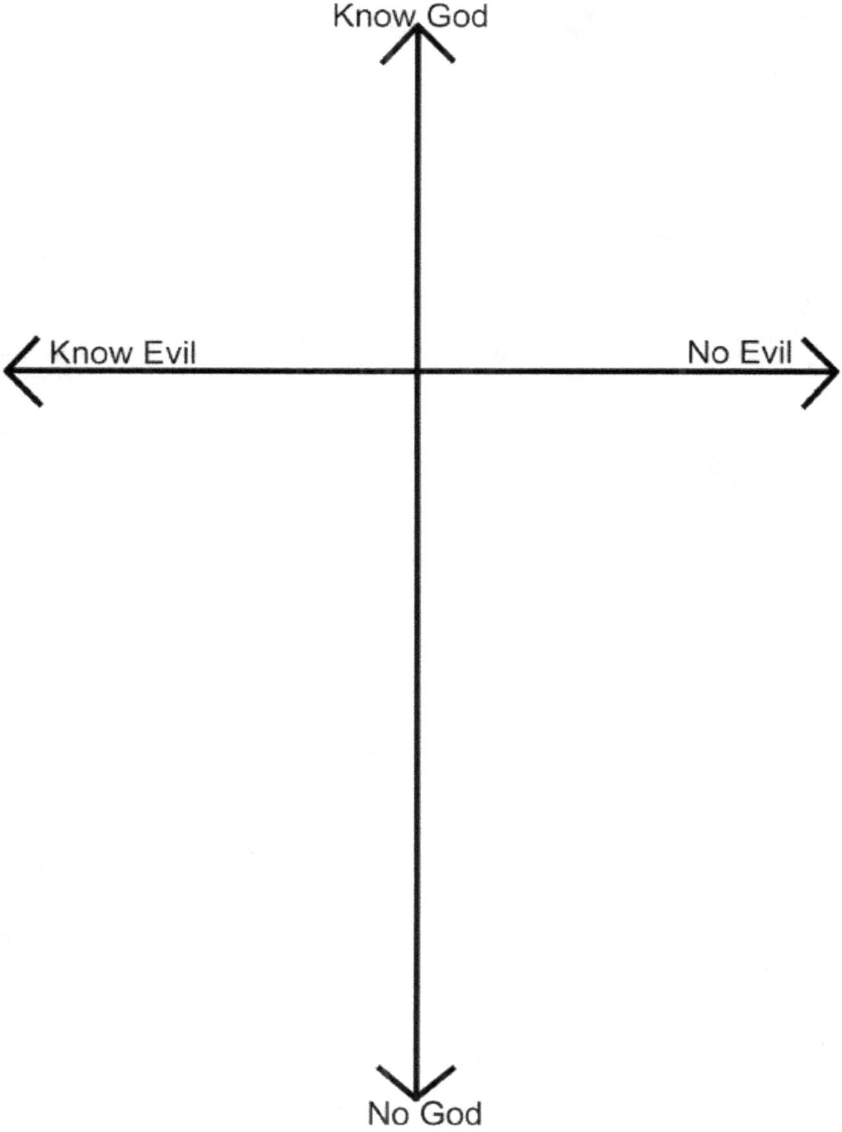
Know God
Know Evil
No Evil
No God

APPENDIX B

Process

Suspicion	Spirituality
Internal Process	Internal Process
Severcide	Science
External Process	External Process

Responses

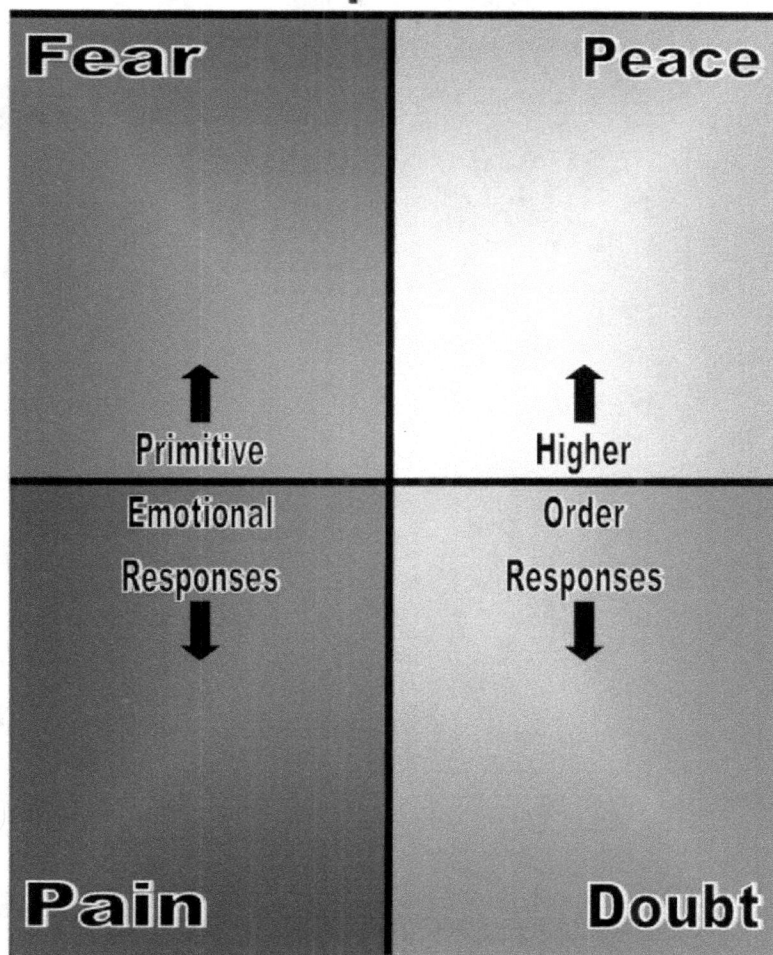

Fear	Peace
↑ Primitive	↑ Higher
Emotional	Order
Responses ↓	Responses ↓
Pain	Doubt

APPENDIX D

Hierarchy of Evil

Perfect Possession
Demonic and Satanic

Imperfect Possession
Demonic and/or Satanic

Human Evil
Progression to Hurtful Actions

Strong Holds
Inner & Outer Conflict

Oppression
Inner Directed

Fear - Confusion - Rebellion - Anger

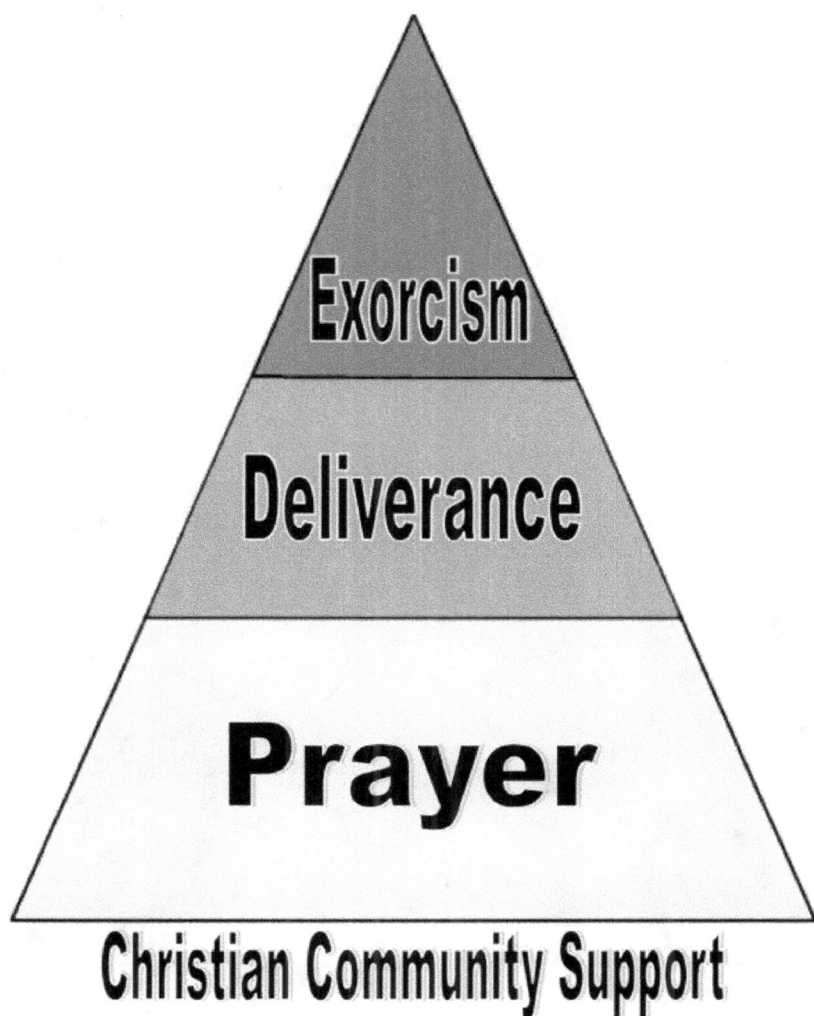

Exorcism

Deliverance

Prayer

Christian Community Support

SELECT BIBLIOGRAPHY

American Psychiatric Association. *Diagnostic and Statistical Manual IV (DSM-IV)*, 1994.

Bernstein, Albert, J. *Emotional Vampires, Dealing with People Who Drain You Dry*. New York: McGraw-Hill, 2001.

Carlin, Sr. Paul W. *Spirit, Soul and Body*. Counselor Certification Program.

Eliot, George. *Silas Marner*.

Erickson, Eric. *The Eight Stages of Man*. Theory of Personality.

Gaines, Ernest. *A Lesson Before Dying*.

Hawthorne, Nathaniel. *The Scarlet Letter*.

Lewis, C.S. *The Screwtape Letters*. New York: HarperOne, 2001.

Martin, Malachi. *Hostage to the Devil*. New York: Reader's Digest, 1976.

McCarthy, Kevin. "Relational Victimization Theory."

McCarthy, Kevin. *Surviving the Justice Experience: An Essential Christian Resource for Families of Offenders*. Ambassador International, Greenville, South Carolina, (2013).

McCarthy, Kevin. "The Psychology of Desperation."

Peck, M. Scott. *People of the Lie: The Hope for Healing Human Evil*. New York: Simon & Schuster, 1983.

Peck, M. Scott. *Glimpses of the Devil*. New York: Free Press, 2005.

Salinger, J.D. *The Catcher in the Rye*.

Schwartz, Peter. *The Art of the Long View* (1991).

Steinbeck, John. *East of Eden*.

The Holy Bible, New International Version (NIV) Biblica, Inc. 2011.

Tutu, Desmond. *God has a Dream: A Vision of Hope for our Time* (Image Books Doubleday 2004).

Twain, Mark. *Tom Sawyer*.

For more information about
Kevin J. McCarthy, Ph.D.
&
A Change of Heart
please visit:

www.dismasproject.com
dismasproject@gmail.com
www.facebook.com/DismasProject
twitter.com/Knowetics

....

For more information about
AMBASSADOR INTERNATIONAL
please visit:

www.ambassador-international.com
@AmbassadorIntl
www.facebook.com/AmbassadorIntl

www.ingramcontent.com/pod-product-compliance
Lightning Source LLC
Chambersburg PA
CBHW072107270326
41931CB00010B/1481
* 9 7 8 1 6 2 0 2 0 2 3 7 1 *